POLITICAL COMMUNICATION
IN A NEW ERA

Recent years have seen a dramatic increase in the number of political issues and events that resonate across borders, and politicians have had to adapt the content of their messages, as well as their modes of transmitting them, to address an ever-widening audience. This book seeks to provide readers with a cross-national perspective concerning the art of political communication in a field increasingly affected by globalization, fragmentation of political audiences, and the rise of professional communications experts – a field concerned not only with how leaders are chosen, but also with how they govern.

Structured in two Parts, *Political Communication in a New Era* examines both methods of gathering and disseminating information in a time of technological transformation, and developments in the uses of political communication across the globe. Contributors offer perspectives from Canada, France, Germany, Israel, Italy, and the US, addressing such issues as: the effects of the technological revolution on journalists and the construction of news, possible directions for "digital democracies" in Europe and the US, the Americanization of European political campaigns, attempts to increase local government participation through new technologies, and the varying role of the news media both in conflict and in peace. This book provides a timely overview of modern political communication at all levels.

Contributors: Christina Holtz-Bacha, Gerald M. Kosicki, Michael Kunczik, Guy Lachapelle, Sabine Lang, Philippe J. Maarek, Gianpietro Mazzoleni, David L. Swanson, Thierry Vedel, Gadi Wolfsfeld.

Philippe J. Maarek is Professor of Information and Communication Sciences, and Director and Co-founder of the Political Communication Department at University Paris 12. He is Chair of the Research Committee in Political Communication of the International Political Science Association and of the similar section of the International Association for Media and Communication Research. He serves on the editorial boards of *The European Journal of Communication, The Journal of Political Marketing* and *Communicazione Politica*. His publications include *Political Marketing and Communication* (2nd edition in French, 2001, also published in English and Spanish).

Gadi Wolfsfeld is Professor of Political Science and Communication at the Hebrew University in Jerusalem. He has served on the editorial boards of *Communication Research, Political Communication* and *The Harvard International Journal of Press/Politics*. He is the author of *Media and Political Conflict* (1997), *The News Media and the Peace Process* (2001), and soon to be published *Media and the Path to Peace*.

ROUTLEDGE RESEARCH IN CULTURAL
AND MEDIA STUDIES
Series advisors: David Morley and James Curran

POLITICAL COMMUNICATION IN A NEW ERA

A cross-national perspective

Edited by
Philippe J. Maarek and
Gadi Wolfsfeld

This book is published with the support of the Political
Communication Research Committee of the
International Political Science Association (IPSA)

Routledge
Taylor & Francis Group

LONDON AND NEW YORK

First published 2003
by Routledge
11 New Fetter Lane, London EC4P 4EE

Simultaneously published in the USA and Canada
by Routledge
29 West 35th Street, New York, NY 10001

Routledge is an imprint of the Taylor & Francis Group

© 2003 Editorial matter and selection, Philippe J. Maarek and
Gadi Wolfsfeld; individual chapters, the contributors

Typeset in Galliard by
Florence Production Ltd, Stoodleigh, Devon
Printed and bound in Great Britain by
Biddles Ltd, Guildford and King's Lynn

British Library Cataloguing in Publication Data
A catalogue record for this book is available
from the British Library

Library of Congress Cataloging in Publication Data
A catalog record has been requested

ISBN 0-415-28953-X

CONTENTS

CONTENTS

CONTRIBUTORS

Christina Holtz-Bacha is Professor in Communication at the University of Mainz, Germany. She is a Co-editor of the German journal *Publizistik* and a member of the editorial boards of *Political Communication, Journal of Communication*, and *European Journal of Communication*.

Gerald M. Kosicki is Director of the Center for Survey Research in the College of Social and Behavioral Sciences at the Ohio State Univesity. he is also Associate Professor in the School of Journalism and Communication, and author of over twenty-four publications in scholarly journals such as *Communication Research, Political Behavior, Journal of Communication, Journalism and Mass Communication Quarterly*, and *Keio Review*.

Michael Kunczik is Professor at the Institute of Communications, Johannes Gutenberg University, Mainz in Germany. His areas of research include mass media effects, theories of mass communication, international communication, public relations, and media economies. He has published numerous articles in both American and European journals.

Guy Lachapelle is Full Professor in the Department of Political Science at Concordia University. He is Secretary General of the International Political Science Association (2001–2004), author of *Polls and the Media in Canadian Elections: Taking the Pulse* (1991), and Co-author of *Quebec Democracy: Structures, Processes and Policies* (1993).

Sabine Lang is Assistant Professor in the Department of Political and Social Sciences at the Free University in Berlin. From 1991 to 1994 she was Director of the Media and Public Relations Department and the Head of the Executive Office of the State Secretary for Labour and Women's Issues in Berlin.

Philippe J. Maarek is Professor of Information and Communication Sciences, and Director and Co-founder of the Political Communication Department at University Paris 12. He is Chair of the Research Committee in Political Communication of the International Political Science Association and of the similar section of the International Association for Media and Communication Research. He serves on the editorial boards of *The European Journal of Communication*, *The Journal of Political Marketing*, and *Communicazione Politica*. His publications include *Political Marketing and Communication* (2nd edition in French, 2001, also published in English and Spanish).

Gianpietro Mazzoleni is Professor of Sociology of Mass Communication and Political Communication at the University of Milan. He is the Editor of *Communicazione Politica* and serves on the editorial boards of *The European Journal of Communication* and *Political Communication* and is Chairman of the EuroMedia Research Group and Vice-Chairman of the Centre d'Etudes Comparées en Communication Politique et Publique of the Université Paris XII.

David L. Swanson is Associate Provost and also Professor of Speech Communication and of Political Science at the University of Illinois at Urbana-Champaign, USA. He was Editor of *Political Communication* from 1999 to 2001. His research on politics and the media has been published in numerous scholarly journals and volumes in the USA, Europe, and elsewhere, in English and in Spanish, Italian, Greek, Japanese, and German translations. His major works include *New Directions in Political Communication* (1990, with Dan Nimmo) and *Politics, Media and Modern Democracy: An International Study of Innovations in Electoral Campaigning and Their Consequences* (1996, with Paolo Mancini).

Thierry Vedel is a Researcher with the National Center for Scientific Research in Paris, and teaches at the Université Paris II and at the Institut d'Etudes Politiques de Paris. He is a member of the editorial boards of *Information, Communication and Society*, *Résaux*, and *Communication and Stratégies*.

Gadi Wolfsfeld is Professor of Political Science and Communication at the Hebrew University in Jerusalem. He has served on the editorial boards of *Communication Research*, *Political Communication*, and *The Harvard International Journal of Press/Politics*. He is the author of *Media and Political Conflict* (1997) and *The News Media and the Peace Process* (2001).

INTRODUCTION

Philippe J. Maarek and Gadi Wolfsfeld

Someone once said that social scientists should confine themselves to making predictions about the past. Even then, many would argue, they are just as likely to get it wrong as right. Attempting to make such predications in the field of communication represents one of the most perilous challenges. It is humbling to recall for example that videophones were invented in the 1960s. It was assumed that these marvelous inventions would quickly become as commonplace as radios and televisions. It turned out, however, that most people do not really want to be seen when they talk on the telephone. It seemed like a good idea at the time.

The problem becomes even more acute when we consider the interface between communication and the world of politics. Communication is and always has been a central component in political processes whether it is leaders communicating with the public, candidates competing for votes, combatants struggling for international attention and sympathy, or citizens debating public issues. Changes in communication technology inevitably have a significant influence in all of these areas. Our ability to predict the direction, intensity, and form of that influence, however, is rather limited. Like many financial investors, by the time we understand where the trend is going, it has already begun to change.

Consider for example the proliferation of the Internet, clearly one of the most important technological developments of the last decades. At first sight, the Internet represents a revolution for democracy. Citizens and groups have greater access to political information than ever before, and there has also been an exponential rise in the ability to distribute information, views, images, and sounds around the world. Everyone with a computer can become a mass medium. It would seem clear that this would lead to a certain redistribution of political power as the public becomes less dependent on either leaders or the mainstream media.

There are, however, equally good reasons to believe that the Net may push societies in a very different direction. As with any technology, those with resources are in a much better position to exploit the Internet than those without. Thus, governments and wealthy corporations are able to

1

build elaborate web sites and to develop distribution networks that allow them to reach the widest possible audience. In addition, the Internet may very well exacerbate the already large information gap between rich and poor on both the national and international level. If information is power, the Internet may simply make it even more difficult for the weak to compete for power. As Dahlgren (2001) has put it: "The growing gap between information haves and have-nots in the digital age threatens to become a serious destabilizing factor for democratic life" (p. 48).

Let us start by asking what exactly has changed in the way people communicate about politics. Blumler and Kavanaugh (1999) present a helpful division between three major ages in political communication that took place in Western democracies during the past half century. The first age took place before the start of television when the primary communication channels were strong and stable political institutions such as political parties. As might be expected, this form of communication was essentially ideological. In the second age the focus shifted to passing on messages through the mass media and increased the demand for communication professionals who were adept at exploiting these channels. In the third (and still emerging) age of media abundance, the professionalization of political communication becomes even more pronounced. Political actors find themselves attempting to send messages through a multitude of channels each of which has its own set of demands and formats. The challenges of communicating in this new age are compounded by the fact that the entire process has speeded up; political actors are expected to react to every issue in real time. Blumler and Kavanagh (1999) put it this way:

> To politicians, the third-age media system must look like a hydra-headed beast, the many mouths of which are continually clamoring to be fed. When something happens, they are expected to tell the media what they are going to do about it well before they can be fully informed themselves. For journalists, the news cycle has accelerated, since more outlets combined with increased competition across them piles pressure on all involved to keep the story moving and to find fresh angles on it. Journalists' "feeding frenzies" become yet more frantic. Time for political and journalistic reflection and judgment is squeezed.
>
> (p. 213)

The increasing use of outside professionals combined with the increasing demand for real time responses leaves less room for substance or ideology. In order to stand out among the crowd, political messages must be especially pithy and entertaining. The blurring of the lines between information and entertainment has become a major concern in the field (Blumler & Kavanagh, 1999; Brants, 1999; Delli Carpini & Williams, 2001; Graber

1994; Newton, 1999; Owen 2000). The term "infotainment" is one of the more useful constructs to emerge from this line of research. Most of these works center on the same point: the greater the influence of commercialism on news content, the less likely the media can serve as serious and responsible forums for public debate.

There is another important discussion going on about this new era that also focuses on the quality of public discourse. A number of scholars have asked whether the massive rise in the number of networks has led to the creation of a new public sphere. The notion of a public sphere originates in the work of Habermas (1989) who wrote about an ideal place in which all citizens communicate freely without governmental interference. Habermas argued that that the public sphere emerged in Western Europe during the latter part of the eighteenth century and the early part of the nineteenth. He describes this period in rather nostalgic terms where many people came to exchange ideas through both interpersonal contacts – such as coffee houses – and through more mass media such as newspapers. The increasing emphasis on commercialism in later years, Habermas claimed, had a destructive influence on the quality of public discourse.

One thing is clear: many citizens living in Western democracies do have an unprecedented number of opportunities to freely exchange ideas and information. Whatever the charms of the coffee house and pub, true freedom must also take into account the number of people who can communicate with each other. Nevertheless, a true public sphere also requires that a significant number of individuals *want* to communicate about politics (Dahlgren, 2001). A study by Hill and Hughes (1998) for example suggest that only a small percentage of all Usenet groups are devoted to politics. The number of groups devoted to sex was, not surprisingly, far higher. To put it differently, it is hard to have a digital revolution if no one shows up.

There is another important trend that can also have an important impact on the nature of public discourse: *fragmentation*. As technology moves forward, citizens are better able to choose the kinds of information that they do and do not want to receive. Perhaps the most telling demonstration of this point is the increasing references to the idea that "narrow-casting" is replacing broadcasting. While such a development certainly has important advantages, it is likely lowers the overall sense of community among people. Citizens may find themselves increasingly divided along ethnic, religious, political, and class lines with enclaves speaking mostly among themselves. The notion of a public sphere makes little sense unless all members of a community participate in the discussion (Gandy, 2001). The process of democratic deliberation over an issue necessitates an *exchange* of ideas between different groups and institutions.

Here too however, it is far too early to make any serious predictions about the impact such a trend will have on communities. On the one hand, one may find increasingly homogeneous groups with little interest in communicating with one another. Yet at the same time people will find themselves forming new communities that are no longer limited by geography. This in turn could lead to *greater* civic engagement rather than less. Robert Putnam (1995) may be correct in his assertion that the age of television served to reduce civil engagement because people found themselves spending an increasing amount of leisure time as individuals ("bowling alone"). The effects of the Internet might run in exactly the opposite direction. The creation of virtual communities could lead to an increasing level of "social capital" as citizens create new groups and institutions.

The new era in political communication is also marked by an increasing amount of globalization in the flow of political information. The first adjustments in this area had to do with the creation of international news media that made a concerted effort to attract a global audience. This was a far-reaching change for it provided political actors with an unprecedented opportunity to promote themselves and their positions to internationally. The advent of the Internet added a new dimension in the area of globalization. One important ramification was that political movements were in a much better position for mobilizing members from different countries and coordinating their international activities. Ironically, the anti-globalization movement may be one of the chief beneficiaries of this change.

One of the most important questions is whether the global reach of the Internet will increase international awareness or diminish national loyalties. As with the example of the videophone, one cannot really answer that question without thinking about whether there is a sizeable market for information about the world. As pointed out by Sparks (2001) the proportion of people who tune into the international news media is minuscule. Thus, while people may become more aware of what is happening all around the world, they will always be more interested in what is happening not just nationally, but locally, in their immediate community. Perhaps the term "glocalization" best captures these contradictory influences.

It can be said then that while we have a rough idea about the major differences between the old communication technology and the new, we have much less understanding about the impact such changes will have on politics. One important reason for this gap is that comprehending social and political behavior is a far more daunting challenge. Hopefully, the articles in this work should provide some direction for those efforts.

This volume

This volume attempts to provide readers with a cross-national perspective concerning where political communication is heading in the new era. It is imperative that researchers look beyond their national borders in order to understand the whole picture. Changes in political communication are taking place throughout the world and only a comparative approach allows us to understand the similarities and differences in these processes.

The scholars that have contributed to this effort come from six different countries: Canada, France, Germany, Israel, Italy, and the US. A five-day workshop was convened in Quebec City in 1999 within the framework of the Research Committee in Political Communication of the International Political Science Association (IPSA). The goal of that workshop was to provide an overview of the field on the eve of the third millennium. The final products of those efforts are presented here.

The book is divided into two major sections. Part 1 looks at transformations in the ways information is gathered and disseminated and the impact of such changes on political communication. In the first chapter David L. Swanson tries to understand the effects of a changing technological environment for journalists on the construction of political news. His work provides an important reminder that the new technology may have some of its most profound effects on the traditional press. Swanson argues that while the growth of on-line news threatens traditional news providers in numerous ways it also offers journalists new opportunities to improve their craft.

Gianpietro Mazzoleni looks at a related question by examining how the "digital revolution" is likely to affect the production of *television news*. Without buying the enthusiasts' visions nor the apocalyptics' skepticism, he argues that there will be significant changes affecting the three main actors involved: the medium itself, the politicians, and the citizenry. Mazzoleni deals directly with the issue of fragmentation and its possible effects on citizens' political involvement. While there are some inherent dangers, he sees no reason to assume that it will increase political disengagement among citizens.

The third piece is written by Thierry Vedel and tries to suggest some possible directions for policies to deal with "digital democracies" in Europe and the US. In order to open the way to a digital democracy, he claims public action is necessary. Only such action can insure that new forms of political communication will adopt the core values associated with democracy. This too is a significant point for researchers to bear in mind. It is just as important to think about how politics can influence the new media as it is to consider the more typical question about the impact of the new media on politics. Just as the political process is transformed when it passes through technological filters, technology is transformed when it is adapted to meet political needs.

The final two chapters in Part 1 deal with the flow of political information from the citizens' vantage point. Gerald M. Kosicki provides an update on what we know about the perennial question concerning the influence of the mass media on public opinion. Among other findings, the author finds that recent studies linking media to opinion have been reinvigorated through the perspective of framing analysis, and this trend is likely continue far into the future. Guy Lachapelle deals with the oldest form of political communication: people talking to one another about politics. Lachapelle grapples with the important question about whether or not we need to change some of our assumptions about "personal influence" in this new era.

Part 2 of this book attacks the issue by examining changes in the uses of political communication, especially by political leaders. Christina Holtz-Bacha provides an important review of European and American research on political advertising during election campaigns. She demonstrates how claims about the "Americanization" of political campaigns in Europe fail to take into account important cultural differences in the way political campaigns are conducted in those environments.

The next four chapters all deal with relatively new issues in the field of political communication. The emergence of these topics can be traced to important changes in the ways in which governments and other institutions deal with modern media. Michael Kunczik shows how many countries invest considerable resources in an attempt to bolster their international image. As he points out, public diplomacy has become an essential element in foreign policy. Gadi Wolfsfeld deals with a related question having to do with the role of the news media in conflict and peace. This struggle over the news media has become an increasingly important part of the political process. He attempts to explain some of the rules that dictate how national and international antagonists compete over the media.

The chapter by Philippe J. Maarek discusses another way in which government communication has changed. Local and national authorities have placed an increasing emphasis on new technologies in their efforts to provide citizens better access to a wealth of official information. Finally, Sabine Lang looks more directly at research concerning local political communication. She tries to understand the extent to which technological developments are likely encourage increasing amounts of political participation.

There are two major themes from these chapters that stand out from the rest. The first is that the rising level of professionalization is one of the most profound changes in political communication. As noted, the increasing use of such professionals constitutes both threats and opportunities for modern democracies. The most interesting question is whether researchers in the future will be in a better position to determine which of these prospects carries more social and political weight.

The second major theme that unites these chapters is a fierce opposition to any form of technological determinism. It makes little sense to ask only about the effects of the new technology on political communication. A better question would be to ask: "Who is using the new communication technology in what ways, within what social and political context and with what effects?" Although this represents a much more complicated question, it is also a more realistic one. Leaders, citizens, groups, and institutions are the ones who will ultimately determine not only how to exploit the new channels but also how to react to them.

References

Blumler, J. G. and D. Kavanaugh (1999). The third age of political communication: influences and features. *Political Communication*, 31, 741–761.

Brants, K. (1998). Who's afraid of infotainment? *European Journal of Communication*, 13, 315–338.

Dahlgren, P. (2001). The public sphere and the net: structure, space, and communication. In W. L. Bennett and R. M. Entman (eds), *Mediated politics: communication and the future of democracy*. New York: Cambridge University Press.

Delli Carpini, M. and Williams, B. (2000). Let us entertain you: politics in the new media environment. In W. L. Bennett and R. M. Entman (eds), *Mediated politics: communication in the future of democracy*. New York: Cambridge University Press.

Gandy, O. H. (2001). Dividing practices: segmentation and targeting in the emerging public sphere. In W. L. Bennett and R. M. Entman (eds), *Mediated politics: communication in the future of democracy*. New York: Cambridge University Press.

Graber, D. (1994). The infotainment quotient in routine television-news – a director's perspective. *Discourse and Society*, 483–508.

Habermas, J. (1989). *The structural transformation of the public sphere*. Cambridge, MA: Polity Press.

Hill, K. A. and Hughes, J. E. (1998). *Cyberpolitics: citizen activism in the age of the internet*. Lanham, MD: Rowman & Littlefield.

Newton, K. (1999). Mass media effects: mobilization or media malaise? *British Journal of Political Science*, 29, 577–599.

Owen, D. (2000). Popular politics and the Clinton/Lewinsky affair: the implications for leadership. *Political Psychology*, 21, 161–177.

Putnam, R. D. (1995). Bowling alone: America's declining social capital. *Journal of Democracy*, 6, 65–78.

Sparks, C. (2001). The internet and the global public sphere. In W. L. Bennett and R. M. Entman (eds), *Mediated politics: communication in the future of democracy*. New York: Cambridge University Press.

Part 1

GATHERING AND DISSEMINATING POLITICAL INFORMATION IN THE NEW ERA

1

POLITICAL NEWS IN THE CHANGING ENVIRONMENT OF POLITICAL JOURNALISM

David L. Swanson

For at least the last half-century, scholars have understood that news in its modern forms, cloaked in authority and claims to privileged status, is a construction – can interpretive representation be produced in each instance, within a particular matrix of historical circumstances, cultural traditions, institutional imperatives and relationships, and professional practices? This fundamental quality of news has been described in various ways by writers from Schramm (1949) to Schudson (1995). The processes by which news is constructed were revealed in the 1970s in a series of famous studies (e.g. Altheide, 1976; Epstein, 1973; Fishman, 1980; Gans, 1979; Roscho, 1975; Tuchman, 1978), and they continue to be explored in more recent work (e.g. Hachten, 1998; Kaniss, 1991; Manoff & Schudson, 1986; Schudson, 1995).

Ever since Walter Lippmann (1922) explained the critical importance of news to twentieth-century citizens perceptions of the political world more than seventy years ago, the nature and consequences of news about politics have been a special focus of study and concern. A generation of scholars, in tandem with some of journalism's more reflective practitioners, has gauged the quality and growing influence of political journalism.[1] Their work has affirmed the power of journalism in modern politics but often found its quality inadequate to the needs of democratic citizenship (to cite but a few examples, Bennett, 1996; Entman, 1989; Fallows, 1997).

Explanations for the failure of news to fulfill its presumed civic role usually have cited various typical features of the content of news stories about political subjects, features which, in turn, reveal much about both the process and product of constructing political news. Well-known examples of such analyses include, in the US, Patterson's (1993) study of the corrosive effects of increasingly negative political journalism, and Cappella and Jamieson's (1997) argument that political journalism which is cynical about politics and politicians fosters the same cynicism in the public. In Europe, we have, for example, Dahlgren's (1995) discussion of how the political economy of television limits the medium's possibilities for contributing to the public sphere, and in the UK, Negrine's (1996) demonstration of how some of political reporting's civic shortcomings reflect the institutional structures and requirements of modern mass media. When researchers have looked beyond the content of news to its reception by audiences, however, they often have produced more optimistic assessments, such as constructionist arguments for the ability of citizens to find meaning and relevance in political journalism despite its shortcomings and self-absorbed priorities (e.g. Neuman *et al.*, 1992), following on the heels of earlier demonstrations of the public's capacity to turn the information tide to their own needs and uses (e.g. Graber, 1984c).

As the foregoing indicates, we have a considerable research literature concerning the construction of political news, and we know a lot about the subject. However, we have entered a period of sweeping, perhaps even fundamental changes that are remaking the environment of political journalism. Understanding these changes and their consequences for the nature, role, construction, and civic effects of political news is the great challenge that now faces researchers. This essay offers some observations and suggestions that, it is hoped, might help to guide our efforts along paths that are especially interesting and important.

The changing environment of political journalism

In an important essay, Blumler and Kavanagh (1999) proposed that political communication has entered a third age. To greatly simplify their detailed analysis: they suggest that, in the post-World War II period, politicians used their ready access to the media to offer substantive messages that had little effect on voters who were guided in most instances by enduring party loyalties. Beginning in the 1960s, political communication became potentially more determinative of voting choices as party loyalty declined, but the content of political communication became less substantive as marketing models and strategies began to be employed to win the temporary support of newly volatile electorates. The still-emerging third age, suggest Blumler and Kavanagh, is "more complex than its predecessors, molded more by conflicting cross currents than by a dominant tendency" (1999, p. 213). Among the features of the current age are proliferation of both traditional and new communication media outlets, an abundance of news sources and forms, 24-hour news services and cycles, intensified professionalization of political communication, increased competitive pressures on the media, popularization of political journalism and discourse, diversification and fragmentation of media, and an enhanced ability of citizens to include messages about politics in their media diet in the forms, at the times, and to the extent they prefer.

12

Most of the elements of Blumler and Kavanagh's synoptic diagnosis of the current scene have been noted by others and documented at length. For purposes of this essay, Blumler and Kavanagh's particular contribution is their integration of these diverse elements within an overarching framework that reveals more comprehensively the upheaval going on in the environment and generative institutions that produce political news, and the uncertain futures these institutions face. Upheaval and uncertainty have led to a widespread sense of anxiety, if not of crisis. It was this sense that led BBC News (1998) to undertake a "fundamental review of its networked journalism" in 1998, noting "it is clear we are entering a period of hyper-competition where increased availability of distribution and falling production costs are leading to an explosion of competing news providers" (p. 2). The pattern in the UK of declining audiences (on a per capita basis) for traditional mainstream journalism – television news and newspapers – with market share moving over time from newspapers to television, and from former monopoly television services to their new competitors has been repeated to differing degrees in most post-industrial countries (Modoux, 1997). Further compounding the worries of traditional news media is concern about the news media's declining credibility with a public that increasingly is cynical toward institutions of all kinds and blames the media for many defects seen in governments that seem less effective and able to solve problems of general concern (Cappella & Jamieson, 1997; Dogan, 1997; Giddens, 1999; Goldfarb, 1991; Norris, 1999; Patterson, 1993).[2]

To scholars who are interested in the construction of political news, the changing environment of political journalism is of great significance because it may alter the forces which shape the construction of political reporting, and thereby alter the nature of the reporting itself. As discussed in the next section of this essay, the traditional analytical strategy for investigating processes of news construction is designed to explore just this relationship.

From institutional context to news content: an analytical strategy

Over the years, most studies of the construction of political news, and most of the best studies of the subject, have attempted to relate features of news construction to its wider context. The model of an analytical strategy for doing so was in place by 1950 and clearly displayed in Berelson and Janowitz's influential volume, *Reader in public opinion and communication* (1953). In that anthology, the treatment of the role of communication media in the formation of public opinion considered, in turn, the institutional organization and management of mass media (where important research topics would include the "relationship between control structure and communication content," p. 191), the media relation to government (that is, "government as a party to the mass communication process," p. 233), and the content of mass media. Institutional features of the wider environment of journalism were considered to be important primarily because of the way they affected the construction of political news, and close examination of the content of the news was the ultimate evidence of the effect of journalism's environment. Today the changing environment of political news, although quite different from the more or less stable patterns of some earlier decades, does not require a new analytical research strategy. The strategy that has served us well in the past will continue to point us in at least a general way toward the essential questions that now confront us.

The new context of media institutions

Three developments in the nature and operating environment of media institutions may shape the construction of political journalism along new lines that already are beginning to be apparent: intensified competition among proliferating traditional media, increasing commercialization of media, and the rapid growth of so-called cybermedia.

Intensified competition among traditional media

The world of news is becoming more competitive everywhere, placing greater pressure on news providers to find strategies that will insure their future success. This development continues a trend that has been evident for a long time but has become much more intense in recent years. In 1948, Raymond Nixon observed that a decline in the number of newspapers in the US and "a tendency toward concentration of ownership has been manifesting itself since the 1890s" (p. 43). Newspaper readership in the US has declined steadily since the 1960s (Baum & Kernell, 1999). The competitive pressure resulting from concentration of newspaper ownership and the declining numbers and readership of newspapers has been noted in many countries, and it has been mirrored in the television industry by increased competition caused by the rapid proliferation of terrestrial, cable, and satellite broadcasters. Between 1980 and 1997 in Western Europe, for example, the number of terrestrial public television channels increased from thirty-six to forty-six while the number of commercial channels grew from three to fifty-nine (McQuail & Siune, 1998). At the same time there has been steady growth in the availability of, and audiences for, television channels delivered by cable and by satellite broadcasting received directly or via cable. In the late-1990s there existed in Europe sixty-two separate French-speaking thematic satellite television channels (Guyot, 1998). In India, the number of television channels grew from one state-controlled terrestrial channel in 1991 to nearly seventy – mostly satellite and cable-delivered – channels in 1998 (Thussu, 1999). In Taiwan, cable television was legalized in 1993 and, by 1996, attracted 70 percent of households (Lo et al., 1998). In the US,

68 percent of households now subscribe to cable television (up from 6 percent in 1969), and they receive from cable an average of forty-five different channels. As a result of the expansion of cable, the three major US television networks (ABC, CBS, and NBC) combined viewership has declined over the same period from nearly 60 percent of households in 1969 to less than 30 percent in 1998 (Baum & Kernell, 1999).

Increasing commercialization of media

As the foregoing suggests, the rapid proliferation of traditional media has resulted from expansion of privately owned, commercial media. In Europe, this reflects a 20-year process in which public television monopolies began to be challenged by new commercial channels; it has resulted in what Mazzoleni and Schulz (1999) describe as a "rush to commercialized communication and news" (p. 257). Although public broadcasters in a number of countries remain in a strong position, it is generally true that public broadcasting nowadays is pressed increasingly to prove its claims to continued support amidst proliferating viewing alternatives that may undermine both the public broadcasters audience and the distinctiveness of some of their traditional programming fare (e.g. Siune *et al.*, 1992).

The media environment has been made even more competitive by the growth of conglomerates which control large numbers of print and broadcast media organizations within vertically integrated, often multinational structures of communication media and other activities (see Alger, 1998; Murdock, 1990; Smith, 1991). This change in patterns of media ownership through mergers and acquisitions has intensified further the pressure on news media to compete for audiences and profitability in a market in which it is increasingly difficult to do so, and consequently is changing in some respects the character and content of news (e.g. Hvitfelt, 1994; McManus, 1994; Pfetsch, 1996; Rosenblum, 1993; Underwood, 1995).

The most general description of the changes in the construction of political news brought about by intensified competition and commercialization of the media sphere concerns a growing infusion of entertainment values into editorial decisions and political reporting, covering politics "only in the ways, and to the extent, that it is good business to do" in order to attract and hold a profitable audience share (Swanson, 1997, p. 1269). These entertainment values include the often-noted practices of covering policy disputes and elections with horse race or game schemas which focus on conflict, drama, and heightened suspense over outcomes rather than the substantive issues involved (e.g. Cappella & Jamieson, 1997; Patterson, 1993).

On some analyses, the desire to attract audiences to news occasionally has led to tabloidization (e.g. Bird, 1998): focus on "personal narratives about individuals," "increasing predominance of the visual image over analysis and rational description," and "the growing use of dramatic techniques" (p. 36).

"More and more," notes Sparks (1992) in one of the most strongly worded descriptions of this phenomenon, "the tabloidised US media offer stories whose aim is simply to engage our emotions, with no other purpose in mind" (p. 40). The personalization that is a particular hallmark of tabloidization has been noted especially, and often critiqued, as a widespread convention of contemporary political news.

In the US, tabloidization has been noted not only in the steadily increasing number of non-traditional forms of news such as numerous political television talk shows, talk radio, and TV news magazine shows but also in traditional forms of serious or quality news. Elsewhere, practice of a more entertainment-focused, sensational style of journalism has been attributed to commercial pressures in India (Thussu, 1999) and noted as a trend in various countries in Europe and other regions (Mazzoleni & Schulz, 1999). One of the most extensive recent analyses of the phenomenon is that of Franklin (1997), who introduces his detailed examination of the rise of "Newszak" in Britain in this way:

> Since the late 1980s, the pressures on news media to win viewers and readers in an increasingly competitive market have generated revised editorial ambitions. News media have increasingly become part of the entertainment industry instead of providing a forum for informed debate of key issues of public concern.
>
> (p. 4)

Franklin finds these developments to be general across all news media, albeit to different degrees: tabloid newspapers and quality broadsheets, the BBC as well as the satellite channels.

The mingling of traditional news conventions and entertainment values sometimes is described as infotainment (Brants et al., 1998; Graber, 1990, 1994). In a poll of 552 US news executives, editors, producers, and reporters conducted in late 1998 and early 1999, two-thirds of respondents said that pressure to attract audiences is pushing their industry too far in the direction of infotainment, blurring the line between entertainment and news, that the most important problem facing journalism today is its lack of credibility, and that the chief cause of declining standards is growing business and financial pressures (Pew Research Center, 1999). In a recent study of hybrid infotainment elements in a range of Dutch television genres from news programs to talk shows, entertainment shows, and variety programs, Brants and Neijens (1998) confirmed Franklin's claim that the infotainment elements exist in serious news programs as well as in other program genres. In a review of research conducted in a number of European countries, however, Brants (1998) found mixed evidence concerning the spread of particular infotainment elements in news formats, and he defends the value of "narratives centered around individual [political] characters"

16

in "a society where ideologies disappear and differences between political parties become less important and visible" (p. 332).

Concern about the mingling of journalism and entertainment is hardly new. Indeed, the need to strike just the right balance between the two is the special challenge that arose with the creation of mass news media in the nineteenth century. In each generation, concerns have been voiced about the two goals not being properly balanced. In 1925, one of the pioneers of the systematic study of journalism and mass communication, Chicago sociologist Robert Park, worried that "'news story' and 'fiction story' are two forms of modern literature that are now sometimes so like one another that it is difficult to distinguish them. *The Saturday Evening Post*, for example, writes the news in the form of fiction, while the daily press frequently writes fiction in the form of news" (Park, 1925/1947, p. 17). However, today's media environment and its possible consequences for political journalism seem to raise this traditional concern with particular urgency.

The preceding makes it clear that researchers in several countries who are interested in the construction of political news have been attempting to determine in what ways and to what extent the increasingly competitive and commercial media environment is affecting the construction of political news by traditional print and broadcast media. As the trends in the media environment we have noted continue, we might expect to find stronger and more consistent manifestations of the influence of competition on news than have been seen thus far. Comparative research on the performance of news providers in different sorts of national media systems can be especially illuminating about these issues and is badly needed. Building on the contributions of Brants and others, such work can take us closer to answering a whole range of interesting and important questions: to what extent are the effects on political news of increasing media competition and commercialization mediated by a strong tradition of public broadcasting? Can we calibrate the degree of effect on news to the degree of competition and commercialization in a country media system? What other factors disrupt the general relationship between news practices and competitive pressures? Across countries, we need to know if new manifestations of competition will emerge in the content of news as competition continues to intensify. Will news aimed at the mass market continue to lose some of its distinctiveness, while serious news becomes marginalized as just another special-interest offering for a small taste culture, equivalent to The Food Channel and The Travel Channel in the US? And, will public service norms assert themselves more forcefully to distinguish public service broadcasters, or will the presumed differences between private and public news providers fail to hold over the long run in an era of fierce media competition? Our best research suggests contradictory answers to such questions.[3] The issues involved are central to the nature of political news, and they deserve our attention.

17

Cybermedia

Political communication researchers have been intensely interested in the possibilities created by the explosive growth of computer-based communications media. Access to and use of these media is expanding at an exponential rate, but not a uniform one: more in technologically advanced and affluent societies than in less advanced societies of more modest means; within each country, more among educated and higher income groups; more in the North than the South; more in the West than the East. But in time, continued expansion and diffusion bid to make these media ubiquitous (although inequalities in access between different social strata seem likely to remain, if in diminished magnitude), and we are yet in the infancy of their development.

Because of their already evident possibilities for interactive communication, information gathering, opinion sharing and registering, persuasion, and mobilizing like-minded citizens across great distances with few resources, the new media have been described as opening opportunities for fundamental changes in political life (e.g. Friedland, 1996; Groper, 1996; Hacker, 1996). At the same time, many of those who focus less on the theoretical possibilities of new media and more on their actual performance to date envision a future not of revolutionary change but rather of change within a framework of continuity with the present (e.g. Barnett, 1997; Davis, 1999; Hill & Hughes, 1998).

The issues raised by new media are much wider and more complex than what will be the future of news or even of traditional forms and institutions of democratic representation, of course.[4] Some of these issues have been described by Carey (1998) in an article entitled The Internet and the End of the National Communication System:

> The Internet is at the center of the integration of a new media ecology which transforms the structural relations among older media such [as] print and broadcast and integrates them to a new center around the defining technologies of computer and satellite. ... This new media ecology develops in relation to new physical ecology among peoples represented by world-wide migrations over national borders, the formation of diasporic groups and by what we might call the diaspora of the Internet itself wherein new social groupings are formed and organized. In turn, and at the cultural level, there is a struggle over new patterns and forms of identity, new representations of nations and transnational associations, and the eruption of "identity politics." The end point of all these changes is quite uncertain.
>
> (p. 34)

Certainly the possibility of profound changes across the next generation enabled by new communications technologies in concert with social, cultural, economic, and political forces is real. At the moment, however, those possibilities can be envisioned but dimly, and we are concerned here with the more mundane question of the effects of the new technologies on the construction of political news. Still, it is useful to recognize that this question is implicated in much larger issues and that our experience is too brief to allow us more than hesitant, temporary answers and speculations about the future. Our experience is, however, long enough and diverse enough to suggest some of the key questions that deserve a place on the research agenda.

Some of these questions concern the effects of new technologies on traditional print and broadcast media as we have known them. The number of newspapers published on the Internet around the world reached nearly 5,000 in 1998. More than 2,000 newspapers were publishing on the Internet in the US in 1997, of which 492 were general-circulation newspapers offering a full range of news that updated their content at least every day (Meyer, 1999). Yet as Sparks (1996) has pointed out, the business model on which newspapers depend is threatened by Internet newspapers, which are unlikely to produce subscription revenue and in principle are no longer essential to advertisers who can transmit their messages directly to consumers. Mainstream television news organizations have been even more active than newspapers in creating their own on-line news services. Although they do not face the newspapers' threat of loss of subscription revenue, they share with newspapers the disastrous consequences that would result from advertisers' migration to direct communication with consumers via the Internet. To this point, most studies have shown that, across all age groups, those who use the Internet for news are deeply interested in current affairs and also follow newspapers and television news (Davis & Owen, 1998; Pew Research Center, 1998). However, research also indicates that those who are most comfortable with Internet technology are young people of 18–25 who watch television less than their older counterparts and among successive cohorts of whom newspaper reading has declined dramatically across the last twenty years (Davis, 1999).

Also worrisome to the future of mainstream media is the success that alternative providers have enjoyed in offering on-line news services to compete with those of traditional newspapers and television news organizations. The sensation caused by the on-line Drudge Report breaking the Monica Lewinsky–Bill Clinton story and the circulation given far-fetched conspiracy theories, and other allegations by on-line "information" services have been causes of concern. The presence of partisan advocates, amateur journalists, and crackpots of all kinds on the Internet may hardly seem to challenge traditional news sources, but it does resonate with a spirit of populism in the most populist medium yet devised. Some have praised this very development as offering, at least in principle, a new form of civic participation (e.g. Bucy *et al.*, 1999), and perhaps creating the conditions for greater diversity in the viewpoints and information offered to the public.

In addition, the easy access of users anywhere to newspapers and other media published everywhere widens the field of competitors to include hundreds of mainstream news providers that before could be read or viewed by citizens in any given location not at all or only through great trouble and expense. Thus, the level of competition faced by news providers in the on-line world is greater by orders of magnitude than is produced by the simple proliferation of traditional media outlets discussed earlier.

Given the rush of traditional news media to the Internet, where they face new competitors and the possibility of long-term threats to their business model, it is important to ask how the construction of political (and other) news may change in the new technological environment. Davis (1999) has pointed out some of the reasons why we might expect change to occur. In the world of the 24-hour news cycle created by all-news channels, migration to the Internet increases further the already high premium on speed in reporting. Those who complain that the 24-hour news cycle led to a decline in journalistic standards resulting from loss of time for editorial judgment, corroborating facts, and the like may point with even greater concern to instances of respected media publishing stories on-line that later had to be retracted when found to be false. To what extent might the erosion of traditional news standards already evident as a consequence of intensified media competition be exacerbated in the intense, expanded competition of the on-line world? Davis (1999) argues against worry about the standards of journalism and future of journalism institutions, but we have little data on the question, and the question is important.

There are also reasons to expect that some of the traditional effects of news may be eroded in the on-line world, perhaps to be replaced by others. As examination of the most sophisticated news sites on the Internet shows, advanced news sites present menus that allow readers to go directly to individual stories of interest with one click of the mouse. This feature is thought to be part of the unique appeal of on-line news services. Yet the reverse of this coin is that, except for one or two top stories given photographs or other displays on the home page, the news provider has given up some tools that have been important to sustaining the well-known agenda-setting function of the press. As more than two decades of research have shown, a key to journalistic agenda-setting is the differential prominence given to various stories, as signaled by space or length, placement, and use of video or photographs. On sophisticated news sites, many stories are equally prominent. The user's ability at the end of every story to click on additional information and visit other relevant sites provides access to a wealth of material, but it does little to convey editorial judgment about the relative importance of topics covered in the news. Some of the scant research that is available on this question suggests that on-line newspaper readers in fact read fewer stories, and notice fewer of the heavily emphasized stories, than do readers of paper versions of the same newspapers (Tewksbury & Althaus, 1999). The agenda-setting effect may rank as our most secure generalization about journalism's effects, but on their face, the tools available for constructing political news for on-line distribution would seem to undercut editors' ability to shape the priorities of their audiences. Here, too, is an important question we need to study.

Not all of the effects of the new technologies are corrosive to journalistic standards or disempowering to news media. The Internet provides reporters ready access to unprecedented quantities of information that could not have been imagined only a few years ago, along with new and easy means of communicating with sources. Some of the benefits of this technology to the newsgathering process already have shown themselves to be substantial (e.g. DeFleur, 1997; Garrison, 1998) and also to pose some dangers such as granting credibility to false or incomplete information or creating unreliable on-line opinion polls (e.g. Borden & Harvey, 1997; Wu & Weaver, 1997). The Internet is regarded as a leading information source in 92 percent of US newsrooms, and its routine use by journalists is spreading at differential rates in every country (e.g. Gómez Fernández, 1997). In spring, 1999, both *The Miami Herald* and the *Washington Post* earned Pulitzer prizes for reporting that depended heavily on computer-assisted data analysis (Boyer, 1999). As these examples suggest, the construction of news may well improve as a result of new technology.

Moreover, the Internet allows reporters the possibility of greatly increased interaction with the public that is fully in the spirit of, and can carry to new levels, efforts to implement the philosophy of public or civic journalism.

At this point, then, it appears that new communications technology presents both concerns and opportunities for journalism, and these possibilities may shape the construction of political news in various ways. However, our enthusiasm, curiosity, and concern for the possibilities outstrip our research efforts to date. This is obviously an important research challenge for the future.

Changing relationships between politicians and the media

The practice of political journalism is shaped profoundly by the relationship between political journalists and politicians. A lot of excellent work across the last two decades, especially, has illuminated this relationship. The general findings emerging from this work are well known and can be summarized briefly.

Across most democracies and for various reasons that have been well documented, the relationship between political parties and voters has become less one of identity and long-term mutual commitment and more a relationship of persuasion in which fickle consumers with rapidly changing tastes and little brand loyalty are induced to buy a product at the point of purchase. In order to win voters momentary support in elections and to maintain public support when in government, politicians have adopted marketing strategies focused heavily on the sophisticated use of communications (see, for example, Bennett, 1992; Kavanagh, 1995; Mayhew, 1997; Newman, 1994; Swanson & Mancini, 1996). This general trend, which is seen to different degrees in different countries and political systems, makes access to mass communications and frequent and favorable news coverage essential for political success, creating what Blumler (1990) described as "the modern publicity process." Professional experts in media use, marketing, fund-raising, and opinion polling have come to play important roles in the constantly intensified efforts of parties and government officials and agencies to manipulate news media to their partisan advantage (see, for example, Asp & Esaiasson, 1996; Blumler & Kavanagh, 1999; Caspi, 1996; Cook, 1998; Franklin, 1994; Kurtz, 1998; Mancini, 1999; Scammell, 1995).

Political operatives' increasingly sophisticated efforts to manipulate the choices of editors and reporters often have spurred journalists to resist manipulation more strongly and demonstrate their independence, changing the traditional relationship of politicians and the press in many democracies from "cooperative competition" (Blumler & Gurevitch, 1981) to a more adversarial struggle. As a senior political columnist noted recently in the UK, for example, "having come to power by news management, New Labour has created a breed of journalism heavily dominated by its desire not to be managed" (Young, 1999, p. 18). In the US, Zaller (1997) has suggested a Rule of Product Substitution, which holds that the more journalists are challenged for control of news, the more they will resist by developing types of information to substitute for what politicians provide them and affirm journalists control of the news. Equivalent rules have been noted in other countries as well (e.g. Blumler & Kavanagh, 1999; Mancini, 1999).

In countries where journalists' struggle to demonstrate their independence from manipulation is particularly strong and has been documented most fully, important changes in the construction of political news have been observed. A host of studies in the US and elsewhere has found that political news has become more negative toward politics and politicians (e.g. Cappella & Jamieson, 1997; Fallows, 1997; Kepplinger, 1998; Mazzoleni & Schulz, 1999; Patterson, 1993). This tendency is manifest in a number of ways, including journalists use of disdaining commentary in news reports to deflate politicians statements and activities (Semetko *et al.*, 1991), the closely related use by journalists of game or strategy frameworks to interpret politicians statements and actions (e.g. Cappella & Jamieson, 1993), and, intense and melodramatic news coverage of political scandals (e.g. Sabato, 1991).

Journalistic independence is demonstrated also in the increasingly prominent role journalists and their interpretations of events occupy in their own news stories, and the correspondingly reduced opportunities given to politicians to express themselves in their own words. This tendency has been seen in a series of studies of diminishing sound bites of politicians in news stories over the years (e.g. Hallin, 1992; Kurtz, 1996; Lowry & Shidler, 1995) and the increasing amount of attention devoted to the reporters themselves and their interpretations of the events they are reporting in both print and broadcast news (e.g. Barnhurst & Steele, 1997; Patterson, 1993; Steele & Barnhurst, 1996; Westerstähl & Johansson, 1986).

Another expression of journalists desire for autonomy is growing efforts of news organizations to actively shape the agenda of issues. These efforts, combined with the shrinking time and attention given to politicians in political news, result in a growing divergence between the agendas of politicians and the agendas stressed in political news. Studies of the last British campaign, for example, found that only 17 percent of campaign news was devoted to what the politicians were saying, and that correlations between the substantive campaign agendas of the press and the politicians continued to decline from the levels of the 1980s campaigns (Blumler & Kavanagh, 1999; Harrison, 1997; Norris *et al.*, 1999). The British findings are consistent with more general observations that "a number of news media organizations try to compete with the political parties and political actors for public consent and legitimation in the same political arena" (Mazzoleni & Schulz, 1999, p. 257; see also Mancini & Swanson, 1996). Whether one regards the move of journalists to the forefront of their own stories as a negative backlash to politicians' efforts to manipulate the press or as a constructive effort to serve the public by not deferring to politicians' judgments, the effect of interest here is the same: politicians' voices are diminished in the media.

Some of the ways in which the changing relationship between politicians and the media appears to be changing the construction of political news are: more negative coverage of politics; more frequent resort to interpretive frameworks that discount the substantive content of politicians' statements and actions; more engagement in interpretive reporting, giving more prominence to journalists themselves, and advancing independent agendas. These phenomena vary substantially between countries and between different kinds of media systems and political systems, of course, but researchers have found manifestations of them in most of the western democracies.

These phenomena are consequential. On balance, they are thought by many to be corrosive to the quality of politics as politicians increasingly adapt their actions and statements to the superficial and suspicious reporting frames of political news. They are also thought by many to undermine public support for the political system by depicting it in judgmental, skeptical, and negative terms.

The challenge for the future is to understand where the continuously evolving dynamic linking political news to politicians will lead and how it will continue to shape the construction of political news. Over time, will differences between countries, political systems, and media systems in this dynamic and its consequences for news widen or narrow, reflecting developmental changes in media systems and political practices? Will the dynamic become less central to the practice of politics as mainstream political news loses its monopoly position as an information source to non-traditional news forms, sources, and media? Concerned about its diminished credibility and its indictment by many members of the public as responsible for many of the defects of government, will political news seek a more constructive independent path, as suggested by proposed reforms such as civic journalism and by the BBC coverage of the last British election, or will it retreat further from political coverage, as US media did during the last American presidential campaign? Or will political journalism perhaps try to recoup its audience and power by going even farther down present paths, producing an even more entertaining, dramatic, and sensational product for the mass market?

An especially interesting question concerns the parallel developments noted in several countries of citizens becoming disenchanted with politics but steadfastly supportive of democratic processes, and engaging increasingly in forms of political activity outside the formal structures and traditional frameworks of politics (e.g. Bennett, 1998; Giddens, 1999). Recognition of these parallel developments came to the fore in the research and exchanges stimulated by the Putnam civic engagement thesis (Putnam, 1993, 1995a, 1995b; see also Brehm & Rahn, 1997; Levi, 1996; Mondak & Mutz, 1997; Norris, 1996). Some interpret the upsurge of activity and volunteerism as a reflection of the irrelevance of traditional politics to issues that most concern citizens, and regard these developments as signaling the rise of a new form of political expression, a kind of politics without politics. A useful question for those who study the construction of political news concerns whether news will continue to hew to (some might say, enforce) a traditional, formal definition of politics, or whether political news will broaden its horizons to devote attention to new, non-institutional forms of political expression. The choice will have significant consequences for how the public understands politics, for the relevance of the political system in the future, and perhaps for the relevance of political news to its consumers.

Conclusion

The very important topic that is missing from this essay is, of course, study of the effects of news content on the consumers of news, which was the third element of Berelson and Janowitz's research strategy. The rationale for most studies of political news rests in part, directly or indirectly, on assumptions about the relationship between news content and news consumers' beliefs, sentiments, and behavior. By most accounts, but not all, qualities of political news have little significance if they do not shape the public's perceptions. There is a large, complex, multidisciplinary research literature concerned with news effects, but it is beyond the scope of this essay. For most students of political communication most of the time, questions about how political news is constructed and why it is as it as have led to examination of the relationship between the content and generative context of news.

Beyond the particular questions for future research this essay has raised, a broader and more fundamental question forms our subtext. It is the same question that is raised today in one form or another in most if not all subfields of political communication: will this century's forms of democratic political institutions, processes, and practices survive the future? The most interesting and pressing question about political news is a more narrowly drawn form of that question: will political news endure in a form we can recognize, with its functions for the public and for political actors more or less intact, and its defining qualities preserved? If not, what will be the consequences?

In the late twentieth century, our very conception of democracy was inextricably intertwined with our understanding of modern communications and news as an institution. A future of continuing rapid and probably fundamental change to news and its contexts seems certain. Moreover, contextual developments we have reviewed suggest the possibility, but by no means the probability, of change that is genuinely revolutionary. Understanding this change and its consequences is the challenging agenda of studies of political journalism.

Notes

1 Some representative works charting the influence of media in chiefly print and, later, television journalism in politics over the decades are: Berelson & Janowitz 1953; Blumler & McQuail, 1969, Graber, 1984a, 1984b; Graber et al., 1998; Iyengar, 1991; Kraus & Davis, 1976; G. E. Lang & K. Lang, 1984; K. Lang & G. E. Lang, 1968.

2 The US is a glaring case in this regard. In a nationwide poll of 1,214 US adults conducted between May 21 and June 1, 1999 for the Council for Excellence in Government (3.2 percent margin of error), 64 percent of respondents reporting feeling disconnected from government, only 25 percent believed that government pursues the people agenda, and only 29 percent trusted the government in Washington to do the right thing. Much of the blame for what is wrong with the government was placed on the media (29 percent), more than either elected officals (24 percent) or political parties (24 percent), and second only to special interest groups (38 percent) (Council for Excellence in Government, 1999).

3 Semetko and Canel (1997) found private television news following more closely than its public counterpart the conventions of serious political reporting in Spain 1996 election campaign, while Scammell (1997) found that the BBC's effort to provide serious coverage of the 1997 British general election met high standards of quality but failed spectacularly to attract an audience in the media marketplace.

4 As we try to imagine what the new media portend, it is an interesting exercise to re-read Belville's essay on "The challenge of the new media" which concludes: "The new meda present us with unrivalled [sic] opportunities to overcome public ignorance and apathy concerning crucial issues of our times" (Belville, 1948, p. 141). The new media of which Belville wrote were FM radio, television, and facsimile.

References

Alger, D. (1998). *Megamedia: how giant corporations dominate mass media, distort competition, and endanger democracy.* Lanham, MD: Rowan and Littlefield.

Altheide, D. L. (1976). *Creating reality: how TV news distorts events.* Beverly Hills, CA: Sage.

Asp, K. and Esaiasson, P. (1996). The modernization of Swedish campaigns: individualization, professionalization, and medialization. In D. L. Swanson and P. Mancini (eds), *Politics, media, and modern democracy: an international study of innovations in electoral campaigning and their consequences* (pp. 73–90). Westport, CT: Praeger.

Barnett, S. (1997). New media, old problems: new technology and the political process. *European Journal of Communication,* 12, 193–218.

Barnhurst, K. G. and Steele, C. A. (1997). Image-bite news: the visual coverage of elections on US television, 1968–1992. *Harvard International Journal of Press/Politics,* 2(1), 40–58.

Baum, M. A. and Kernell, S. (1999). Has cable ended the golden age of presidential television? *American Political Science Review,* 93, 99–114.

BBC News (1998). *BBC News: the future – public service news in the digital age.* London: Author.

Belville, H. M. Jr (1948). The challenge of the new media. In W. Schramm (ed.), *Communications in modern society* (pp. 126–141). Urbana, IL: University of Illinois Press.

Bennett, W. L. (1992). *The governing crisis: media, money, and marketing in American elections.* New York: St. Martin.

Bennett, W. L. (1996). *News: the politics of illusion* (3rd edn). White Plains, NY: Longman.

Bennett, W. L. (1998). The uncivic culture: communication, identity, and the rise of lifestyle politics. *PS: Political Science and Politics,* 31, 741–761.

Berelson, B. and Janowitz, M. (eds) (1953). *Reader in public opinion and communication* (enlarged edn). Glencoe, IL: Free Press.

Bird, S. E. (1998). News we can use: an audience perspective on the tabloidisation of news in the US. *The Public,* 5(3), 33–49.

Blumler, J. G. (1990). Elections, the media and the modern publicity process. In M. Ferguson (ed.), *Public communication: the new imperatives* (pp. 101–113). London: Sage.

Blumler, J. G. and Gurevitch, M. (1981). Politicians and the press: an essay on role relationships. In D. D. Nimmo and K. R. Sanders (eds), *Handbook of political communication* (pp. 467–493). Beverly Hills, CA: Sage.

Blumler, J. G. and Kavanagh. D. (1999). The third age of political communication: influences and features. *Political Communication*, 16, 209–230.

Blumler, J. G. and McQuail, D. (1969). *Television in politics: its uses and influences.* Chicago, IL: University of Chicago Press.

Borden, D. L. and Harvey, K. (eds) (1997). *The electronic grapevine: rumor, reputation, and reporting in the new on-line environment.* Mahwah, NJ: Erlbaum.

Boyer, T. (1999, July/August). Playing catch-up. *American Journalism Review* [On-line]. Available URL: http://ajr.newslink.org/ajrboyerja99.html.

Brants, K. (1998). Who afraid of infotainment? *European Journal of Communication*, 13, 315–335.

Brants, K., Hermes, J. and Van Zoonen, L. (eds) (1998). *The media in question: popular cultures and public interests.* London: Sage.

Brants, K. and Neijens, P. (1998). The infotainment of politics. *Political Communication*, 15, 149–164.

Brehm, J. and Rahn, W. M. (1997). Individual-level evidence for the causes and consequences of social capital. *American Journal of Political Science*, 41, 999–1023.

Bucy, E. P., D'Angelo, P. and Newhagen, J. E. (1999). The engaged electorate: new media use as political participation. In L. L. Kaid and D. G. Bystrom (eds), *The electronic election: perspectives on the 1996 campaign communication* (pp. 335–347). Mahwah, NJ: Erlbaum.

Cappella, J. N. and Jamieson, K. H. (1997). *Spiral of cynicism: the press and the public good.* New York: Oxford University Press.

Carey, J. W. (1998). The Internet and the end of the national communication system: uncertain predictions of an uncertain future. *Journalism and Mass Communication Quarterly*, 75, 28 54.

Caspi, D. (1996). American-style electioneering in Israel: Americanization versus modernization. In D. L. Swanson and P. Mancini (eds), *Politics, media, and modern democracy: an international study of innovations in electoral campaigning and their consequences* (pp. 173–192). Westport, CT: Praeger.

Cook, T. F (1998). *Governing with the news: the news media as a political institution.* Chicago, IL: University of Chicago Press.

Council for Excellence in Government (1999, July 12). *America unplugged: citizens and their government – survey conducted by Hart-Teeter.* Available URL: http://www.excelgov.org/ecel/pressrelease.htm.

Dahlgren, P. (1995). *Television and the public sphere: citizenship, democracy and the media.* London: Sage.

Davis, R. (1999). *The web of politics: the Internet's impact on the American political system.* New York: Oxford University Press.

Davis, R. and Owen, D. (1998). *New media and American politics.* New York: Oxford University Press.

DeFleur, M. H. (1997). *Computer-assisted investigative reporting: development and methodology.* Mahwah, NJ: Erlbaum.

Dogan, M. (1997). Erosion of confidence in advanced democracies. *Studies in Comparative International Development*, 32(3), 3–29.

Entman, R. M. (1989). *Democracy without citizens: media and the decay of American politics*. New York: Oxford University Press.

Epstein, E. J. (1973). *News from nowhere: television and the news*. New York: Random House.

Fallows, J. (1997). *Breaking the news: how the media undermine American democracy*. New York: Vintage.

Fishman, M. (1980). *Manufacturing the news*. Austin: University of Texas Press.

Franklin, B. (1994). *Packaging politics: political communications in Britain's media democracy*. London: Arnold.

Franklin, B. (1997). *Newszak and news media*. London: Arnold.

Friedland, L. A. (1996). Electronic democracy and the new citizenship. *Media, Culture and Society*, 18, 185–212.

Gans, H. J. (1979). *Deciding what's news: a study of CBS Evening News, NBC Nightly News, Newsweek, and Time*. New York: Pantheon.

Garrison, B. (1998). *Computer-assisted reporting* (2nd edn). Mahwah, NJ: Erlbaum.

Giddens, A. (1999, May 5). *Democracy*. BBC Reith Lectures, London.

Goldfarb, J. C. (1991). *The cynical society: the culture of politics and the politics of culture in American life*. Chicago, IL: University of Chicago Press.

Gómez Fernández, P. (1997, February–March). Changes in the news service processes with the Spanish audiovisual media: difficulties and expectations facing the new technologies. Paper presented at the workshop on New Media and Political Communication, European Consortium for Political Research, Bern.

Graber, D. A. (1984a). *Mass media and American politics* (2nd edn). Washington, DC: CQ Press.

Graber, D. A. (ed.) (1984b). *Media power in politics*. Washington, DC: CQ Press.

Graber, D. A. (1984c). *Processing the news: how people turn the information tide*. New York: Longman.

Graber, D. A. (1990, June). The infotainment quotient in routine television news. Paper presented at the meeting of the International Communication Association, Dublin.

Graber, D. A. (1994). The infotainment quotient in routine television news: a director perspective. *Discourse and Society*, 5, 483–509.

Graber, D., McQuail, D. and Norris, P. (eds) (1998). *The politics of news and the news of politics*. Washington, DC: CQ Press.

Groper, R. (1996). Electronic mail and the reinvigoration of American democracy. *Social Science Computer Review*, 14, 157–168.

Guyot, J. (1998). Rethinking regional television: intercultural challenge in the face of media profusion. *The Public*, 5(2), 61–71.

Hachten, W. A. (1998). *The troubles of journalism: a critical look at what's right and wrong with the press*. Mahwah, NJ: Erlbaum.

Hacker, K. L. (1996). Missing links in the evolution of electronic democratization. *Media, Culture & Society*, 18, 213–232.

Hallin, D. C. (1992). Sound bite news: television coverage of elections, 1968–1988. *Journal of Communication*, 42(2), 5–24.

Harrison, M. (1997). Politics on the air. In D. Butler and D. Kavanagh (eds), *The British general election of 1997* (pp. 133–155). Houndmills: Macmillan.

Hill, K. A. and Hughes, J. E. (1998). *Cyberpolitics: citizen activism in the age of the internet*. Lanham, MD: Rowan and Littlefield.

Hvitfelt, H. (1994). The commercialization of the evening news: changes in narrative technique in Swedish TV news. *The Nordicom Review*, 2, 33–41.

Iyengar, S. (1991). *Is anyone responsible? How television frames political issues.* Chicago, IL: University of Chicago Press.

Kaniss, P. (1991). *Making local news.* Chicago, IL: University of Chicago Press.

Kavanagh, D. (1995). *Election campaigning: the new marketing of politics.* Oxford, UK: Blackwell.

Kepplinger, H. M. (1998). *The dismantling of politics in the information society.* Freiburg, Germany: Alber.

Kraus, S. and Davis, D. (1976). *The effects of mass communication on political behavior.* University Park, PA: Pennsylvania State University Press.

Kurtz, H. (1996, October 12). Does the evening news still matter? *TV Guide*, pp. 20–23.

Kurtz, H. (1998). *Spin cycle: inside the Clinton propaganda machine.* New York: Free Press.

Lang, G. E. and Lang, K. (1984). *Politics and television re-viewed.* Beverly Hills, CA: Sage.

Lang, K. and Lang, G. E. (1968). *Politics and television.* Chicago, IL: Quadrangle.

Levi, M. (1996). Social and unsocial capital: a review essay of Robert Putnam's *Making democracy work. Politics and Society*, 24, 45–56.

Lippmann, W. (1922). *Public opinion.* New York: Macmillan.

Lo, V., Neilan, E. and King, P. (1998). Television coverage of the 1995 legislative election in Taiwan: rise of cable television as a force for balance in media coverage. *Journal of Broadcasting and Electronic Media*, 42, 340–355.

Lowry, D. T. and Shidler, J. A. (1995). The sound bites, the biters, and the bitten: an analysis of network TV news bias in campaign 92. *Journalism and Mass Communication Quarterly*, 72, 33–44.

Mancini, P. (1999). New frontiers in political professionalism. *Political Communication*, 16, 231–245.

Mancini, P. and Swanson, D. L. (1996). Politics, media, and modern democracy: Introduction. In D. L. Swanson and P. Mancini (eds), *Politics, media, and modern democracy: an international study of innovations in electoral campaigning and their consequences* (pp. 1–28). Westport, CT: Praeger.

Manoff, R. K. and Schudson, M. (eds) (1986). *Reading the news.* New York: Pantheon.

Mayhew, L. H. (1997). *The new public: professional communication and the means of social influence.* Cambridge, UK: Cambridge University Press.

Mazzoleni, G. and Schulz, W. (1999). "Mediatization" of politics: a challenge for democracy? *Political Communication*, 16, 247–261.

McManus, J. H. (1994). *Market driven journalism.* London: Sage.

McQuail, D. and Siune, K. (eds) (1998). *Media policy: convergence, concentration and commerce.* London: Sage.

Meyer, E. K. (1999, July 20–26). An unexpectedly wider Web for the world newspapers. *American Journalism Review NewsLink* [On-line]. Available URL: http://ajr.newslink.org/emcol10.html.

Modoux, A. (1997). *World communication report: the new media and the challenge of the new technologies.* Paris: UNESCO.

Mondak, J. J. and Mutz, D. C. (1997, April). What's so great about league bowling? Paper presented at the meeting of the Midwest Political Science Association, Chicago, IL.

Murdock, G. (1990). Redrawing the map of the communications industries: concentration and ownership in the era of privatization. In M. Ferguson (ed.), *Public communication: the new imperatives – future directions for media research* (pp. 1–15). London: Sage.

Negrine, R. (1996). *The communication of politics.* London: Sage.

Neuman, W. R., Just, M. R. and Crigler, A. N. (1992). *Common knowledge: news and the construction of political meaning.* Chicago, IL: University of Chicago Press.

Newman, B. I. (1994). *The marketing of the president: political marketing as campaign strategy.* Thousand Oaks, CA: Sage.

Nixon, R. B. (1948). Implications of the decreasing numbers of competitive newspapers. In W. Schramm (ed.), *Communications in modern society* (pp. 43–55). Urbana, IL: University of Illinois Press.

Norris, P. (1996). Does television erode social capital? A reply to Putnam. *PS: Political Science and Politics*, 29, 474–480.

Norris, P. (1999). *Critical citizens.* Oxford: Oxford University Press.

Norris, P., Curtice, J., Sanders, D., Scammell, M. and Semetko. H. A. (1999). *On message: communicating the campaign.* London: Sage.

Park, R. E. (1947). The natural history of the newspaper. In W. Schramm (ed.), *Mass communications* (pp. 7–22). Urbana, IL: University of Illinois Press. (Original work published 1925).

Patterson, T. E. (1993). *Out of order.* New York: Knopf.

Pew Research Center for the People and the Press (1998). *Internet takes off* [Online]. Available URL: http://www.people-press.org/tec96sum.htm.

Pew Research Center for the People and the Press (1999). *Striking the balance: audience interests, business pressures and journalists values.* Available URL: http://www.people-press.org/press99rpt.htm.

Pfetsch, B. (1996). Convergence through privatization? Changing media environments and televised politics in Germany. *European Journal of Communication*, 11, 427–451.

Putnam, R. D. (1993). *Making democracy work: civic traditions in modern Italy.* Princeton, NJ: Princeton University Press.

Putnam, R. D. (1995a). Bowling alone: America declining social capital. *Journal of Democracy*, 6, 65–78.

Putnam, R. D. (1995b). Tuning in, tuning out: the strange disappearance of social capital in America. *PS: Political Science and Politics*, 28, 664–683.

Roscho, B. (1975). *Newsmaking.* Chicago, IL: University of Chicago Press.

Rosenblum, M. (1993). *Who stole the news?* New York: Wiley.

Sabato, L. J. (1991). *Feeding frenzy: how attack journalism has transformed American politics.* New York: Free Press.

Scammell, M. (1995). *Designer politics: how elections are won.* Basingstoke: Macmillan.

Scammell, M. (1997, August). Old values versus news values: the media in the 1997 British general election. Paper presented at the meeting of the American Political Science Association, Washington, DC.

Schramm, W. (1949). The nature of news. *Journalism Quarterly*, 26, 259–269.

Schudson, M. (1995). *The power of news.* Cambridge, MA: Harvard University Press.

Semetko, H. A., Blumler, J. G., Gurevitch, M. and Weaver, D. H. (with Barkin, S. and Wilhoit, G. C.) (1991). *The formation of campaign agendas: a comparative analysis of party and media roles in recent American and British elections.* Hillsdale, NJ: Erlbaum.

Semetko, H. A. and Canel, M. J. (1997). Agenda-senders versus agenda-setters: television in Spain 1996 election campaign. *Political Communication*, 14, 457–479.

Siune, K., McQuail, D. and Truetzschler W. (1992). From structure to dynamics. In K. Siune and W. Truetzschler (eds), *Dynamics of media politics: broadcast and electronic media in Western Europe* (pp. 1–7). London: Sage.

Sparks, C. (1992). Popular journalism: theories and practice. In P. Dahlgren and C. Sparks (eds), *Journalism and popular culture* (pp. 24–44). London: Sage.

Sparks, C. (1996). Newspapers, the Internet, and democracy. *The Public*, 3(3), 43–57.

Smith, A. (1991). *The age of behemoths: the globalization of mass media firms.* New York: Priority Press.

Steele, C. A. and Barnhurst, K. G. (1996). The journalism of opinion: network news coverage of US presidential campaigns, 1968–1988. *Critical Studies in Mass Communication*, 13, 187–209.

Swanson, D. L. (1997). The political-media complex at 50: putting the 1996 presidential campaign in context. *American Behavioral Scientist*, 40, 1264–1282.

Swanson, D. L. and Mancini, P. (eds) (1996). *Politics, media, and modern democracy: an international study of innovations in electoral campaigning and their consequences.* Westport, CT: Praeger.

Tewksbury, D. and Althaus, S. L. (1999, May). Differences in knowledge acquisition among readers of the paper and on-line versions of a national newspaper. Paper presented at the meeting of the International Communication Association, San Francisco.

Thussu, D. K. (1999). Privatizing the airwaves: the impact of globalization on broadcasting in India. *Media, Culture and Society*, 21, 125–131.

Tuchman, G. (1978). *Making news: a study in the construction of reality.* New York: Free Press.

Underwood, D. (1995). *When MBAs rule the newsroom.* New York: Columbia University Press.

Westerståhl, J. and Johansson, F. (1986). News ideologies as molders of domestic news. *European Journal of Communication*, 1, 126–145.

Wu, W. and Weaver, D. (1997). On-line democracy or on-line demagoguery? Public opinion "polls" on the Internet. *Harvard International Journal of Press/Politics*, 2(4), 71–86.

Young, H. (1999, February 11). Skeptical journalists, Parliament committees – all are swept aside. *The Guardian*, p. 18.

Zaller, J. (1997, August). A theory of media politics: the struggle over news coverage in presidential campaigns. Paper presented at the meeting of the American Political Science Association, Washington, DC.

2

POLITICAL COMMUNICATION AND TELEVISION

Between old and new influences

Gianpietro Mazzoleni

An obsolete question?

To discuss television and politics today, when political communication relies increasingly on alternative channels, may sound a tired academic exercise, leading the discussants onto a terrain where little seems still worth being discussed. It may also appear itself an obsolete topic, which generations of scholars have repeatedly dealt with since television made its spectacular and threatening ingress into the political arenas around the world.

Every aspect of the role, meaning, power, good, and bad of television in politics has been passed under thorough inspection by political communication research. The amount of scientific (letting alone the opinionated) works produced in so many years by so many researchers and theorists is almost beyond imagination, hardly matched by that of the printed press, and well exceeding that on radio.

This is a doubtless sign of the huge importance gained by the "old" medium in the political process of modern democracies. Television can well be picked out as one of the dozen most important inventions of the second millennium, as symbol of modernization of society. In our case it can be said that television has markedly changed politics and political leadership to such an extent that future historians will perhaps mark the introduction of television as a milestone in the history of politics and democracy, very much like, in its far-reaching effects, the French Revolution and the fall of the Berlin Wall. Politics in the television era has turned into a quite different reality from the one known in pre-television times! Surely politics has not lost its inner nature of competition for power, but competition is played on completely different grounds.

All this is well familiar to the academic community. So, what's the purpose of chewing over the matter for the hundredth time? To put it in different words: what's new under the sun of tele-politics that is worth the boredom of resuming looking at the phenomenon? Are there symptoms that the well established kind of relations between television and politics is somehow changing?

The questions may also seem idle, especially to a young researcher who has not personally lived the years when television was diffusing in the political arena, and, taking as certain its impact on politics, prefers speculating around the impact of the Internet.

The questions, however, are all but trivial, as television is turning into a quite different thing than the one most of us started to watch in the 1950s. Of course, it has changed since: it got colors, the number of channels soared to hundreds in many countries, it turned into a powerful industry, its news provision is round-the-clock, its audience is little less than global, and so on. But, now, there are powerful signs that the "old lady" – without passing away – is going to metamorphose into a new creature, of which we can only imagine the features. One of these signs is the passage from analogic to digital technology – apparently one of the several technical leaps (most of which of little interest to untrained users) scored by television in its first life, but in reality an epochal revolution, capable of triggering in the next few years a far-reaching change in people's lives comparable to the one brought about in the post-war Western countries.

This is not the place for embroidering around the technicalities of the "digital revolution" – bookstores and news-stands overflow with works and magazines dedicated to them. Here there is the risk of enjoying in striking scenarios, how the digital house will look in the future, what a digital newspaper will offer, how marvelous digital-democracy will be, etc., perhaps a gratifying exercise for visionary technology-determinists – such as N. Negroponte – but indeed a sterile one for down-to-earth social and political scientists. What interests us are simply the political implications of television's new technical life.

Among the several effects of the digitalization of communications, the enormous multiplication of communication opportunities is the most pregnant of consequences on the mediatized public sphere. In the future there will be more channels, more communicators and more content, however, audience fragmentation means that political communicators will struggle to reach large numbers of people. This affects the whole media complex, but especially television. Digital television will mean an infinity of broadcasting, cable, satellite, and web providers and provisions of television material: news, entertainment, information, educational contents, etc., all with the unprecedented asset of interactivity, itself foreboding thrilling future worlds of communication!

The digital metamorphosis of television seems to represent a mighty challenge to the very concept of mass communication, to the "one-to-many" structure of the media that developed in contemporary times, since the mass diffusion of the printed press, cinema, radio, and lastly of broadcast television. To be sure, the first significant blow has come from pay-TV, that allowed users to *choose* which programs to watch. The traditional scheme of mass communication was and still is someone else choosing what to offer to the mass audiences. The example of pay-TV shows that television is already changing its nature today, anticipating some of the features that will characterize the era of full-digital-TV, when it is married to mobile communications and to the Internet. The coming of that era, characterized by interactive global communications, will most probably mean the end of the mass media, television included. The traditional media will not die, but will be transformed into outlets of a very different sort.

If the public sphere and its major activity – politics – changed so deeply when broadcast television stepped into it, is politics changing also as television is turning into a different medium? It might be too early to make sensible conjectures on the relation between changes in one field and changes in the other; nevertheless as political communication analysts we must pay attention to all signs of change and assess what the implications might be. The question whether the (undeniable) developments in the television industry entail significant drifts in the mediatized political world makes a discussion on a topic such as "political communication and television" necessary and timely, surely not old fashioned or obsolete!

Political communication in the television age

Before discussing the changes in the political domains initiated by television's recent mutation, it is useful to give an overall assessment of the weight of television in politics in what Blumler and Kavanagh (1999) name "Age 2" of political communication's history, that is, "when limited-channel nation-wide television became the dominant medium of political communication".

Kurt and Gladys E. Lang (1968) gave us a masterful illustration of how television intruded into political events in its early years. That was only the beginning of a successful march into political institutions, political leadership, political language, that is in the world of political communication.

Ever since those times every major national as well international political event has been marked – and transformed – by the presence of television (Dayan & Katz, 1992). It has been *co-protagonist* of those events together with the personalities who used (and abused) it; it played the role of *witness* of terrible or exceptional events; it was itself an *agent* of small and big happenings that turned the course of history. From the parade in honor of Gen. MacArthur, to the Great Debates Nixon–Kennedy, from the crowning of Queen Elizabeth to the funeral of Lady Diana, from the air-attack on Baghdad to the signing of peace between Arafat and Rabin, from the hammering down of the Berlin Wall to the rally of Boris Yeltsin on a tank in the Red Square, from the introduction of TV cameras into the

British Parliament to the victory of TV mogul Berlusconi, we have the direct experience of how tenaciously television has rooted in the dynamics of the public and political spheres.

A simple but meaningful reflection can be made here: "contemporary politics needs television, politics without television is unimaginable". Even if it sounds a bit peremptory, the statement is not a denial of the autonomy of political action – it would be an absurd simplification – it rather emphasizes the intimate association existing between political action and its public dimension and practice mainly carried out through television. In other words, when politics seeks the legitimation of persons and decisions, the consensus of citizens, the public representation of conflict of interests – things that are at the heart of political action – it has to go through the communication channels offered by the media, and in particular by television. It is mostly the grammar of the television medium and its proteus-like nature of medium for entertainment and information, for emotions as well as education, in a word, it is its unique "logic" that affects – and upsets – the rules of the political game.

Television to politics means mostly broadcast journalism, itself conditioned by the peculiar grammar of the medium, the grammar of image and spectacle, and – with the growth of commercialism – of the audience ratings. Television news has been often blamed (e.g. by Entman, 1989; Jamieson, 1992; Patterson, 1993) for having turned electoral campaigns into "horse races", coverage of political leaders into search for tele-genie, political debate into "sound-bites". Its preference for and insistence on personalities, show biz, image, sensationalism and even scandalism, that is on the dramatic dimensions of politics, in the long run affected the nature of the relations among political actors, between political leaders and public opinion, between politicians and news professionals. To a certain extent, politics has become an hostage of the news media.

Politicians and political institutions have not resisted the inroad of television into their arena. On the contrary, politics has swiftly adjusted to the medium, perhaps without realizing that it would overturn most of the traditional patterns of public performance.[1]

The reference here is to the process of mediatization, i.e. the adaptation of political language and of political action to the constraints of what J. G. Blumler calls the "modern publicity process" (1990). The way politics is performed publicly, the content of communications by government and party leaders, the conquest and exercise of political leadership, the scheduling of political events, and several other facets of political reality, all have adapted to the production values and formats of television and to the consumption patterns of television audience (Mazzoleni & Schulz, 1999).

On the audience side, the diffusion of the "old" television meant an enlargement of the number of people accessing political communication contents, an increase of "incidental exposure among people previously more difficult to reach" and a shift in "the balance from long-term influences on political outlook [...] toward more short-term ones" (Blumler & Kavanagh, 1999). This did not mean however an overall increase in the political information and participation levels in the electorate, as dozens of scholars have repeatedly tried to demonstrate.

The fruits of the long-lasting marriage between politics and the "old" television can be briefly outlined in the control of the agenda by journalists, spectacularization, fragmentation of political discourse, personalization of political debate, selection of political elites (winnowing power).

Tele-politics today

The picture of political communication that we have been familiar with in past decades is now slowly losing its sharpness and through a process of technological "morphing" is taking new features. Again all three actors of political communication, i.e. medium, politicians, viewer-citizens, are affected by the metamorphosis, even if to different extents.

As hinted above, one of the main changes in the television medium is the multiplication of its outlets, content and, mostly, of its functions: from a traditional mass-medium offering entertainment and news it is turning into a multi-channel vehicle of all kinds of contents.

Using the information traffic typology (Bordewijk & van Kaam, 1986), we observe that the broadcast media, without losing their *natural* "allocution" pattern, are increasingly becoming media characterized by new, *interactive* patterns, such as "consultation," "conversation," and "registration." These changes bear important implications for political communication: they might mean a "broad shift of balance of communicative power from sender to receiver, although this may be counterbalanced by the growth of registration" that is the capacity by the controllers of the communication channels to extend their powers of surveillance on the users (McQuail, 1994; pp. 57–59). In other words, television as it becomes more and more a "fragmented" and multi-faceted entity, controlled by a myriad of senders and fueled by a myriad of services, loses some of its traditional assets and powers in the political arena, as it is no longer that interlocutor clearly-identifiable by political actors which was once capable of influencing the features and the functioning of the political system.

If one adds to this process the trend – indirectly linked to the structural change of television – from "sacerdotal" attitudes towards politics of broadcast news media to "irreverence [and] marginalization" (Blumler & Kavanagh, 1999), because the media industry is increasingly cutting back on politics, for increasingly fiercer competitive constraints, then politicians are eventually going to be less harassed (but also less courted) by television(s).

This bears significant effects on the second actor of political communication: politics starts to emancipate from its previous state of hostage of the media. The diminished "centrality" of television in the political process couples with the resort by political institutions and politicians to alternative, "back" channels to reach their constituencies. Such trend has been illustrated by several recent studies (see Doris Graber on this) in and out election campaigns, it is certainly of great importance for political communication research, as it in some cases it takes the form of an intentional attempt by politicians to "bypass" the (troublesome and uncontrollable) mediation of the news media, a sort of revenge made possible by new communication technology on the long-lasted surveillance power of the mass media.

Nevertheless it is unthinkable, at least for the time being, that politics can get rid altogether of the mass media. Television, even if crippled by its own proliferation, maintains Midas' powers, still crucial in assuring celebrity to unknown political personalities and wide echo to their words and enterprises, something that no Internet web site can guarantee! The novelty lies in the increased difficulty in accessing the too-numerous television channels in the attempt to build *public* visibility. Politicians and candidates will have to develop and implement more sophisticated techniques to exploit at best media fragmentation and to draw attention by the largest number of television channels. The capacity of generating news will need to be multiplied: this will force politicians to invest more money and put up complex organizations to secure wide visibility.

But probably the most interesting and consequences-laden changes are occurring with the third actor of political communication, the citizen spectator. Here the process can be epitomized by the concept (and evidence) of "audience fragmentation": the so far *massified* dimension of the public of the media is somehow being shattered by multiplication and structural change of communication and information outlets, by what has been named "symbolic inflation", hardly digested by audiences of large width. "The captive audience [. . .] with large numbers of viewers tuned in to the same material often because it followed some other popular program – shrinks or disappears" (Blumler & Kavanagh, 1999). One consequence is that people (and voters) can no longer be reached by political leaders and messages by means of a simple appearance on the major channel, as there might be several major channels, all fiercely competing for new fractions of the audience(s). "The more fragmented the audience, the more difficult is the politicians' task of manipulating multiple television services to their advantage and the greater the possibility that viewers can avoid exposure to political programs and advertisements carried on only one or two channels" (Swanson & Mancini, 1996; p. 266). By the same token, the materials eventually reaching the several "niches" of the viewers escape the highly centralized editorial control previously exerted by the few, powerful broadcasting organizations, not to mention the thousands of Internet channels that escape such control, something that in the long run might make possible "media pluralism", so longed by generations of sensible democrats.

What is the impact of this new dynamics on the audience's processing of the (fragmented) political communication provided by (fragmented) television?

Given for granted the evidence of a diminished interest for politics and of a declining popular participation in the traditional forms of political action (but civic engagement is all but declining, argues W. Lance Bennett, 1998), the picture of the processes that political participation is undergoing in many Western post-modern democracies is also of fragmented "consumption" of politics. There will be more research needed to find out how people process the bits and bites of information falling on their heads from hundreds of sources, and if it benefits their political knowledge levels.

Two things seem already clear at this stage of fragmentation of the whole political-media complex:

1 people no longer have television as the "main source" of political information; and
2 given the increasing provision of "populist programs" by television, the chance of exposure to (informative and engaging) political television contents is dramatically decreasing.

The implications of such simple evidence are several, all deserving to be investigated and discussed by political and social science. Among them: more disinterest for "high" politics as well as for *la politique politicienne* (i.e. politicking), political anomie and dispersion of party militancy. But one consequence is by far the most threatening for political communicators (parties and leaders): their diminished capability to mobilize masses and to influence mass opinion.

Less powerful television and less powerful political communication?

John Zaller has recently (and convincingly) argued that television is just one of the least important dynamic factors of the political process: "American politics tends to be driven more by political substance [. . .] than by the antics of Media Politics" (Zaller, 1998; p. 187). He has also contested the alleged power of television: "the effects of Media Politics on political outcomes must be demonstrated on a case-by-case basis, because sometimes the effects are real and lasting and other times they are not" (p. 186). The point he makes is that people might be scarcely affected by the media complex, they might even ignore or disregard political information channels, but they are quite "capable of recognizing and focusing on [their] own conception of what matters" in politics (ibid.).[2]

Zaller's argument clashes with common wisdom held by much scholarly research and by several politicians who developed smart techniques to use television; however it brings further support to the speculation that politics and political communication are undergoing emblematic mutations in connection with the loss of the former (even if pretended, according to Zaller) power of influence of the media and following the structural changes in the television's domains. Political communicators will face a fragmented public in a digitalized-multichannel media landscape and will have to invent new communication devices to get their message across. Perhaps they have most to lose from such mutation, while the third actor of political communication, the citizen-voter, will be less targeted by political messages via television channels but will not necessarily drift toward (antidemocratic) political disengagement (Bennett, 1998), and surely will continue to bring his/her contribution to the political process getting the "not especially complex type of political information needed to function effectively as a citizen" (Delli Carpini & Keeter, 1996; p. 272) through "information short-cuts" (Popkin, 1991; p. 14), and easily recognizing the difference between virtual politics and political substance.

Challenged by such structural as well as cultural changes in political communication, the old tele-politics has to recast itself and return – paradoxically enough – to pre-television patterns of communication, that privileged *substance* over appearance.

Even in the era of virtual politics, people seem to prefer the "politics of substance".

Notes

1 An emblematic (and somewhat prophetic) expertise on the powers of television in politics was given by Peter Mandelson: "TV does more to make or break a politician than any other medium. It is the voter's key source for forming impressions of politicians. They are looking for good judgement, for warmth, for understanding of people's concerns. That can only be demonstrated on television" (quoted in D. Watts, 1997; p. 190).

2 A similar stance is held by E. Diamond and R. A. Silverman (1995) in their book *White House to your house. Media and politics in virtual America.* They write that in 1992 Bill Clinton's campaign "benefited not so much from art but from reality" (p. 30), and tell of a Clinton's political consultant who printed a sign for the campaign headquarters in Little Rock that read "It's the Economy, Stupid" (p. 31).

References

Bennett, L. W. (1998). The uncivic culture: communication, identity, and the rise of lifestyle politics. *PS: Political Science and Politics*, XXXI, 741–761.

Blumler, J. G. (1990). Elections, the media, and the modern publicity process. In M. Ferguson (ed.), *Public communication – the new imperatives: future directions for media research* (pp. 101–113). London: Sage.

Blumler, J. G. and Kavanagh, D. (1999). The third age of political communication: influences and features. *Political Communication*, XVI, 3, 209–230.

Bordewijk, J. L. and van Kaam, B. (1986). Towards a new classification of tele-information services. *Intermedia*, XIV, 1, 16–21.

Dayan, D. and Katz, E. (1992). *Media events. The live broadcasting of history.* Cambridge, MA: Harvard University Press.

Delli Carpini, M. X. and Keeter, S. (1996). *What Americans know about politics and why it matters.* New Haven, CT: Yale University Press.

Diamond, E. and Silverman, R. A. (1995). *White House to your house. Media and politics in virtual America.* Cambridge, MA: The MIT Press.

Entman, R. E. (1989). *Democracy without citizens. Media and the decay of American politics.* New York: Oxford University Press.

Jamieson, K. H. (1992). *Dirty politics. Deception, distraction, and democracy.* New York: Oxford University Press.

Lang, K. and Lang, G. E. (1968). *Politics and television.* Chicago, IL: Quadrangle Books.

Mazzoleni, G. and Schulz, W. (1999). Mediatization of politics: a challenge for democracy? *Political Communication*, XVI, 3, 247–261.

McQuail, D. (1994). *Mass communication theory. An introduction.* London: Sage.

Patterson, T. E. (1993). *Out of order.* New York: Kopf.

Popkin, S. L. (1991). *The reasoning voter. Communication and persuasion in presidential campaigns.* Chicago, IL: The University of Chicago Press.

Swanson, D. L. and Mancini, P. (1996). Patterns of modern electoral campaigning and their consequences. In D. L. Swanson and P. Mancini (eds), *Politics, media and modern democracy* (pp. 247–276). Westport, CT: Praeger.

Watts, D. (1997). *Political communication today.* Manchester: Manchester University Press.

Zaller, J. (1998). Monica Lewinsky's contribution to political science. *PS: Political Science and Politics*, XXXI, 182–189.

3

POLITICAL COMMUNICATION IN THE AGE OF THE INTERNET

Thierry Vedel

Introduction

When a first draft of this chapter was presented in 1999, research on the political uses of ICTs (Information and Communication Technologies), and particularly the Internet, was in a nascent state. This was partly due to the lack of commitment of political organizations. Although they foresee a time when political communication could be electronic, political organizations have been slow in going online. It was only in 2000 that the Internet was used in election campaigning in a visible fashion.

It can also be argued that political communication scholars have not been prompt in seizing the changes brought about by ICTs. In many countries, political science has not paid sufficient attention to the evolution of communication means. Some fields which are being deeply affected by the development of ICTs – for example, communication processes in the design of public policies, or the use of the media by social movements – remain somewhat neglected and left to the students of media and technology.

Another reason is that the study of ICTs raises difficult methodological problems. Due to the rapidity of technological change, ICTs define objects that are not easy to characterize. The uses of ICTs are still under construction and are not stable. Added to that, political communication scientists are often uncomfortable in responding to questions on the impacts of ICTs: when asked whether the Internet will change the ways of campaigning, voting, or debating, they can only reply that it is much too early to know, that the history of communication has shown that the impacts of the new media are often ambivalent, that they take place over a long period and that, all things considered, communication tools are just one among the many factors that shape political behavior, structures, and processes.

However, recent years have seen an impressive mobilization of political scientists on Internet issues and given rise to important studies and books which I would like to present in this chapter.

41

The potential impact of ICTs on political communication

As shown in Table 3.1, ICTs – and especially the Internet – have several properties which, compared to traditional means of communication, can change the processing of information (Abramson *et al.*, 1988; van de Donk *et al.*, 1995; Boncheck, 1997). Depending on the context in which information processes take place, this might affect political communication in various ways.

ICTs can enhance the information of citizens

The development of ICTs for political communication basically rests on the traditional argument that citizens in a democracy need full information and an enlightened understanding of situations to contribute to democratic deliberation and make good decisions (Dahl, 1989). ICTs make enormous quantities of information available to the public. This change in quantity may result in a change in quality. Instead of getting limited and

Table 3.1 The potential impact of ICT on political communication

Properties of ICTs	Potential benefits	Problems or issues
Low costs of producing, storing and, especially, disseminating information	Easy access to the production of information Big amounts of information can be made available to the public	Information overload
Direct link between sender and receiver	Direct communication: media can be bypassed	Risks of propaganda Lack of mediators able to play a critical function
Selection of receivers	Targeted communication Closed group communication	Privacy
Speed of information	Possibility of constant updating Enhanced data gathering	Costs of maintaining systems Push-button decision-making
Interactive capabilities	Feedback from receivers Information can be customized to receiver's needs	Privacy
Decentralized architecture	Possibility of designing systems independent from geographical boundaries	Fragmentation of public sphere Regulation is difficult
Global dimension	Diversification of sources	Cultural conflicts or homogenisation

general information on a public project (for instance, the adoption of new health regulations), citizens can be provided with detailed data, preparatory reports, experts' advice, and accounts of previous experiences in other countries, and can examine in depth the value of this project. In the same way, instead of getting abstracts of politicians' statements or political platforms, citizens can get the full text and, therefore, have a better knowledge of what politicians really propose.

Second, citizens can be active. Instead of being the passive recipients of news from a limited number of sources, citizens can actively search out the information they want, compare sources, and look for alternative views. Again, this should enhance the quantity and the quality of information that citizens can use to make up their minds about political matters.

ICTs might enhance the strategies of communications by political actors

ICTs give political actors an easy access to people. First, they reduce the costs of information production and, above all, of information dissemination. By setting up a web site (an investment which starts at €8,000), any political group can be in a position to communicate its views to the rest of the world.

Second, and possibly more importantly, ICTs provide a means of direct communication. By bypassing the media, ICTs might dramatically change the conditions of political communication. So far, a significant part of political communication strategies has been devoted to catching the attention of the media gatekeeper. In order to maximize their access to, and exposure in the media, political forces have developed techniques of media management – for example, pseudoevents, press releases, establishing regular contacts with journalists. More generally, ICTs seem to put an end to all intermediaries between senders and receivers (see p. 45).

ICTs facilitate the process of political mobilization

First, ICTs allow people who share common interests to get in touch despite distance or social barriers. People can escape geography (and marginality) through global forums based on specialized narrow interests. For example, it is difficult for people who belong to a minority to really count in a small city; but, through the Internet, those people can acquire a sense of their identity and of their social or political weight at the global level.

Second, once these people have set up a group, they can more easily exchange ideas in order to define a platform and decide the kinds of action they want to engage in. E-mail updates can be sent regularly to members, and discussion forums can be established to discuss options.

Finally, ICTs can be used as a means of influencing decision-makers or public opinion – for instance, by organizing email campaigns directed at government officials or politicians. So far, a large part of advocacy efforts has been related primarily to the Internet (e.g. the Blue Ribbon campaign in the US to fight the restrictions on the freedom of speech, and actions to get cheaper local telephone rates in Europe). But it seems that the Internet is being increasingly used as a tool for general advocacy. There are many accounts of uses of the Internet by advocacy and interest groups. Thus, in Canada, Citizens for Local Democracy in Toronto used e-mail announcements and discussion lists to accelerate information sharing and strategy development in order to organize an efficient opposition to the provincial government.

ICTs can also improve communication within political organizations

Another possible impact of ICTs might be to reinvigorate the internal activities of political forces. Over the last thirty years, the traditional mass-party model, built on a large membership, has been replaced by a new form of party. This change is linked in part to the development of TV which has reduced the importance of local campaigning and moved the focus of activity to central party staff. This has resulted in an increased centralization of parties and the marginalization of grassroots.

ICTs allow party members to be provided with more information on what their leaders are doing and thus can allow a better accountability of parties' elites, but also a better efficiency in the external communication of parties by a better synchronization and coordination of local actions – for instance, local members can be informed about the message to be delivered. Through ICTs, members parties can participate more actively, frequently, and quickly in the decision-making process of the central leaders. They can communicate their opinions on parties' platforms, and express disagreements with parties' strategies.

Besides the redistribution of power between local members and elites, ICTs might result in the decentralization of political forces. Minority groups within parties may communicate their views independently to the other members and express dissent, and, link up with other minority groups to challenge parties elites.

The end of intermediaries?

With the Internet, it seems that gatekeepers no longer exist. However, it is much too early to say that ICTs means the end of the intermediation role that the media has played in political communication. It is likely that traditional media will continue to play an important role in political communication for several reasons:

- The Internet does not eliminate the need for mediators. While ICTs are eliminating scarcity of space (which justified in part the editing function of the media), they make scarcity of time more acute. A major problem for information and service providers on the Internet is to catch the attention of millions of people who have a limited time-budget. In order to cope with information overload, Internet users increasingly use tools to obtain the information they want and services that quickly digest political news (search engines, portals, etc.).
- As potential candidates to this mediating function, media have strong advantages (Grossman, 1995). Among the various actors engaged in information provision, they are certainly the ones that have made the largest investment in making content available on the Internet. They have a great deal of expertise in editing information and a good knowledge of people's needs. People know the kind of editorial service that they can expect from one given media and are likely to trust the media more than other intermediaries. For instance, if you get on the *Le Monde* site, you get an idea of how political news will be presented to you. Finally, the media have the ability to advertise for their own Internet services. As long as they remain the primary means of communication, TV and newspapers can direct the major Internet users towards their own sites.

To sum up, the impacts of ICTs – and primarily the Internet – on political communication processes can be broken down into two categories:

1 ICTs significantly reduce the costs associated with political communication. Traditionally, engagement in politics and political participation have been limited by the barriers of time, money, or space. With ICTs, the costs of entry on the public sphere are lowered and the communication of ideas is much less dependent on financial and material resources. It is no longer necessary to be physically present at a certain place and time to take part in a political action. People can exchange ideas, build up political organizations, and coordinate their actions without face-to-face contact, which allows dispersed individuals to get involved in collective actions (Myers, 1994).
2 ICTs also generate new ways of interactions between individuals, which in turn produce qualitative effects on political activism. ICTs contribute to intensify the actors' sense of involvement for at least two reasons. First, people have the impression of counting more than with traditional means of communication. Second, ICTs give the organization in which they are applied an image of a powerful and efficient agent, able to exert influence on its environment. ICTs also increase the formation of collective identities. Through networks-based exchanges and

interactions, individuals get a better perception of what they have in common. In addition, because of the procedures they establish (codes, private mail-boxes, scrambling systems, closed discussion groups, etc.), ICTs give people the feeling of belonging to a specific group, of being part of a special community (Schmidtke, 1997).

The state of literature

General sources on ICTs and politics

A number of books provide a general overview of the relationship between ICTs and politics, dealing in most cases with political communication:

- *The electronic commonwealth* edited by Abramson *et al.* (1988) describes how changes in the media have affected elections throughout history. The essential part of the book is about how ICTs can be used to befriend or belittle democratic processes (since, according to the authors, technology does not determine a model of society). Against electronic plebiscitary democracy – based on electronic voting at home, they argue in favor of an electronic commonwealth based on electronic town meetings and communities conferencing.
- *Orwell in Athens* edited by van de Donk *et al.* (1995) provides a good review of the literature, cover the political uses of ICTs by political parties, administrations, and especially local governments, and address some of the issues that ICTs raise (such as the privacy issue). One of the merits of this book is to combine analytical and theoretical reflection with well-documented case studies. Overall, this book demonstrates that ICTs tend to be used to strengthen the position of powerful actors, be they bureaucracies or elected individuals. This book has recently been complemented by two others – *Digital democracy*, edited by Hacker and van Dijk (2000) and *Democratic governance and new technology*, edited by Hoff, Horrocks and Tops (2000) – which similarly discuss the conceptual and practical dimensions of the Internet and political systems through theoretical chapters and case studies. In addition to their European focus, these books are especially interesting for the link they make between ICT developments and models of democracy.
- *Digital divide* edited by Norris (2001) is to date the most comprehensive book on the Internet and politics. After discussing the theories of digital democracy, it provides an outstanding array of cross-national data on the political virtual system and documents the uses of the Internet by governments, parliaments, parties, advocacy, and grassroots

organizations worldwide. The book ends up with a reflection on civic engagement in the age of information and suggests the idea of a virtuous circle (developed in Norris's earlier work, 2000) to explain that, in its present state, the Internet largely serves to reinforce the activism of the activists. Yet, with appropriate policies, "politics as usual" may be altered by digital technologies and the Internet could positively contribute to the flourishing of a strong civil society in countries which lack stable party organizations and strong opposition movements.

Political institutions on line

An increasing number of political institutions are using the Internet. They include parliaments, administrations, regulatory agencies, and other governmental bodies.

Parliamentary projects have in general several goals (Coleman *et al.*, 1999; Owen & Striker, 1999; Taylor *et al.*, 1999): they aim at making legislative processes more transparent and ensuring the publicity of laws; enhancing MPs' work in their relationship to their constituents and colleagues; and associating citizens to law-making (for instance, in the form of forums or discussion groups where citizens can voice their concerns or suggest ideas). Of special interest among parliamentary sites is the project of the new Scottish parliament (almost created from *ex nihilo*) which is probably one of the most ambitious and most advanced in technical terms (CSTAG, 1998). In the US, Casey (1996) has given a good account of the difficulties in introducing new information systems within old organizations and described the politics of technological change in a bureaucracy.

In most industrialized countries, programs to establish on-line administrations have been launched (especially after the G7 meeting on information super highways in Brussels, in February 1995).[1] Studies (Diamond & Silverman, 1995), show that beyond the rhetoric about citizen empowerment and the improvement of the quality of public services, government sites have also more trivial objectives: reducing administrative costs (as in the case of the so-called tele-procedures which allow administrative forms to be filled in online, bypassing traditional media (Bellamy & Taylor, 1994). It can also be suspected that government sites are a means to establish a tighter social control on citizens through a kind of electronic panoptic machine (Gandy, 1993): by facilitating the collection of personal data and data coupling and sorting, ICTs might lead to a surveillance society in which citizens are transparent to the state rather than states being transparent to citizens (Bekkers & Van Duivenboden, in van de Donk *et al.*, 1995). The issue of privacy is the object of a growing concern among social scientists (Lyon, 1994; Agre & Rotenberg, 1998).

Local governments and ICTs

At the local level, many cities have established web sites. Some of them, including Amsterdam, Bologna, Issy-les-Moulineaux, Manchester, Parthenay, and Santa Monica, have been the object of in-depth studies (Schalken & Tops, 1995; Carter, 1997; Tsagarousianou *et al.*, 1997; Hale *et al.*, 1999). Cities which use the internet to enhance local democracy follow three defferent approaches (Vedel, 2000): the open city model which is based on the ideal of an enlightened citizen and consists in disseminating information about the operation of local authorities; the forum model which seeks to enlarge and stimulate the local public sphere; the consultative model, which aims to allow citizens to take part in the decision-making process. Using a similar framework in their survey of 290 Californian municipalities, Hale and others (1999) have found that the interactive function of local web sites was often underdeveloped and that many sites did not even provide basic civic information. Based on a study of 89 Flanders cities, Steyaert (2000) found that local officials tend to consider their constituencies as clients rather than as citizen or electors. Pratchett (1995) has also shown that ICTs have unanticipated consequences and are frequently unsuccessful in achieving their original objectives. Instead of strengthening local democracy, they reinforce the power of local elites and contribute to a recentralization of local management. As a result, it appears that behind the rhetoric of electronic democracy, little has been done to extend democratic practices and to broaden the public sphere (Tsagarousianou, 1997). Most municipal sites are top-down and executive-initiated projects which focus on the provision of practical services and information and simply modernize the forms of publicness.

In the US, the notion of Electronic Town Meetings – or Halls – (ETM) were heavily promoted by 1992 presidential candidate Ross Perot. With ETM, direct links between voters and representatives are created at the level of local communities and ICTs allow citizens to decide on pre-selected public policy options. ETM have been the object of much criticism (Nimmo, 1994) as they can appear as just a new version of plebiscites and push-button referenda that discourage serious consideration of the issues.[2]

Political parties and campaigning

Dozens of parties have now established web sites. Studies on these (Gibson & Ward, 1998; Roper, 1999) show that the potential of the Internet for parties (Smith & Webster, 1995) is not fully used. Web sites are used primarily as a top-down information-disseminating tool rather than as a means to increase internal democracy or to enhance relationships between citizens and politicians. Contrary to the hopes of cyberoptimists, the Internet is not a fully open battlefield. Because they have more resources to create and maintain web sites, large parties are more present online than fringe or small parties (Norris, 2001).

While the potential of ICTs for election campaigning has been described as early as 1985 (Neustadt), it was only in 1996 that the use of the Internet during elections became visible, especially in the US and in Britain. Studies available on such applications (Margolis, 1997; Ward & Gibson, 1998; Kamarck, 1999; Coleman, 2001) provide interesting insights. The Internet primarily reaches people who are already well informed and serves to preach to the converted (Norris, 2001). There is a lack of a strategical approach in using the Internet: most campaign managers are unaware of the effects of using the Internet, but they nevertheless climb on to the bandwagon. Bimber (1999) drew interesting findings from a study of Internet users. While education, income, and age are the strongest predicators of voting participation, the active use of the Internet is associated with a small increase in the likelihood of voting. It also seems that the Internet exacerbates differences between politically active and inactive people by providing new resources and new pathways of influence for traditional political participators. Yet in terms of causality, it seems that the same set of factors that influence political participation (social networks, civic skills) also shape access and use of the Internet. Overall, studies in this area show that the Internet has not revolutionized political communication and tends to reproduce traditional politics (Margolis & Resnick, 2000; Norris, 2001).

Social movements, collective action, and the Internet

Besides TV and traditional media, the use of the new electronic means of communication by social movements has been rarely studied. However, in the 1970s and 1980s, a number of studies scrutinized the use of fax, telephone, local FM radios, and cable TV by protest groups. For example, in France, Kergoat (1994) examined how public hospital nurses were able to use the Minitel in their efforts to set up coordinations, apart from traditional unions. Marchand (1987) showed how the Minitel allowed students, spread in dozens of locations, to organize their 1986 movement and discuss its objectives.

The development of the Internet is changing the situation and a growing number of studies are paying attention to the way it may be applied for collective action (for general considerations, see Meyer & Tarrow, 1998; Della Porta *et al.*, 1999). Several studies have underlined how the Internet might favor the building of cross-national coalitions and the adaptation of civil society to the globalization of economies (Frederick, 1992 and 1993; Lee, 1997; Ayers, 2001; Georges, 2001). Others have pointed out how the Internet helps to recruit new members (Boncheck, 1995), or to rein-force solidarity among organizations' members (O'Donnell, 1995a, 1995b).

Overall, research in this area tends to emphasize the instrumental func-tion of the Internet and to focus on internal communications of social movements and interest groups. ICTs are primarily considered as a means to reduce coordination costs, to integrate new members within organiza-tions, and to increase the frequency and effectiveness of intra-organization exchanges (with the possible effect of flattening existing hierarchies between members and leaders). According to some observers, the Internet is an excellent tool for short-term opposition, but is more difficult to use over the long term. No real Internet-based interest groups have emerged yet. In most cases, advocacy applications are tied to a dedicated volunteer and only a few organizations have moved towards a strategic or coordinated approach. On-line discussions are rarely successful in generating group consensus and there needs to be a consensus on positions from the start (Clifts, 1998). Yet other functions should be taken into account. Of special interest here is Melucci's approach: Melucci underlines the symbolical dimension of collective action and views ICTs as contributing to the construction of organizations' identities and codes (Melucci, 1996).

By contrast, the application of the Internet to express views and dissem-inate information in the direction of the general public or of targeted groups (including the media) is less often scrutinized. However, surveys have begun to explore this aspect: Cleaver (1998) showed how the Zapa-tistas used the Internet to reach the international public opinion and popularize their uprising (see also Gingras, 1999); Derville (1997) thor-oughly examined the struggle between Greenpeace and the French government to control satellite links that fed the media images of nuclear tests in Polynesia as they happened.

The Internet and the transformation of the public sphere

Following Hiltz and Turoff (1978), an important body of literature has attempted to characterize the nature of cyberspace, the new forms of sociability and identity which are appearing through networks, and the style of exchange among Internet users, especially in newsgroups. A common question is whether cyberspace is a world apart from the real world which generates specific politics (Tepper, 1997). Many studies – often dominated by a post-modernist perspective – have described the Internet as an auto-nomous space, governed by its own logic, which is separated from nation-states and the real world, and produces a peculiar culture with specific codes and norms of behavior, forms of identity and modes of sociability (Morley & Robins, 1995; Jones, 1997; Poster, 1997; Smith & Kollock, 1999). In other words, the Internet would give rise to virtual communities, a notion popularized by Howard Rheingold, and defined as "the social aggregations that emerge from the Net when enough people carry on those public discussions long enough, with sufficient human feeling to form webs of personal relationships in the cyberspace" (Rheingold, 1993, p. 5). However, this notion is criticized by some students of the Internet who consider that virtual communities, being the voluntary association of like-minded people, differ from "traditional" communities (in the sense of Tönnies) for at least three reasons (Healy, 1997): they are chosen by their members, whereas traditional communities (family, village, etc.) originate in fate; they do not oblige their participants to deal with diversity and heterogeneity, and there is no relational imperative except when they are connected with physical communities (e.g. PEN, the San Francisco WELL); and they do not have any degree of permanence and are volatile since users can freely get in and out of a virtual community.

From a political communication perspective, a recurrent question is whether the Internet brings about a new public sphere. As cafés and salons in the eighteenth century, print media and popular newspapers in the nineteenth century, television and polls in the twentieth century were the dominant tools or places for public debate, will the Internet become the public sphere of the twenty-first century, where social issues are constructed and discussed (Thompson, 1995; Miège, 1997). According to Poster (1997), the Internet enables new political groupings: "Internet communities function as places of difference from and resistance to modern society. In a sense, they serve the function of a Habermasian public sphere without intentionally being one. They are places (. . .) of the inscription of new assemblages of self-constitution (p. 113)." On empirical grounds, a number of studies have focused on newsgroups and public forums (Schneider, 1996), with contrasted results: these parts of the Internet are viewed as places which contribute to a certain degree of political socialization and where people learn principles of democratic exchange; others describe them as exacerbating individualism and being a sort of new opium for people (Woolley, 1992). Studies also point out the conflicting function of the Internet: both fragmenting and globalizing the public sphere (Morley & Robins, 1995).

Agenda for future research

For many years, the literature on the political uses of the Internet has been essentially speculative. Books and articles have tried to describe the possible impact of the Internet on political systems, but these forecasts were rarely documented and grounded on case studies, and they often lacked the distance with the object required in social sciences (to such an extent that their authors looked sometimes more as propagandists who were diffusing the ideology of the information society). Since 1995–1996, the situation has positively changed and field surveys as well as case studies have multiplied. While this empirical effort should be continued, it is also necessary to take new directions.

Improve empirical research by bringing in additional approaches

So far, empirical studies devoted to the political uses of ICT have tended to focus on the supply-side. As a result, numerous articles providing content analysis of web sites or presenting actors strategies regarding ICTs are available. However useful these studies are, they often have two drawbacks. They rarely deal with the way information services are used by people (for a good counter-example, see the outstanding work by Bimber, 1999); they lack a theoretical perspective. Thus, studies of web sites rarely investigate the visions of citizenship or the conceptions of polity which are embodied in these sites. The information age enables the enhancement of all forms of democracy as well as permitting a new synthesis to occur among them (cyber-democracy). An important issue for social scientists (as well as decision-makers) lies in the clarification of what forms of democracy are promoted electronically (see Hague and Loader, 1999; Hacker & van Dijk, 2000; Hoff *et al.*, 2000). In addition, it is important that researchers make clear their own values and preferences (for instance by indicating what their definition of "good" or "hard" political communication is.

While many students of ICTs agree with the necessity to inquire into the impact of ICTs on political behaviors, structures, and processes, such an objective raises difficult theoretical and methodological problems. ICTs are still changing and their usage is not stabilized. Their social appropriation takes time (generally, one or two generations). As long as the political uses of ICTs is a moving object, the lessons that can be drawn from their observation are limited. For instance, whether on-line forums will change the relationship between citizens and representatives is impossible to determine at the moment; once the ado about the Internet has vanished, news groups might turn out in places in which only a tiny part of the population is interested.

Consider the whole field of ICTs and not just the Internet

The study of the political uses of ICTs primarily focus on the Internet, which is quite understandable given the properties of the network of networks (see Table 3.1, p. 42). Yet there are other ICTs which deserve attention. For instance, the political impacts of television by satellite (such as its effects on the homogenization of cultures, its possible uses as an alternative source of information in countries in which media are tightly controlled by governments, or its application by immigrants to access identity referents and get back to their cultural roots) should be studied in further detail (on this matter see, for instance, the reader edited by Sreberny-Mohammadi *et al.*, 1997). Cable TV – which was the object of much attention in the 1970s as a medium for local communities – should also be reconsidered as the interactive capacities of cable have increased with changes in technology.

Engage in comparative and international research

It will soon be time to go beyond case studies and the assessment of local experiments and to engage in their comparison so that common trends and global logics can be identified. However, comparative research is a difficult exercise. As we have shown elsewhere (Dutton & Vedel, 1992), many comparative studies, which pretend to provide cross-national analysis of political systems, are actually a simple juxtaposition of national cases studies and look like inventories which have little, if any, analytical value. Genuine comparative research requires strong analytical frameworks.

Besides comparative research, there is now a need for international research. By that I mean research dealing with communication processes and structures in a global world. ICTs are opening new ways of information, allowing citizens to search for information in other countries and information providers to design global strategies. For instance, regulations restricting the access to some contents on the Internet can be bypassed by the delocalization of sites. More importantly, as political systems are interpenetrating and as new forms of global governance are emerging, politics is to some extent becoming global (as is economics). This globalization raises new issues: the possible emergence of a global civil society, and the sophistication and transnationalization of government policies.

Globalize research on political communication and ICTs

Research on political communication and ICTs is to date concentrated in a small number of countries. That a huge part of the literature originates from the US does not come as a surprise. This domination is obviously linked to the early development of the Internet in this country, to the traditional weight of American political science in the discipline, and perhaps also to the strength of American publishers. Yet significant work has been produced in the UK, and to a lesser extent in the Netherlands and Germany. By contrast, research in other parts of Europe is notably insufficient. In the case of France, some surveys of the (foreign) literature and position papers are available (Massit-Follea, 1997; Rodota, 1999), but fresh research on the topic is almost non-existent. It is a pity that previous research dealing with Minitel has not been extended to the Internet. Studies in the 1980s drew interesting lessons regarding the behavior of ICT users and their social usage that remain useful for an understanding of the Internet. They also led to original approaches which provide a stimulating theoretical framework to analyze the social dynamics of ICT development (Flichy, 1995).

Notes

1 ICT can also be used internally by governments. Some studies have documented the use of satellites in foreign policy (Eldon, 1994; Holma, 1998).
2 Fishkin (1995) in particular has challenged the Perot's concept of ETM for being neither representative nor deliberative and stressed the need for deliberative opinion polls (on these, see also Mayer, 1997).

References

Abramson, J. B., Arterton, F. C. and Orren, G. R. (1988). *The electronic commonwealth: the impact of new media technologies on democratic politics*. New York: Basic Books.

Agre, Philip E. and Rotenberg, Marc (eds) (1998). *Technology and privacy: the new landscape*. Cambridge, MA: The MIT Press.

Arterton, F. Christopher (1987). *Teledemocracy. Can technology protect democracy?* Newbury Park, CA: Sage.

Ayers, Jeffrey (2001). Transnational activism in the Americas: the Internet and mobilizing against the FTAA. Paper presented at the Annual Meeting of the APSA, San Francisco.

Barber, Benjamin (1984). *Strong democracy*. Los Angeles, CA: University of California Press; French edition: *Démocratie forte* (1997). Paris: Desclée de Brower.

Bellamy, Christine and Taylor, John (1994). Towards the information polity? Public administration in the information age. *Public Administration*, 72, pp. 1–12.

Benjamin, Gerald (ed.) (1982). *The communications revolution in politics*. New York: The Academy of Political Science.

Bimber, Bruce (1999). The Internet and citizen communication with government: does the medium matter? *Political Communication*, 16, pp. 409–28.

Boncheck, Mark (1995). Grassroots in cyberspace: recruiting members on the Internet. Paper presented at the 53rd Annual Meeting of the Midwest Political Association, Chicago, IL.

Boncheck, Mark (1997). *From broadcast to netcast: the Internet and the flow of political information*, Ph.D. dissertation, Harvard University. Available at http://institute.strategosnet.com/msb/thesis/download.htm.

Burnham, David (1983). *The rise of the computer state*. New York: Random House.

Carter, Dave (1997). Digital democracy or information aristocracy? Economic regeneration and the information economy. In Brian Loader (ed.), *The governance of cyberspace*. London: Routledge, pp. 136–154.

Casey, Chris (1996) *The hill on the net. Congress enters the information age*. Boston, MA: AP Professional Age.

Cleaver, Harry (1998). The Zapatistas and the electronic fabric of struggle. In J. Holloway and E. Peláez (eds), *Zapatistas reinventing revolution in Mexico*. London: Pluto Press, pp. 81–103.

Coleman, Stephen (2001). *2001 cyberspace odysssey: the Internet in the UK election*. London: The Hansard Society.

Coleman, Stephen, Taylor, John and van de Donk, Wim (1999). *Parliament in the age of the Internet*. Oxford: Oxford University Press.

CSTAG, Glasgow Caledonian University (1998). *Parliamentary devolution in the information age. Telematics and the Scottish parliament: transferable democratic innovations*. Report commissioned by the Scottish Office on behalf of the Consultative Steering Group (CSG) on the Scottish Parliament, September.

Dahl, Robert A. (1989). *Democracy and its critics*. New Haven, CT: Yale University Press.

Della Porta, Donatella, Kriesi, Hanspeter and Rucht, Dieter (eds) (1999). *Social movement in a globalizing world*. New York: Macmillan Press.

Derville, Gregory (1997). Le combat singulier Greenpeace-SIRPA, *Revue française de science politique*, 47 (5), October, pp. 589–629.

Diamond, Edwin and Silverman, Robert (1995). *White House to your house. Media and politics in virtual America*. Cambridge, MA: MIT Press.

Docter, Sharon and Dutton, William H. (1998). The First Amendment on line. Santa Monica's public electronic network. In Roza Tsagarousianou, Damian Tambini and Cathy Bryan (eds), *Cyberdemocracy. Technology, cities and civic networks*. London: Routledge, pp. 125–151.

Dutton, William and Vedel, Thierry (1992). The dynamics of cable television in the US, Britain and France. In Jay Blumler *et al.*, *Comparatively speaking: communication and culture across space and time*. London: Sage, pp. 70–93.

Eldon, S. (1994). *From quill pen to satellite. Foreign ministries in the information age*. London: Royal Institute of International Affairs.

Electronic democracy (1996). *Media Culture & Society*. 18, (2), April.

Fishkin, James (1995). *Democracy and deliberation. The voice of the people*. New Haven, CT: Yale University Press.

Flichy, Patrice (1995). *L'innovation technique. Récents développements en sciences sociales. Vers une nouvelle théorie de l'innovation*. Paris: La Découverte.

Frederick, Howard H. (1992). Computer communications in cross-border coalition-building: North American NGO networking against NAFTA. *Gazette: the International Journal for Mass Communication Studies*, 50 (2–3), pp. 217–241.

Frederick, Howard (1993). Computer networks and the emergence of global civil society. In Linda M. Harasim (ed.), *Global networks: computers and international communication*. Cambridge, MA: MIT Press.

Gandy, Oscar H. Jr (1993). *The panoptic sort*. Boulder, CO: Westview Press.

Georges, Eric (2001). De l'utilisation d'Internet comme outil de mobilisation: les cas d'Attac et de Salami. *Sociologie et Sociétés*, 32 (2), pp. 171–189.

Gibson, R. and Ward, S (1998). UK political parties and the Internet: politics as usual in the new media. *The Harvard International Journal of Press/Politics*, 3 (3), pp. 14–38.

Gingras, Anne-Marie (1999). Démocratie et nouvelles technologies de l'information et de la communication: illusions de la démocratie directe et exigences de l'action collective. *Politique et Sociétés*, 8 (2), pp. 37–60.

Greenman, Ben and Miller, Kristin (1996). *Netvote*. New York: Michael Wolff & Cy Publishing.

Grossman, Lawrence K. (1995). *The electronic republic. Reshaping democracy in the information age*. New York: Penguin Books.

Hacker, Kenneth L. and van Dijk, Jan (eds) (2000). *Digital democracy. Issues of theory and practice*. London: Sage.

Hague, Barry and Loader, Brian (eds) (1999). *Digital democracy: discourse and decision-making in the information age*. London: Routledge.

Hale, Matthew, Musso, Juliet and Weare, Christopher (1999). Developing digital democracy: evidence from Californian municipal Web pages. In Barry Hague and Brian Loader (eds) *Digital democracy: discourse and decision-making in the information age*. London: Routledge, pp. 96–115.

Healy, Dave (1997). Cyberspace and place. The Internet as middle landscape on the elecronic frontier. In David Porter (ed.), *Internet culture*. New York, London: Routledge: pp. 55–68.

Hiltz, Starr Roxane and Turoff, Murray (1978). *The network nation*. Reading, MA: Addison-Wesley.

Hoff, Jens, Horrocks, Ivan and Tops, Pieter (2000). *Democratic governance and new technology: technologically mediated innovations in political practice in western Europe*. London: Routledge.

Holma, J. (1998). Information technology as a factor in foreign policy making. Paper presented at 26 the ECPR Joint Sessions of Workshops, University of Warwick.

Holmes, David (ed.) (1997). *Virtual politics. Identity & community in cyberspace*. London: Sage.

Jones, Steven (ed.) (1997). *Virtual culture*. London: Sage.

Kamarck, Elaine (1999). Campaigning on the Internet in the elections of 1998. In Elaine Kamarck and Joseph Nye Jr (eds), *Democracy.com? Governance in a networked world*. Hollis, NH: Hollis Publishing, pp. 99–123.

Kergoat, Danièle (1994). De la jubilation à la déréliction. L'utilisation du Minitel dans les luttes infirmières (1988–1989) in *Les coordinations de travailleurs dans la confrontation sociale*. Paris: Futur Antérieur/L'Harmattan, pp. 73–101.

Kitchin, Rob (1998). *Cyberspace*. Chichester: Wiley & Sons. (See especially Chapter 5, Cyberspace, politics and polity.)

Kubicek, Herbert, Dutton, William H. and Williams, Robin (eds) (1997). *The social shaping of information superhighways*. New York: St Martin Press.

Kubicek, Herbert and Wagner, Rose (1998). Community networks in a generational perspective. Paper presented at the Workshop Designing Across Borders: The Community Design of Community Networks, Participatory Design Conference, Seattle, Washington, November 12–14.

Lee, Eric (1997). *The Labour movement and the Internet. The new internationalism*. New York: Pluto Press.

Licklider, J. C. R. (1979). Computers and government. In Michael Dertouzos and Joel Moses (eds), *The computer age*. Cambridge, MA: The MIT Press.

Lyon, David (1994). *The electronic eye. The rise of surveillance society*. Cambridge: Polity Press.

Mann, William (1995). *Politics on the net*. Indianapolis, IN: Que Corporation.

Marchand, Marie (1987). *La grande aventure du Minitel.* Paris: Larousse.

Margolis, M. *et al.* (1997). Campaigning on the Internet: parties and candidates on the World Wide Web in the 1996 Primary Season. *Press/Politics,* 2 (1), 59–78.

Margolis, Michael and Resnick, David (2000). *Politics as usual: the cyberspace "revolution".* Thousand Oaks, CA: Sage.

Massit-Follea, Françoise (1997). La démocratie électronique: mise en perspectives. In Jean Mouchon (dir.), *Information et démocratie. Mutation du débat public.* Paris: ENS Editions.

Mayer, Nonna (1997). Le sondage délibératif au secours de la démocratie. *Le Débat,* 96, September–October, pp. 67–72.

Melucci, Alberto (1996). *Challenging codes. Collective action in an information age.* Cambridge, MA: Cambridge University Press (especially Chapter 10).

Meyer, David and Tarrow, Sidney (eds) (1998). *The social movement society. Contentious politics for a new century.* Lanham, MD: Rowman & Littlefield.

Miège, Bernard (1989 and 1997). *La société conquise par la communication.* Grenoble: Presses universitaires de Grenoble, vols 1 and 2. (Especially, vol. 1, pp. 105–167 and vol. 2, pp. 109–140.)

Morley, David and Robins, Kevin (1995). *Spaces of identity. Global media, electronic landscapes and cultural boundaries.* London: Routledge.

Myers, D. J. (1994). Communication technology and social movements: contributions of computer networks to activism. *Social Science Computer Review,* 12, (2), pp. 250–260.

Neustadt, Richard M. (1985). Electronic politics. In Tom Forrester (ed.), *The information technology revolution.* Oxford: Basil Blackwell, pp. 561–570.

Nguyen, Dan Thu and Alexander, Jon (1996). The coming of cyberspacetime and the end of the polity. In Rob Shields (ed.), *Cultures of internet. Virtual spaces, real histories, living bodies.* London: Sage, pp. 99–124.

Nimmo, Dan (1994).The Electronic Town Hall in Campaign '92: interactive forum or carnival of Buncombe? In Robert E. Denton (ed.), *The 1992 presidential campaign. A communication perspective.* Westport, CN: pp. 207–226.

Norris, Pippa (2000). *A virtuous circle. Political communications in postindustrial societies.* Cambridge: Cambridge University Press.

Norris, Pippa (2001). *Digital divide. Civic engagement, information poverty, and the internet worldwide.* Cambridge: Cambridge University Press.

O'Donnell, Susan (1995a). Solidarity on the Internet: a study of electronic mailing lists. MA thesis, Center for Journalism Studies. Cardiff: University of Wales, August.

O'Donnell, Susan and Guillermo, Delgado (1995b). Using the Internet to strengthen the indigenous nations of the Americas. *The Journal of Media Development,* 3.

Oliver, Pamela E. and Marwell, Gerald (1992). Mobilizing technologies for collective action. In Aldon D. Morris and Carol McClurg Mueller (eds), *Frontiers in social movement theory.* New Haven, CT: Yale University Press, pp. 251–272.

Owen, D., Davis, R. and Strikler, V. J. (1999). Congress and the Internet. *The Harvard International Journal of Press-Politics,* 4 (2), pp. 10–29.

Pool, Ithiel de Sola (1983). *Technologies of freedom: on free speech in an electronic age.* Cambridge, MA: Belknap/Harvard University Press.

Poster, Mark (1997). Cyberdemocracy: Internet and the public sphere. In David Porter (ed.), *Internet culture*. London: Routledge, pp. 201–218.

Pratchett, Lawrence (1995). Democracy denied: the political consequences of ICTs in UK local government. In W. B. H. J. van de Donk, I. Th. M. Snellen and P. W. Tops (eds), *Orwell in Athens. A perspective on informatization and democracy*. Amsterdam: IOS Press, pp. 127–154.

Raab, Charles D. (1997). Privacy, democracy information. In Brian Loader (ed.), *The governance of cyberspace*. London: Routledge, pp. 155–174.

Reingold, Howard (1993). *The virtual community: homesteading on the electronic frontier*. Reading, MA: Addison-Wesley (the subtitle of the book varies in different editions).

Rodota, Stefano (1999). *La démocratie électronique. De nouveaux concepts et expériences politiques*. Rennes: Éditions Apogée (especially Chapter 6).

Roper, J. (1999). New Zealand political parties on line: the World Wide Web as a tool for democracy or for political marketing? In C. Toulouse and T. Luke (eds), *The politics of cyberspace*. London: Routledge, pp. 69–83.

Schneider, Steven M. (1996). Creating a democratic public sphere through political discussion: A case study of abortion conversation on the Internet, *Social Science Computer Review*, 14 (4), winter, pp. 373–393.

Schuler, Douglas (1996). *New community networks*. Reading, MA: Addison-Wesley.

Sclove, Richard (1995). *Democracy and technology*. New York: The Guilford Press.

Sheldon, Annis (1991). Giving voice to the poor. *Foreign policy*, 84, autumn, pp. 93–106.

Smith, C. and Webster, W. (1995). Information, communication and new technology in the political parties. In J. Lovenduuski and J. Stanyer (eds), *Contemporary political studies*. York: UK Political Studies Association.

Smith, Marc A. and Kollock, Peter (eds) (1999). *Communities in cyberspace*. New York: Routledge (especially Chapter 8, Invisible Crowds in Cyberspace).

Sreberny-Mohammadi, Annabelle *et al.* (1997). *Media in global context. A reader*. London: Arnold.

Steyaert, Jo (2000). Local government on line and the role of the residents. *Social Science Computer Review*, 18(1), spring, pp. 3–16.

Taylor, John *et al.* (1999). Special issue on parliaments and the ICT. *Parliamentary Affairs*.

Theranian, Majid (1990). *Technologies of power. Information machines and democratic prospects*. Norwood, NJ: Ablex Publishing Company (especially pp. 217–227).

Thompson, John B. (1995). *The media and modernity. A social theory of the media*. Cambridge: Polity Press (especially Chapter 8, The Reinvention of Publicness).

Tsagarousianou, Roza, Tambini, Damian and Bryan, Cathy (1998). *Cyberdemocracy. Technology, cities and civic networks*. London: Routledge.

van de Donk, W. B. H. J., Snellen, I. Th. M. and Tops, P. W. (1995). *Orwell in Athens. A perspective on informatization and democracy*. Amsterdam: IOS Press.

Vedel, Thierry (2000). Internet et les villes: trois approches de la citoyenneté. *Hermès*, nos. 26–27, pp. 247–262.

Ward, S. and Gibson, R. (1998). The first internet election? UK political parties and campaigning in cyberspace. In I. Crewe *et al.* (eds), *Political communications: why Labour won the 1997 General Election*. Ilford: Frank Cass, pp. 93–112.

Woolley, B. (1992). *Virtual worlds.* London: Blackwell.

4

MASS COMMUNICATION
AND PUBLIC OPINION

Gerald M. Kosicki

Introduction

This paper addresses the twin puzzles of public opinion and mass communication, as well as their inter-relationships. Public opinion is fundamental in democratic societies, as is media discourse, and yet both remain confusing as research concepts.

Mass communication scholars have been engaged in empirical research on the nature of mass communication effects on audiences for many decades. These studies have included dependent variables that range from aggressive behavior through various psychological constructs to emotions and fright responses to scary materials. Many of these studies have implications for the study of mass communication and public opinion in that they have pioneered new ways of measuring media use or attention, intervening variables found helpful in understanding media effects generally, or have solved some other knotty problems of methodology. The study of mass communication and public opinion, however, has become an important topic in its own right, with its own set of preoccupations, practitioners, theoretical perspectives and methods. Each of these may be broader than is commonly thought. The field has in recent years coalesced around several major theoretical positions. The study of these is pursued rigorously with a variety of methods. The field is small in terms of the practitioners who work only or even mainly on such problems. But it is augmented by a rather large and growing group who do their primary work in other areas. Often these individuals have worked off and on in the media-public opinion nexus, sometimes with lasting effect.

Scope of this chapter

The main concern of this chapter is to discuss the central topics that constitute the study of communication and public opinion today. This will begin with a statement of the theoretical tradition, some of the key studies and findings and in some cases integrative reviews. Finally, I will comment upon and review a few other issues that are important for the continued success of this enterprise, as well as a few comments about the future of this research area.

Public opinion is a concept that can be seen to encompass a series of subtopics that cut across many classic problems and fields of study. The general competence of citizens in a democracy is one of the key issues in public opinion, examining knowledge held by citizens, the informed nature of decision making in political life, and the sources of such knowledge are all important matters in democratic society. There is a long history in our field of studying levels of political knowledge and how it varies across social strata and among audience members with various levels of media use and attention. The knowledge gap hypothesis remains a major domain for organizing such work in the field, and there are signs this is being brought to bear on questions involving new media and the on-line world in general.

A second matter is the treatment of political issues. Once exclusively the province of agenda-setting theorists, the study of public issues in the field is now considerably broader, encompassing the way political issues are framed and understood by citizens and the process by which such determinations are made. The latter point gets us into the realm of the ingredients of public opinion, priming.

Third, we enter into the realm of models of opinion formation and change, according to the integration of new information. As in some of the matters above, work in this area, using information-processing theories borrowed from cognitive and social psychology, has done much to revolutionize thinking in this area over the past twenty years.

There are, of course, many things left out of this essay. The large and growing influence of social marketing campaigns aimed at the improvement of public health in terms of anti-smoking, anti-cancer, anti-violence, anti-binge drinking, anti-HIV campaigns. This specialized area would require its own chapter. Similarly, the entire realm of political campaign communications can only be dealt with here as part of the larger themes and frameworks of media effects. Many important questions are left out on which there is important literature. The effects of media in social contexts such as election campaigns and comment on the role of media in elections, debates, and advertising and negative campaigning is similarly beyond the scope of this essay.

Influence of psychology

One of the more notable features of recent work in public opinion is the unmistakable influence of social psychology. Theories, concepts and methods from social psychology are major factors in the flood of work that has been published in the past twenty years, and this trend is accelerating rapidly. All this is part of the cognitive revolution that is sweeping through much of political science, communication, and many other fields, bringing both realistic assumptions about human thinking abilities, and a veritable treasure trove of theories and hypotheses that have been for the most part worked out in laboratory studies. The borrowing fields have found this attractive for many reasons, but mainly because the cognitive approaches have produced real benefits in a common vocabulary that provides wide access to the borrowers work across many disciplines and fosters a true interdisciplinary perspective. These theories, concepts and hypotheses have proven to be very robust, and have produced considerable benefits for both the borrowing and the lending fields. See, however, Krosnick and McGraw (2002) for more on the asymmetrical contributions of political psychology to psychology and political science.

An unexpected aspect of this cognitive revolution in the field of public opinion has been the emergence of a great wave of methodological innovation in survey research (Groves et al., 1988; Schwarz et al., 1998; Weisberg et al., 1996). This is important because survey remains the typical ways that public opinion is empirically assessed. In this case, models from cognitive psychology have been used to produce substantial insights into question wording variations (e.g. Krosnick, 1999; Schwarz & Sudman, 1996; Schwarz et al., 1999; Shuman & Presser, 1996; Sudman et al., 1996; Tanur, 1992; Tourangeau et al., 2000; Willis, 1994). Some of this work may have profound implications for what "public opinion" really is (Feldman, 1995). Other methodological work reinterprets many other aspects of survey research from measurement issues to interviewing and data analysis (Sirken et al., 1999). Still other innovations have resulted from technology, such as the shift in reliance from in-person to computer-assisted telephone interviewing, which has improved the management, efficiency and quality of information gathered by controlling virtually all aspects of the interaction of interviewer and interviewee (Couper et al., 1998). Many of the management strategies and insights balancing costs and error are known as the Total Survey Error Approach (e.g. Groves, 1989; Lavrakas, 1993). There have been advances in computer assisted interviewing software (Couper et al., 1998), and even in seemingly mundane or static areas such as sampling (Levy & Lemeshow, 1999), and survey administration (Biemer et al., 1991; Lyberg et al., 1997). Sophisticated work has revolutionized our thinking about non-response (Groves & Couper, 1998; Groves et al., 2002) and other types of non-sampling errors (Lessler & Kalsbeek, 1992). Available evidence suggests this work of reinventing the sample survey is just beginning. Combined with innovative on-line technologies and powerful theories of human cognition and response, we can expect continued innovation from this area for many years as this methodological area becomes a self-conscious field of study (Groves, 1996) with its own training programs. Continued methodological innovations will be needed to keep pace with the development of the World Wide Web and the research potential implied by this technology (Dillman, 2000). Useful at the moment mainly for surveys of technology rich environments, this may change rapidly in the coming years. The web also contains the promise of being a platform upon which many new and unique research innovations can be created. For example, the possibility of delivering multimedia materials to a random sample of people on-line and getting detailed response to their reactions and use of such materials could revolutionize the study of the field.

Definition of public opinion

V. O. Key (1961; p. 14) defined public opinion as "those opinions held by private citizens which governments find it prudent to heed." By this he meant to call attention to the fact that governments may or may not choose to pay attention to every whim of citizens, and may well ignore many trendy blips in opinion polls. Officials may be able to take a casual attitude toward certain opinions because some are not fully formed, carefully thought out opinions. Some views are formed of careful study, experience and discussion; others are not. Wise leaders learn to detect the difference and pay attention to whether views are held by a few or are more widely shared. Strength of opinion is another dimension that has received considerable research attention in recent years (Petty & Krosnick, 1995).

Interdisciplinary character of the field

The conception of the field of communication and public opinion discussed so far cannot fall within the province of any single academic discipline. It is a subfield of many disciplines in the social sciences, ranging from the level fields of psychology and sociology to the so-called variable fields of political science, communication, economics, and public policy. One practical result of this is that scholarly work relevant to the problem is hard to locate as it is spread over many journals in a given field, and over many fields. Funding tends to be problem- or variable-specific, as do publications. This means that it can be difficult to find funding. Publication outlets tend to be discipline-specific, with all the complications that entails for interdisciplinary work. Here I'm speaking not only of specific courtesies such as reciprocal citations, but reviewing practices and the prevalence of the not-invented-here syndrome.

Scholars from big fields looking out tend to see this as less of a problem than those from little fields looking in.

Survey research and public opinion

The contemporary study of public opinion is certainly heavily dependent upon survey research. This is a two-edged sword. On the one hand, survey research is today a highly sophisticated tool with a well-developed empirical and technical literature treating virtually all aspects of the method. On the other hand, it dominates the study of public opinion in such a way that barely allows for challenges or diverse perspectives, leading in some extremes to a Law of the Hammer mentality in certain circles in which everything needs hammering because a hammer is the only tool available. Critics (e.g. Bourdieu, 1979; Herbst, 1999) have pointed out various shortcomings and drawbacks, as well as assumptions made in standard survey research that question the reliance on this method.

Of course, other tools besides surveys are available, most notably the intensive interview and ethnographic methods (e.g. Chong & Marshall, 1999; Graber, 1984; Herbst, 1999; Lane 1962), analysis of voting records (e.g. Kelley, 1983) and most prominently, the analysis of social movement organizations and their interactions with policymakers and journalists (e.g. Gitlin, 1980; Hilgartner & Bosk, 1988; Pan & Kosicki, 2001).

Mass communication and media content

Defining mass communication

While there are many ways to define mass communication, a particularly useful one seems to be provided by Turow (1992; p. 107). In this brief but important article, he suggests the following definition:

> Mass communication is the industrialized [mass] production, reproduction and multiple distribution of messages through technological devices.

In this definition "messages" can be either linguistic or pictorial representations that appear purposeful. The word "industrialized" indicates that the process is carried out by mass media firms – that is, by "conglomerations of organizations that interact regularly in the process of producing and distributing messages."

The definition means that industrial application of technology is a key defining feature of mass communication and this is crucial in separating mass communication from other forms of communication. The industrial process suggests that large numbers of messages and audience members are involved. The definition calls special attention to the industrial nature of message creation, particularly the relationships among media and other sources of social, political, and economic power.

A key element of this perspective is that in stressing attention to the production and distribution processes, along with the considerations that shape news, information and entertainment, there is a recognition that these cultural patterns lead to similar cultural models across stories may be as important as individual stories. As Turow notes:

> Even when the specific subjects that media carry are not the same, the similarity with which creators approach the world can still yield similar perspectives. . . . When local TV stations across the country daily fill their 7:25 a.m. newscasts with tales of overnight murders, robberies and accidents, the general knowledge and world view gleaned from those patterns might be the same, even though individual stories might not be.
>
> (Turow, 1992; p. 108)

Framing news and public affairs

Public deliberation is fundamental in democratic societies (e.g. Kinder & Herzog, 1993). Framing is one perspective from which to approach the study of this, which includes the "discursive process of strategic actors utilizing symbolic resources to participate in collective sense-making about public issues" (Pan & Kosicki, 2001). Framing analysis is an analytical approach to connect normative propositions from "deliberative democracy" and the empirical questions of collective decision making and to understand political participation and experiences in democratic society (Baumgartner & Jones, 1993; Kingdon, 1984).

Public deliberation is the process of collective and open reasoning and discussion about the merits of public policy (Page, 1996). It is fundamental for the study of public opinion and political communication because of its intimate connection with democratic ideals. Furthermore, political communication is being democratized, as seen through the opportunities for public participation in many spheres of activity, ranging from media talk shows (Pan & Kosicki, 1997a), to public opportunity to question candidates directly in debates.

Goffman (1974) defined frames as "schemata of interpretation" that enable individuals to locate, perceive, identify and label occurrences in everyday life. Framing analysis deals with how various social actors act and interact to produce organized ways of making sense of the world (Pan & Kosicki, 1993). Fames are "central organizing ideas to understand and organize political reality" (Gamson & Modigliani, 1987).

Framing also owes much to its roots in cognitive science. Price and Tewksbury (1997) and Price, Tewksbury and Powers (1997) review this literature well and it will not be repeated here. Others such as Iyengar (1991), Cappella and Jamieson (1997) and Scheufele (1999) make this case in the area of media effects. But the effects tradition does not exhaust what framing brings to the study of public opinion and communication.

Frames define the boundaries of discourse surrounding an issue and categorize each political actor involved in the issue in a particular way. Heated political contestation surrounds these boundaries, as well as what an acceptable definition of a given issue really is. Pan and Kosicki (2001) argue that framing analysis needs to place political and social actors in the center of the process. The framing potency of any actor comes from the resources one can bring to bear, one's strategic alliances and one's stock of skills and knowledge in the arts of frame sponsorship and management. Through such resources, they argue, political actors weave "webs of subsidies" to privilege the dissemination and packaging of information in the most advantageous directions.

The combination of a frame and its symbolic devices or "package" functions as a narrative that may resonate in the minds of other actors under certain conditions, which include credibility and shared experiences that form the basis for "frame alignment" (Snow & Benford, 1988). This alignment is enhanced to the extent that an actor can link his or her frame to some enduring values in the society, and thus subsidizing other actors in processing and packaging information concerning a given issue. Framing potency is also determined by certain sociological factors, such as the size and depth of an actor's web of subsidies and the framing actor's ability to mobilize such subsidies with strategic targeting (Pan & Kosicki, 2001). In general, the broader a discursive community becomes, and the more clear its identity becomes, the greater the likelihood of achieving its goals.

This type of framing analysis requires the use of tools and strategies for analysis quite different from those in public opinion analysis, although public opinion analysis might be one part of the total picture. Developing an understanding and empirical verification of such framing efforts requires data about the various framing actors and groups, their communication and other organizing strategies, as well as their messages to other groups as well as the public. This implies that case history approaches may be favored for this part of the story (e.g. Gamson & Modigliani, 1987; Gitlin, 1980).

Pan and Kosicki (1997b) have also introduced the notion of "issue regime" to denote "periods in which a news story is so big that it dominates the amount of total media attention available." These giant stories occupy so much time and space, and consume so many media resources that they tend to crowd out other news items and thus has a profound impact on public discourse and public attention. Following the work of Hilgartner and Bosk (1988) they rely on the notion of public arena, that is, the totality of channels, forums, and means of public deliberation about public policy and the relevant venues in which such matters are discussed. This is based upon the insight, among others, that there is only so much channel capacity in the public arena and so issues compete for resources. The issue regime concept has proven useful in the analysis of public opinion during and after the Gulf War, in which President Bush went from the most popular American president to one of the least, in part because of declining media attention to the war, and the increasing attention to the economy, which was in recession.

Types of effects

Knowledge of public affairs

One of the major problems of democratic societies has been the issue of citizen competence, a key component of which is knowledge. A persistent criticism of citizens and electorates in democratic societies is that they do not know enough to participate sensibly in governmental decision making. Related to this is the criticism that public opinion, to the extent it is uninformed, is not worth the attention of officials. Putting aside questions of whether politics is worth the effort required to become informed (e.g. Downs, 1957; Lane, 1962; Lippmann, 1922) in favor of the argument that democracy requires an informed citizenry (Dahl, 1998).

Over the years there has been a steady stream of research on what the public knows about politics (e.g. Converse, 1962; 1990; Delli Carpini & Keeter, 1996) and how rational stands on issues are (e.g. Page & Shapiro, 1992). Timing of the acquisition of information may be of special interest, as demonstrated by the work of Brady and Johnston (1987) and Brady (1993) on information and presidential primaries. This work demonstrates that media may sort candidates first by their so-called viability, and then report details about only the viable ones as a way of winnowing the field in multi-candidate elections. Bartels (1988) has written convincingly on the concept of media and momentum in US primary elections as an effect brought on by the avalanche of publicity that follows a successful primary election win in an early state-level contest. This can propel relatively obscure individuals into national prominence.

Of special interest here is research that examines the role of media in citizen acquisition of this knowledge (Becker *et al.*, 1975). In the early days of the field, knowledge acquisition seemed perhaps too humdrum as a dependent variable and focus was instead on persuasion or attitude change or behaviors such as voting. This turned around and it is now understood that learning is a natural, but important consequence of media use. It is now recognized that it is important to understand not only the level of learning, but also the rate of learning, its distribution through populations and across subgroups, and the inequalities of this distribution. These are important social questions that have policy implications for media and governments.

Learning from the news in recent times has focused on making content easier to understand and as well as the information processing characteristics of the audience (e.g. Kosicki & McLeod, 1990; Robinson & Levy,

1986). Davis and Robinson (1989) have produced a masterful essay in which they summarize decades of work in this tradition, along with a variety of other research on unintended audience effects of journalism and news, as well as present some of their own research on news comprehension.

Much of the research in this area over the years might be seen as attempts to improve the measurement of the key independent variables – media use as indicated by frequency of use, exposure to certain public affairs topics (Price & Zaller, 1993), attention (e.g. Chaffee & Schleuder, 1986) or reliance (e.g. McLeod & McDonald, 1985). Other writers have preferred to combine various measures of media use, formal education and knowledge of current affairs and issues into "information" and use that as a construct to predict various aspects of attitude change or stability (Zaller, 1989) is an important statement of this perspective, and deserves careful reading, not only in itself, but because it has been widely influential. Price (1999) gives a very thorough review of the possible conceptual meanings of political information and their empirical counterparts.

In the field of mass communication, a great deal of emphasis has been given to the treatment of inequality of information holding, differential rates at which members of different population subgroups learn new information from media, and factors which tend to increase or decrease these gaps. The knowledge gap hypothesis was first advanced thirty years ago by Tichenor *et al.* (1970; 1980). Over the past decades, it has grown into a major research area in the field, with more than 100 published studies explicitly invoking this perspective (Gaziano, 1997; Viswanath & Finnegan, 1996). Over this time, a great many variations in measurement of dependent and independent variables have been studied, along with an impressive series of contexts such as homogeneous versus heterogeneous communities. Many ways of trying to narrow information gaps have been studied, many in the health communication context (Viswanath & Finnegan, 1996).

The differential rates of adoption of new technologies among certain minority groups and people in rural communities again raises again concerns about inequalities that cast serious doubt on the good life promised by the rapid page of technological invention. Questions have also been raised about the pace of innovation across the globe. These questions remind us that invention is not the same as availability and successful adoption, and that there are many potholes along the road of progress in bringing technology to bear on everyday problems of people, communities, businesses, and government. Innovation in health care practices over the past forty years has been simply stunning, yet even simple matters are not widely understood, and access to high-tech innovations, even in advanced economies, lags. As we stand once again on the brink of a new era in communication, we will do well to remember this fact, as well as to seize the research opportunities afforded us at this critical time. Studies of this sort were never more relevant than they are in today's high-optimism environment for technology. As a field we might also be mindful that studies diagnosing the problems are only part of the way toward successful resolution of them. Careful and creative campaigns and other interventions have the possibility of truly improving lives for our citizens, and communication scholars must be an important part of any such innovations.

Public issues and media effects

Media scholars have had for about thirty years a standard answer for questions about the media and public issues – the agenda-setting hypothesis. This has been presented as an all-purpose response to the role of media in reporting and influencing thinking about public issues. Yet, in recent years, a number of perspectives for dealing with public issues have emerged in the field. This section will take them up one by one.

Agenda-setting

Agenda-setting seeks to establish a causal relationship between the agenda set by the news media and the public agenda as expressed in public opinion about the importance of various issues of the day. The ingredients of this media agenda-setting hypothesis (Kosicki, 1993; p. 101) are a measure of the public agenda derived by content analysis of media, and public opinion expression, typically through survey results, although this could be expressed in alternative ways. In its simplest form, the agenda-setting hypothesis states that the issue priorities of the media come over time to be the issue priorities of the public. Developed by McCombs and Shaw in the late 1960s, this hypothesis has proven to have a great deal of heuristic value in the sense of inspiring studies in this tradition (Rogers *et al.*, 1993).

Agenda-setting at its core is a system for describing the key issues of the day in rather broad, abstract categories such as "the economy," "trust in government," and "environment," and correlating the public and media agendas, sometimes over time. This is an important effect, and empirical support has been found for it in several hundred studies of varying quality (Becker, 1991; Kosicki, 1993). This work seems to have run into something of a rut in the late 1980s and was reinvigorated by the introduction of both information-processing theory and experimental methods (Iyengar & Kinder, 1987). The path-breaking work of political psychologists Iyengar and Kinder not only demonstrated that agenda-setting could indeed be studied experimentally, but also showed that information-processing concepts were useful in understanding this phenomenon and extending it in new, interesting and provocative directions.

Recent major statements in the agenda-setting model (McCombs *et al.*, 1997; Wanta, 1997) point out the impressive volume of work in the area over the years, but do little to explicate the psychological processes involved or build in the direction suggested by Iyengar and Kinder. Ghanem's (1997) efforts, along with Takeshita (1997), for example, to invoke "attribute agenda-setting as the so-called "second level" agenda-setting are worthwhile, but seem to bump into priming (Willnat, 1997) or framing, or both.

Priming and framing hail from different intellectual roots than the agenda-setting model. Agenda-setting is usually discussed as tracing its history from comments of Bernard Cohen (1963) through Walter Lippmann (1922), has been largely innocent of the intellectual lineage of either priming or framing research, which are emerging as more precise and flexible rivals of agenda-setting in terms of ways to think about and study issues in public opinion. Agenda-setting remains a useful perspective, but it should be viewed as one of several perspectives that we might use when thinking about issues. The choice should depend upon the research questions, not tradition.

Priming

Priming, according to Iyengar and Kinder's (1987, p. 63) formulation, is a type of media effects hypothesis that suggests that "By calling attention to some matters while ignoring others, television news influences the standards by which governments, presidents, policies and candidates for public office are judged."

The concept of priming originates with the cognitive revolution in psychology, and is a good example of the application of realistic cognitive assumptions about human thinking powers to applied problems in public opinion and communication. A key assumption is that when making decisions people often simply search for an alternative that is good enough, but not necessarily optimal. This is so because of the limitations of human thinking powers, the great deal of work that optimizing such decisions would require, and limited time and interest. Herbert Simon (1957) coined the word "satisfice" to describe this decision-making process, which characterizes much of human decision making, particularly regarding matters that are not terribly important or consequential. In describing "satisficing" behavior, Simon made the point that people often make decisions on all sorts of matters not on everything they know, but on a rather limited subset of this information, that is, what comes to mind without a great deal of effort. The idea is that if a matter is not particularly important, it does not justify a time-consuming search of all available information and criteria. Instead, we typically seek "good enough" solutions to the choices before us. For most people, most of the time, the world of public affairs, public issues and public officials certainly falls into the realm in which satisficing rather than optimizing is the strategy of choice. Of course, for certain types of decisions of great consequence, humans do attempt to optimize. We might expect this type of decision making style to be more prevalent in circumstances where the consequences of choosing wrongly are expensive or involvement in the decision is high.

As it is applied to problems in public opinion, the priming effects is measured according to an additive model of evaluation as the increased weight associated with the factor that has been made salient by the media during the times subjects are making the required evaluative judgments (Iyengar & Kinder, 1987). In theoretical terms, this is a special case of the general cognitive process called priming, which is derived from the associative network model of human memory, in which a concept is stored as a node on a network and is related to other concepts by semantic paths (e.g. Collins & Loftus, 1975; Higgins & King, 1981; Price & Tewksbury, 1997; Taylor & Fiske, 1978; Wyer & Srull, 1981). Priming is thought to result when a node on the memory network is activated by some stimulus. This node acts as a kind of interpretive framework for further information processing or judgment formation. Once activated, the node may remain active for an undetermined time and thus increases the probability that related thoughts may be activated.

The implications of this for our field are that media coverage of an issue is an indication of the salience of the issue in media content. This may affect the cognitive processes that audience members use to make sense of a given issue. Pan and Kosicki (1997b, p. 10) note that this may happen in at least three ways: increase the ease with which the related thought elements are activated, increase the breadth of the accessible thought elements related to a given topic or issue, and tighten the links of the various thought elements. The upshot is that individuals will be more likely to use issue elements activated by media in their calculations for evaluating a given policy or policy actor such as the president.

Note that this is very different from traditional persuasion research as explained by Miller and Krosnick (1996, p. 81):

> Whereas persuasion focuses on media messages advocating particular positions, priming can be invoked simply by a news story devoting attention to an issue without advocating a position. And whereas persuasion is thought to result from effortful decision-making about a message's likely veracity, priming presumably occurs as a result of automatic and effortless processes of spreading activation in people's minds.

Key predictions based on this theory have been supported strongly by data from both laboratory experiments and population surveys (e.g. Iyengar & Kinder, 1987; Iyengar & Simon, 1993; Iyengar et al., 1984; Krosnick & Kinder, 1990).

Combining data from content analysis, as well as panel surveys, Pan and Kosicki, 1997b have shown, for example, that the rise and fall of President

Bush between August 1990 and November 1992 in public opinion polls was closely tied to changes in the salience of the Gulf War and economic recession.

Study of political attitudes and attitude change

The final area to discuss is persuasion, which is a very active area of research and would require many pages to develop fully. For our purposes, it is noteworthy that this area of study has been completely transformed by the cognitive revolution, largely built around the Elaboration Likelihood Model and its variations (Lau & Sears, 1986; Perloff, 1993; Petty & Cacioppo, 1986). In the realm of public opinion, once again we see the effects of this work in many ways. Sniderman, Brody and Tetlock (1991), in an influential work, articulated a notion of "reasoning chain" which is a kind of metaphor for the reasoning process, particularly one in which people are shown to compensate for missing information by engaging in judgmental shortcuts, often derived from ideology. The areas of political judgment formation (Lodge & McGraw, 1995), persuasion (Mutz, Sniderman & Brody, 1996), and causes and consequences of attitude strength (Petty & Krosnick, 1995) have been particularly active in the 1990s.

The work of Zaller (1992) has been important for his introduction of the R-A-S Model of public opinion formation. In this, the main notion is that public opinion is an outcome of a process in which individuals *receive* new information, decide whether to *accept* it, and then *sample* at the moment of answering questions. Zaller presents a great deal of evidence in varying information environments in support of his rather general model. Zaller has made rather extravagant claims about a return to a powerful media effects paradigm, but empirically has not always taken care to differentiate among various sources of information such as media versus general education, or to take note of "real-world" conditions as alternative sources of influence. Zaller (1992) uses his model to argue that most people, most of the time, make up their attitudes as they go along. This is a significantly different position to take with respect to the problem of "nonattitudes" as it has developed over the years (e.g. Converse, 1964; 1970). Proponents of nonattitudes claim that some issues are so abstract or unrelated to people's concerns that people do not form an attitude about them. See also Sniderman *et al.*, (2001) for a different, more hopeful, perspective on non-attitudes and the incorporation of new information with prior attitudes. Through a series of clever experiments embedded in population surveys, they show that citizens make judgments about issues in part on prior attitudes, but updated with information on the specific problem (p. 284).

Entertainment content and politics

There is one additional literature that is relevant to the world of communication and public opinion about political matters, and that is the rather far-ranging literature of entertainment content and political effects. This is a highly controversial topic, with a large and diverse literature. Most of the work in this area draws upon the seminal work of George Gerbner and his colleagues on cultivation and mainstreaming, a type of media effect in which heavy television viewing contributes to viewers' notions of social reality. Originally confined largely to television and violence, this work has generated very broad findings over many politically and socially significant topic areas (e.g. Shanahan, 1998). The work of Gerbner and his students is massive and a detailed review of this vast literature and its critics is beyond the scope of this essay. There are a number of excellent summaries and extensions of this vast literature, including that of Morgan and Shanahan (1996), Shanahan and Morgan (1999), and Signorielli and Morgan (1990). The work has also drawn its share of critics, e.g. Hirsch (1980, 1981), Hawkins and Pingree (1980), and Potter (1994), among others.

Alternative conceptions of public opinion

Although survey research technology is pervasive in the study of public opinion today, there remain doubts in some quarters about the desirability of this state of affairs. Bourdieu (1979) argued a complex case against public opinion as measured by surveys, charging that pollsters wrongly assume that everyone is capable of producing an opinion, that all opinions measured in a survey are necessarily equivalent, and that simply producing a poll about a particular issue framed in a certain way assumes that there is some agreement about the importance of those issues. These doubts are not new, although they are often treated by critics as if they were, perhaps because the essay appeared without any notes or references. In any case, similar arguments are traceable at least as far back as the work of Lippmann (1922) and Blumer (1948), who argued in part that that opinions of those in powerful positions always matter more than those of common citizens. Bourdieu's arguments are also oddly parallel to those of Lippmann (1922), who harbored grave doubts about the basic competency of citizens. In recent years, research has responded to these critiques in innovative ways. Herbst (1992, 1993, 1994 and 1999) has bolstered this critique in important ways and pointing out significant limitations in polling practices and purposes and showing alternative ways of studying public opinion (Herbst, 1995). Champagne (e.g. 1997) has also emerged as a critic of polling in electoral and other contexts, bringing considerable sophistication to bear on issues of journalism and the use of polling and social science data in general. However, recent American evidence suggests that pollsters and journalists are working hard to understand each other's strengths and limitations and work is being done that suggests some very sophisticated conceptual and methodological tools being brought to bear on the coverage of elections (e.g. Lavrakas & Traugott, 2000).

In addition, significant large-scale social experiments such as the National Issues Convention have been proposed, implemented (Fishkin, 1991, 1995) and studied McCombs and Reynolds (1999). Based in part on critiques of public opinion similar to those voiced by Bourdieu, Blumer and Herbst, we have seen large-scale attempts to improve the measurement of public opinion, including the innovation of tools such as the "choice questionnaire" (Neijens, 1986), a technique for providing an informed basis for survey responses in the context of the Dutch general social debate about the use of nuclear power. These early studies and the later work of Price and Neijens (1997; 1998) have done much to both focus attention on the notion of "quality" in public opinion, but also ways to foster public deliberation, which has in itself become a very significant topic in recent years (e.g. Bohman, 1996; Kinder & Herzog, 1993; Putnam, 2000).

Conclusion

The study of public opinion and mass communication is seen as a complex, interdisciplinary matter, drawing upon the work of many individual disciplines, but being strongly influenced by cognitive and social psychology and various aspects of sociology, among others. This leads to a rich perspective, but also to information scatter and lack of focus for a small field. Fortunately, the number of practitioners continues to increase, and this interdisciplinary nature might be seen as one the major strengths in the years ahead.

The study of media content has been recently reinvigorated by the perspective of framing analysis, and this is likely to continue far into the future. This vigorous tradition strongly suggests that there will be increased opportunity in the future to study the relationships among media content and public opinion in very satisfying ways.

Pan and Kosicki (1996) have suggested four major ways that media content relates to the opinion formation process. First, media function as sources of information. This information, interpreted in various ways by recipients and learned with various degrees of completeness, is nonetheless helpful in enhancing the importance of certain cognitive factors involved in policy reasoning, that is, influencing the ingredients of public opinion. Second, media provide images, instances and episodes that function as examples of abstract principles involved in thinking about various issues. This may well enhance the capacity for ideological thinking, and relating such ideology to concrete examples. Third, the media may help arouse and sustain emotional and affective experiences relevant to public issues. Patriotic feelings engendered by war coverage, or moral outrage developed from portrayals of genocide are powerful motivators and shapers of public opinion. Finally, media portray through the use of examples, appeals to emotions, and other symbolic devices that audiences use to frame public policy issues in specific ways. These portrayals not only limit the scope of discussion, but supply the vocabulary and other ingredients of opinion formation.

Media are thus seen as powerful, but not automatic factors in the public discourse and public opinion formation and change.

Acknowledgments

This chapter was originally presented to the political communication study group, International Political Science Association, Quebec, August 27–31, 1999. The author acknowledges the helpful discussion of the seminar participants and particularly the insightful comments of Philippe J. Maarek, Gadi Wolfsfeld and Peter Golding.

References

Bartels, Larry M. (1988). *Presidential primaries and the dynamics of public choice*. Princeton, NJ: Princeton University Press.

Baumgartner, Frank R. and Jones, Bryan D. (1993). *Agendas and instability in American politics*. Chicago, IL: University of Chicago Press.

Becker, Lee B. (1991). Reflecting on metaphors. *Communication yearbook 14* (pp. 341–346). Newbury Park, CA: Sage Publications.

Becker, Lee B., McCombs, Maxwell E. and McLeod, Jack M. (1975). The development of political cognitions. In Steven H. Chaffee (ed.), *Political communication* (pp. 21–63). Beverly Hills, CA: Sage.

Biemer, Paul P., Groves, Robert M., Lyberg, Lars E. *et al.* (1991). *Measurement errors in surveys*. New York: John Wiley & Sons.

Blumer, Herbert (1948). Public opinion and public opinion polling. *American Sociological Review*, 13(5), 542–549.

Bohman, James (1996). *Public deliberation: pluralism, complexity and democracy*. Cambridge, MA: MIT Press.

Bourdieu, Pierre (1979). Public opinion does not exist. In Armand Mattelart and Seth Singelaub (eds), *Communication and class struggle* (pp. 124–130). New York: International General.

Brady, Henry E. (1993). Knowledge, strategy and momentum in presidential primaries. *Political Analysis*, 5, 1–38.

Brady, Henry E. and Johnston, R. (1987). What's the primary message? Horse race or issue journalism? In Gary R. Orren and Nelson W. Polsby (eds), *Media and momentum* (pp. 127–186). New York: Chatham House.

Cappella, Joseph N. and Jamieson, Kathleen H. (1997). *Spiral of cynicism*. New York: Oxford University Press.

Chaffee, Steven H. and Schleuder, Joan (1986). Measurement and effects of attention to media news. *Human Communication Research*, 13, 76–107.

Champagne, Patrick (1997). Pre-election polls and democracy. In Shella Perry and Maire Cross (eds). *Voices of France: Social, political and cultural identity* (pp. 3–17). London: Pinter.

Chong, Dennis and Marshall, Anna-Maria (1999). When morality and economics collide (or not) in a Texas community. *Political Behavior*, 21(2), 91–122.

Cohen, Bernard (1963). *The press and foreign policy*. Princeton, NJ: Princeton University Press.

Collins, A. and Loftus, E. (1975). A spreading activation theory of semantic memory. *Psychological Review*, 82, 407–428.

Converse, Philip E. (1962). Information flow and the stability of partisan attitudes. *Public Opinion Quarterly*, 26(4), 578–599.

Converse, Philip E. (1964). The nature of belief systems in mass publics. In David Apter (ed.), *Ideology and discontent* (pp. 206–261). New York: Free Press.

Converse, Philip E. (1970). Attitudes and non-attitudes: continuation of a dialogue. In Edward R. Tufte (ed.), *The quantitative analysis of social problems* (pp. 168–190). Reading, MA: Addison-Wesley.

Converse, Philip E. (1990). Popular representation and the distribution of information. In J. A. Ferejohn and J. Kuklinski (eds), *Information and democratic processes* (pp. 367–388). Urbana, IL: University of Illinois Press.

Couper, Mick P., Baker, Reginald P., Bethlehem, Jelke, Clark, Cynthia Z. F., Martin, Jean, Nicholls, William, L. and O'Reilly, James M. (1998). *Computer assisted survey information collection*. New York: John Wiley and Sons.

Dahl, Robert A. (1998). *On democracy*. New Haven, CT: Yale University Press.

Davis, Dennis K. and Robinson, John P. (1989). Newsflow and democratic society in an age of electronic media. *Public Communication and Behavior*, 2, 59–102.

Delli Carpini, Michael X. and Keeter, Scott. (1996). *What Americans know about politics and why it matters*. New Haven, CT: Yale University Press.

Dillman, Don A. (2000). *Mail and internet surveys*. New York: John Wiley & Sons.

Downs, Anthony. (1957). *An economic theory of democracy*. New York: Harper.

Feldman, Stanley (1995). Answering survey questions: the measurement and meaning of public opinion. In Milton Lodge and Kathleen McGraw (eds), *Political judgment* (pp. 249–270). Ann Arbor, MI: University of Michigan Press.

Fishkin, James S. (1991). *Democracy and deliberation: new directions for democratic reform*. New Haven, CT: Yale University Press.

Fishkin, James S. (1995). *The voice of the people: public opinion and democracy*. New Haven, CT: Yale University Press.

Gamson, William A. and Modigliani, Andre (1987). The changing culture of affirmative action. *Research in Political Sociology*, 3, 137–177.

Gaziano, Cecile (1997). Forecast 2000: widening knowledge gaps. *Journalism and Mass Communication Quarterly*, 74(2), 237–264.

Ghanem, Salma (1997). Filling in the tapestry: the second-level of agenda-setting. In Maxwell McCombs, Donald L. Shaw, and David H. Weaver (eds), *Communication and democracy* (pp. 3–14). Mahwah, NJ: Erlbaum.

Gitlin, Todd (1980). *The whole world is watching*. Berkeley, CA: University of California Press.

Goffman, Erving (1974). *Frame analysis*. New York: Harper and Row.

Graber, Doris A. (1984). *Processing the news*. New York: Longman.

Groves, Robert M. (1989). *Survey errors and survey costs.* New York: John Wiley & Sons.

Groves, Robert M. (1996). Presidential address: the educational infrastructure of the survey research profession. *Public Opinion Quarterly,* 60, 477–490.

Groves, Robert M. and Couper, Mick P. (1998). *Nonresponse in household interview surveys.* New York: John Wiley and Sons.

Groves, Robert M., Biemer, Paul P., Lyberg, Lars E. *et al.* (1988). *Telephone survey methodology.* New York: John Wiley and Sons.

Groves, Robert M., Dillman, Don A., Eltinge, John L. and Little, Roderick J. A. (2002). *Survey nonresponse.* New York: John Wiley and Sons.

Hawkins, Robert P. and Pingree, Suzanne (1980). Some processes in the cultivation effect. *Communication Research,* 7, 193–226.

Herbst, Susan (1992). Surveying the public sphere: applying Bourdieu's critique of opinion polls. *International Journal of Public Opinion Research,* 4(3), 220–229.

Herbst, Susan (1993). *Numbered voices: how opinion polling has shaped American politics.* Chicago, IL: University of Chicago Press.

Herbst, Susan (1994). *Politics at the margin.* Cambridge: Cambridge University Press.

Herbst, Susan (1995). On the disappearance of groups: 19th and early 20th century conceptions of public opinion. In Theodore L. Glasser and Charles T. Salmon (eds), *Public opinion and the communication of consent* (pp. 89–104). New York: Guilford Press.

Herbst, Susan (1999). *Reading public opinion.* Chicago, IL: University of Chicago Press.

Higgins, E. Tory and King, G. (1981). Accessibility of social constructs: information, processing consequences of individual and contextual variability. In N. Cantor and J. F. Kihlstrom (eds), *Personality, cognition, and social interaction* (pp. 69–121). Hillsdale, NJ: Erlbaum.

Hilgartner, Stephen and Bosk, Charles L. (1988). The rise and fall of social problems: a public arenas model. *American Journal of Sociology,* 94, 53–78.

Hirsch, Paul (1980). The "scary world" of the nonviewer and other anomalies: a reanalysis of Gerbner *et al.*'s findings on cultivation analysis. *Communication Research,* 7, 403–456.

Hirsch, Paul (1981). On not learning from one's own mistakes: a reanalysis of Gerbner *et al.*'s findings on cultivation analysis, part II. *Communication Research,* 8, 3–37.

Iyengar, Shanto. (1991). *Is anyone responsible?* Chicago, IL: University of Chicago Press.

Iyengar, Shanto and Kinder, Donald R. (1987). *News that matters.* Chicago, IL: University of Chicago Press.

Iyengar, Shanto and Simon, Adam (1993). News coverage of the gulf crisis and public opinion: a study of agenda-setting, priming and framing. *Communication Research,* 20, 365–383.

Iyengar, Shanto, Kinder, Donald R., Peters, M. D. and Krosnick, Jon A. (1984). The evening news and presidential evaluations. *Journal of Personality and Social Psychology,* 46, 778–787.

Kelley, Stanley (1983). *Interpreting elections.* Princeton, NJ: Princeton University Press.

Key, V.O. (1961). *Public opinion and American democracy.* New York: Knopf.

Kinder, Donald R. and Herzog, Don (1993). Democratic discussion. In George E. Marcus and Russell L. Hanson (eds), *Reconsidering the democratic public*. University Park, PA: University of Pennsylvania Press.

Kingdon, John (1984). *Agendas, alternatives and public policies*. New York: Harper Collins.

Kosicki, Gerald M. (1993). Problems and opportunities in agenda-setting research. *Journal of Communication*, 43(2), 100–127.

Kosicki, Gerald M. and McLeod, Jack M. (1990). Learning from political news: Effects of media images and information processing strategies. In Sidney Kraus (ed.), *Mass communication and political information processing* (pp. 69–83). Hillsdale, NJ: Erlbaum.

Krosnick, Jon A. (1999). Maximizing questionnaire quality. In John P. Robinson, Phillip, R. Sharer and Lois S. Wrightsman (eds), *Measures of political attitudes* (pp. 37–57). San Diego, CA: Academic Press.

Krosnick, Jon A. and Kinder, Donald R. (1990). Altering the foundations of support for the president through priming. *American Political Science Review*, 84, 497–512.

Krosnick, Jon A. and McGraw, Kathleen M. (2002). Psychological political science versus political psychology true to its name: a plea for balance. In Kristen R. Monroe (ed.), *Political psychology* (pp. 79–94). Mahwah, NJ: Lawrence Erlbaum Associates.

Lane, Robert (1962). *Political ideology*. New York: Free Press.

Lau, Richard R. and Sears, David O. (1986). Introduction to political cognition. *Symposium on Cognition*, 19.

Lavrakas, Paul J. (1993). *Telephone survey methods: sampling, selection and supervision* (2nd edition). Thousand Oaks, CA: Sage Publications.

Lavrakas, Paul J. and Traugott, Michael W. (eds). (2000). *Election polls, the news media and democracy*. New York: Chatham House.

Lessler, Judith T. and Kalsbeek, William D. (1992). *Nonsampling error in surveys*. New York: John Wiley and Sons.

Levy, Paul S. and Lemeshow, Stanley (1999). *Sampling of populations: methods and applications* (3rd edition). New York: John Wiley & Sons.

Lippmann, Walter (1922). *Public opinion*. New York: Macmillan.

Lodge, Milton and McGraw, Kathleen M. (1995). *Political judgment*. Ann Arbor, MI: University of Michigan Press.

Lyberg, Lars, Biemer, Paul, Collins, Martin *et al.* (1997). *Survey measurement and process quality*. New York: John Wiley & Sons.

McCombs, Maxwell and Reynolds, Ann (1999). *The poll with a human face: the national issues convention experiment in political communication*. Mahwah, NJ: Lawrence Erlbaum Associates.

McCombs, Maxwell, Shaw, Donald L. and Weaver, David (1997). *Communication and democracy: exploring the intellectual frontiers in agenda-setting theory.* Mahwah, NJ: Erlbaum.

McLeod, Jack M. and McDonald, Daniel G. (1985). Beyond simple exposure: media orientations and their impact on political processes. *Communication Research* 12(1), 3–33.

Miller, Joanne and Krosnick, Jon A. (1996). News media impact on the ingredients of presidential evaluations: a program of research on the priming hypothesis. In Diana Mutz, Paul M. Sniderman, and Richard A. Brody (eds), *Political persuasion and attitude change* (pp. 79–99). Ann Arbor, MI: University of Michigan Press.

Morgan, Michael and Shanahan, James (1996). Two decades of cultivation research: an appraisal and meta-analysis. *Communication yearbook 20* (pp. 1–45). Thousand Oaks, CA: Sage Publications.

Mutz, Diana C., Sniderman, Paul M. and Brody, Richard A. (eds), *Political persuasion and attitude change*. Ann Arbor, MI: University of Michigan Press.

Neijens, Peter (1986). *The choice questionnaire: design and evaluation of an instrument for collecting informed opinions of a population*. Amsterdam: Free University Press.

Page, Benjamin I. (1996). *Who deliberates? Mass media in modern democracy*. Chicago, IL: University of Chicago Press.

Page, Benjamin I. and Shapiro, Robert Y. (1992). *The rational public*. Chicago, IL: University of Chicago Press.

Pan, Zhongdang and Kosicki, Gerald M. (1993). Framing analysis: an approach to news discourse. *Political Communication* 10(1), 55–75.

Pan, Zhongdang and Kosicki, Gerald M. (1996). Assessing news media influences on the formation of whites' racial policy preferences. *Communication Research*, 23(2), 147–178.

Pan, Zhongdang and Kosicki, Gerald M. (1997a). Talk show exposure as opinion activity. *Political Communication*, 14(2), 371–388.

Pan, Zhongdang and Kosicki, Gerald M. (1997b). Priming and media impact on the evaluations of the president's performance. *Communication Research*, 24(1), 3–30.

Pan, Zhongdang and Kosicki, Gerald M. (2001). Framing as strategic action in public deliberation. In Stephen D. Reese, Oscar H. Gandy, and August E. Grant (eds), *Framing public life* (pp. 35–65). Mahwah, NJ: Lawrence Erlbaum Associates.

Perloff, Richard M. (1993). *The dynamics of persuasion*. Hillsdale, NJ: Erlbaum.

Petty, Richard and Cacioppo, John (1986). The elaboration likelihood model of persuasion. *Advances in Experimental Social Psychology*, 16.

Petty, Richard E. and Krosnick, Jon A. (1995). *Attitude strength*. Mahwah, NJ: Erlbaum.

Potter, James (1994). Cultivation theory and research: a methodological critique. *Journalism Monogaphs*, 147, 1–35.

Price, Vincent E. (1999). Political information. In John P. Robinson, Phillip R. Shaver, and Lois S. Wrightsman (eds), *Measures of political attitudes* (pp. 591–639). San Diego, CA: Academic Press.

Price, Vincent and Neijens, Peter (1997). Opinion quality in public opinion research. *International Journal of Public Opinion Research*, 9(4), 336–360.

Price, Vincent and Neijens, Peter (1998). Deliberative polls: toward improved measures of informed public opinion? *International Journal of Public Opinion Research*, 10(2), 145–176.

Price, Vincent E. and Tewksbury, David (1997). News values and public opinion: a theoretical account of media priming and framing. In G. Barnett and F. J. Boster (eds), *Progress in communication sciences* (pp. 173–212). Greenwich, CT: Ablex.

Price, Vincent E. and Zaller, John (1993). Who gets the news? An examination of news reception and its implications for research. *Public Opinion Quarterly*, 57, 133–164.

Price, Vincent E., Tewksbury, David and Powers, Elizabeth (1997). Switching trains of thought: the impact of news frames on readers' cognitive responses. *Communication Research* 24(5), 481–506.

Putnam, Robert D. (2000). *Bowling alone: the collapse and revival of American community*. New York: Simon and Schuster.

Robinson, John P. and Levy, Mark (1986). *The main source*. Newbury Park, CA: Sage.

Rogers, Everett M., Dearing, James W. and Bregman, Dorine (1993). The anatomy of agenda-setting research. *Journal of Communication*, 43(2), 68–84.

Scheufele, Dietram (1999). Framing as a theory of media effects. *Journal of Communication*, 49(1), 103–122.

Schuman, Howard and Presser, Stanley (1996). *Questions and answers in attitude surveys*. Thousand Oaks, CA: Sage Publications.

Schwarz, Norbert and Sudman, Seymour (eds) (1996). *Answering questions: methodology for determining cognitive and communicative processes in survey research*. San Francisco, CA: Jossey-Bass.

Schwarz, Norbert, Groves, Robert M. and Schuman, Howard (1998). Survey methods. In Daniel T. Gilbert, Susan T. Fiske and Gardner Lindzey (eds), *Handbook of social psychology* (4th edition, pp. 143–179). New York: Oxford University Press.

Schwarz, Norbert, Park, Denise, Knauper, Barbel and Sudman, Seymour (eds) (1999). *Cognition, aging and self-reports*. Philadelphia, PA: Psychology Press.

Shanahan, James (1998). Television and authoritarianism: exploring the concept of mainstreaming. *Political Communication*, 15, 483–495.

Shanahan, James and Morgan, Michael (1999). *Television and its viewers. Cultivation theory and research*. Cambridge: Cambridge University Press.

Signorielli, Nancy and Morgan, Michael (1990). *Cultivation analysis*. Newbury Park, CA: Sage Publications.

Simon, Herbert A. (1957). *Models of man*. New York: John Wiley & Sons.

Sirken, Monroe G., Herrmann, Douglas J. and Schechler, Susan (eds) (1999). *Cognition and survey research*. New York: John Wiley & Sons.

Sniderman, Paul M., Brody, Richard A. and Tetlock, Philip E. (1991). *Reasoning and choice: explorations in political psychology*. Cambridge: Cambridge University Press.

Sniderman, Paul M., Brody, Richard A. and Tetlock, Philip E. (2001). Public opinion and democratic politics: the problem of nonattitudes and the social construction of political judgment. In James H. Kuklinski (ed.), *Citizens and politics: perspectives from political psychology*. Cambridge: Cambridge University Press.

Snow, David A. and Benford, Robert D. (1988). Ideology, frame resonance and participant mobilization. In Bert Klandermans, Hanspeter Kriesi, and Stanley Tarrow (eds), *From structure to action: comparing social movement research across countries* (pp. 197–217). Greenwich, CT: JAI Press.

Sudman, Seymour, Bradburn, Norman M. and Schwartz, Norbert (1996). *Thinking about answers: the application of cognitive processes to survey methodology*. San Francisco, CA: Jossey-Bass.

Takeshita, Toshio (1997). Exploring the media's roles in defining reality: from issue-agenda setting to attribute-agenda setting. In Maxwell McCombs, Donald L. Shaw, and David H. Weaver (eds), *Communication and democracy* (pp. 15–27). Mahwah, NJ: Erlbaum.

Tanur, Judith M. (ed.) (1992). *Questions about questions: inquiries into the cognitive bases of surveys.* New York: Russell Sage Foundation.

Taylor, Shelley E. and Fiske, Susan T. (1978). Salience, attention and attribution: top of the head phenomena. *Advances in Experimental Social Psychology*, 11, 249–288.

Tichenor, P.J., Donohue, G.A. and Olien, C. (1980). *Community conflict and the press.* Newbury Park, CA: Sage Publications.

Tichenor, Phillip J., Olien, Clarice and Donohue, George A. (1970). Mass media flow and differential growth in knowledge. *Public Opinion Quarterly*, 34, 159–170.

Tourangeau, Roger, Rips, Lance J. and Rasinski, Kenneth (2000). *The psychology of survey response.* Cambridge: Cambridge University Press.

Turow, Joseph (1992). On reconceptualizing mass communication. *Journal of Broadcasting and Electronic Media*, 36, 105–110.

Viswanath, K. and Finnegan, John R. (1996). The knowledge gap hypothesis: twenty-five years later. *Communication Yearbook 19* (pp. 187–227). Thousand Oaks, CA: Sage Publications.

Wanta, Wayne (1997). *The public and the national agenda.* Mahwah, NJ: Erlbaum.

Weisberg, Herbert F., Jon A. Krosnick and Bruce D. Bowen (1996). *An introduction to survey research, polling, and data analysis.* Thousand Oaks, CA: Sage Publications.

Willis, Gordon B. (1994). Cognitive interviewing and questionnaire design: a training manual. Working papers series, No. 7. Office of Research and Methodology, National Center for Health Statistics.

Willnat, Lars (1997). Agenda setting and priming: conceptual links and differences. In Maxwell McCombs, Donald L. Shaw, and David H. Weaver (eds), *Communication and democracy* (pp. 51–66). Mahwah, NJ: Erlbaum.

Wyer, R. S. and Srull, T. K. (1981). Category accessibility: some theoretical and empirical issues concerning the processing of social stiumulus information. *Social Cognition: The Ontario Symposium*, 1, 161–197.

Zaller, John (1989). Bringing converse back in: modeling information flow in political campaigns. *Political Analysis*, 1, 181–234.

Zaller, John (1992). *The nature and origins of mass opinion.* New York: Cambridge University Press.

5

POLITICAL COMMUNICATION AND PERSONAL INFLUENCE

Do the media make a difference?

Guy Lachapelle

The goal of this chapter is to evaluate the pertinence of the social influence model over media influence. The study of the key determinants that shape public opinion has been the central concern of research research in political communication and voting behavior. The contribution of Elihu Katz and Paul Lazarsfeld was vital to the development of the field of political communication; it showed how cross pressures from community leaders (including family and friends) affect political behavior and election outcomes.[1] Attitudinal conflicts can lead, for example, to a reduction of partnership and diminished interest in politics and the policy process. The basis of the authors' study is the 1940 presidential election in the US, they found "that certain people in every stratum of a community serve relay roles in the mass communication of election information and influence."[2]

Katz and Lazarsfeld have also hypothesized a "two-step flow model" of communication and social influence, but subsequent efforts have suggested that this process is probably more a "multi-step process." Political information is mediated by several opinion leaders who then transmit information to the general public and followers. However, the fact that many opinion leaders were not influenced by the mass media caused the impact of the media – press and radio – to become weakened in the political communication process. The "discovery" began with the finding that radio and the printed material appeared to have only negligible effects on actual voting decisions and particularly insignificant effects on *changes* in voting decisions. Here, then, was another finding that lessens the belief in the magic of mass media influence."[3] As they argue, then the key question is: "if the mass media are not the major determinants of an individual's vote decision, then what is?"[4] Katz and Lazarsfeld concluded that "the one source of influence that seemed to be far ahead of all others in determining the way people made up their minds was personal influence."[5]

The key question is therefore who are these "opinion leaders" that influence people? According to their analysis, the "new" opinion leaders "were not at all identical with those who are thought of traditionally as the wielders of influence; opinion leaders seemed to be distributed in all occupational groups, and on every social and economic level."[6] Katz and Lazarsfeld claim that their study simply gives more value to the idea that information is mediated by the "primary group" (family, friends, co-workers). But it raises also the issue of "who or what influences the influentials?" Their results indicated that the mass media play a key role in the lives of opinion leaders and had a lesser influence on people who have no opinion. If a person disagrees with the members or opinion leaders of a community then he or she will be in a conflict situation that can affect participation (opinions, decisions and actions) into the democratic life.[7]

In this chapter – almost sixty years after the "discovery" – we will once again examine the hypotheses formulated by Katz and Lazarsfeld.[8] (1) Do the media influence only opinions leaders? (theory of mininal media effects). (2) Who are those opinion leaders? (theory of elite domination). (3) How do opinion leaders shape public opinion during and outside election periods? (theory of elite domination/manipulation of mass opinion through use of the media). (4) Finally, we will briefly submit our hypothesis that we labelled "the screening theory of communication."

The empirical testing of a philosophical issue: the participation of citizens in a democratic life

Katz and Lazarsfeld's book begins with a quote from John Stuart Mill that reads as follows: "And what is a still greater novelty, the mass do not now take their opinions from dignitaries in Church or State, from ostensible leaders, or from books. Their thinking is done for them by men much like themselves, addressing them or speaking in their name, on the spur of the moment."[9] The ideal-type of democracy as perceived by Katz and Lazarsfeld is one in which citizens can fully participate in the political and policy process. Political participation of the masses is the essential condition for the progress of democracy.

Katz and Lazarsfeld were also influenced by the work of James Bryce.[10] In his book *The American commonwealth*, Bryce argued that the role of public opinion is crucial in the US. Public opinion is at the heart of the behavior of political leaders who are conscious of its significance. Along the lines of the work of Tocqueville, Bryce wants to describe how the pressure of public opinion affects leaders and government. His main thesis is that democracy is achieved when we can observed the birth of "government by opinion." The discussion is therefore based on the strength of public opinion in any society and on what kind of opinion would most benefit the state.[11]

According to Bryce, the ultimate stage of any democracy is when

> the will of the majority can be determined at any time and without
> the prerequisite of having to be routed through a representative
> body, and if possible, even without the presence or requirement
> of the voting machine . . . It is based on this opinion alone that
> the expression "government by public opinion" might adequately
> apply, in that public opinion would not simply prevail, but it would
> control."[12]

In the minds of some authors, such as Loic Blondiaux, Bryce advocated
the creation of certain mechanisms by means of which governments might
regularly monitor the needs of the citizens and act accordingly. Bryce wrote:

> Yet even if the device that measures public opinion from one week to
> the next and from one month to the next were not to exist, or were
> not about to be invented, I would like to surmise that hopefully, and
> no matter what, heads of government – be they ministers or legisla-
> tors – might have the inclination to act as if it truly did exist; which
> is to say that they constantly examine demonstrations of existing
> public opinion, and that they shape their actions according to their
> understanding of these demonstrations." [13]

Bryce is perceived as a prophet given that he recognizes the significance
of finding mechanisms to measure the state of opinions outside the electoral periods. The originality of Bryce's approach is that in any democracy
there should be other means of analyzing public opinion. By this process
we should see the emergence of a larger democratic society which would
facilitate the participation of citizens in political life.

The other significant element of the analysis of Bryce concerns more
specifically the development of public opinion. The circulation of information is a process in which three types of actors play a key role. First,
there are the "practical politicians" (journalists, politicians) who create the
news and who make politics an integral part of their lives. Second, there
are those who follow the action of government closely and who communicate the information; these are members of political associations, the
public relations officers, the opinion leaders who originate from the middle
classes. Finally, the third group is composed of the masses, citizens who
have *no opinion* and negligible interest in public affairs, but who are influenced by the second group. For Elizabeth Noelle-Neumann, Bryce was the
first one to "describe what will later be called the silent majority".[14]
Therefore, Loic Blondiaux argues that we can already see, in Bryce's description, the elements of what Elihu Katz and Paul Lazarsfeld will describe
later as the *two-step flow of communication.*[15]

There are however, four conditions for the implementation of this process of political communication:

1 The opinion leaders should be interested in the information presented in the media;
2 The media (the press, at the time of Bryce) should capable of engaging in a process of exchange with its readers/listeners/viewers;
3 There should be public discussions (arguments, counter-arguments) over a policy issues; and
4 The election will close the debate, since the electorate will either support or reject the proposal.

Determinants of public opinion

Personal influence: the role of community leaders

One of the chief criticisms concerning the Katz and Lazarsfeld hypothesis is that it provides "no mechanism for explaining how interpersonal communications could bring about systematic changes in the distribution of mass opinion independently of elite influence."[16] In the two step flow model, "opinion leaders may be said merely to aid in the diffusion of elite-generated information." As the studies of Sheriff (1936), Asch (1940), and Merton (1948) have indicated, individuals seem to act socially and to support the opinion of community leaders who shared the same vision.[17] One crucial distinction that can be made here is that the significance of the group is particularly central to non-committed information (e.g. who is the best candidate in an election?). The opinion of the group will prevail over personal opinion, since people prefer "to be wrong collectively than right individually." Therefore, the view of citizens as "social actors" involved in interpersonal and social relationships is at the core of the two-step flow model.

The minimal effect of the mass media and the cathodic legitimacy

Opinion leaders are the main source of personal influence and one of the reasons why the early researchers in political communication were unable to find the "direct effects" of the mass media. The hypothesis that purports a limited effect of the mass media on public opinion is the result of what Denis McQuail called the "invisible contribution of opinion leaders."[18]

Meanwhile, each time a new medium (radio, television, and more recently the Internet) appears, there are always a number of observers who are ready to argue for the end of the traditional social communication process.[19] The other vital point of the discussion concerns the media themselves. The definition given by Katz and Lazarsfeld includes not only electronic media but also specialized publications, political meetings, and personal relationships with prominent leaders. Their definition refers to all means used by a community leader to acquire greater *competence*. For example, an article published in a specialized journal no doubt has a significant impact on academic leaders and communities.

This leads us to the argument suggesting that the media have a hypodermic effect on the public.[20] This "discovery" was reassuring for many people, since the "elite domination" of the mass media seems to be limited. But in recent years this hypothesis has been contested. The minimal effects have come under attack; many researchers have found strong evidence of media effects.[21] One of the key elements of their findings is that no single news story or broadcast has great effect on the population. It is the cumulative effect over time that can have a strong influence. Moreover, the idea of elite manipulation of mass opinion through the use of the media is not the dominant paradigm of the actual research. The answer seems to lie between the elite and democratic theory of political communication.

However, in some situations where the objective of the media is to be engaged in a "process of persuasion" (when the media want to modify the people's attitudes, for example, during an electoral campaign) then their impact can be much stronger. The role of community leaders becomes crucial. They then become "agents of social changes." According to Katz and Lazarsfeld, opinion leaders are essentially experts who are loyal to their group and possess a higher level of competency. Political leaders, for example, maintain a certain degree of authority, and those with strong public support and a high level of confidence (competence and honesty) are more likely to be influential leaders. To summarize, let us say that the key finding that can be argued is that the media are part of the social universe of people and they are not as efficient as common wisdom would have us think. There are other means of communication in all societies that are more weighty than the media. During an electoral campaign, personal influence remains a key factor.

The dissemination and persuasiveness of information

Aside from the influence they exert upon political decisions through interpersonal contact, opinion leaders play a key role in the dissemination of political information. News of political events reaches a large section of citizens by way of a two-step flow of information. However, the precise relationship of mass and interpersonal media in the broadcasting of information is hard to determine. The central hypothesis is that "the greater the news value of an event, the more important will be interpersonal communication in the diffusion process."[22] But the central core of most research is that both the media and interpersonal channels play a significant role, but neither of them plays a dominant one.

A great deal of news is transmitted directly from the media to the public. The percentage of the direct impact of the media varies between 19 percent and 97 percent.[23] The most cited example is, no doubt, news of the assassination of John Kennedy in 1963. Fifty-seven percent more people learned about the event through interpersonal means; 32 percent of the population of Colorado found out about it via personal contacts.[24] Moreover, 45 percent of Americans learned about the assassination attempt on Ronald Reagan through interpersonal means.[25] These observations led to the following hypothesis: the more important the event is, the larger the proportion of citizens who will learn about it through interpersonal channels of communication.[26]

Another important point about the *persuasiveness* of the mass media is that many governmental activities lie in the relationships between politicians, interest groups leaders, professional communicators, party activists, and citizens. Those interpersonal channels of communication are more important than the role of the media.[27] In 1999, we studied the governmental decision-making process regarding the preparation of a new budget. In general, journalists perceive the budgetary process as too technical and they rarely make comments or inform citizens about the issues during the pre-budgetary period. Even if the media is thought to be the first source of diffusion people nevertheless regard personal communication as an essential means of obtaining information. In the budgetary example, opinion leaders are instrumental in dispensing information.

What most of the studies indicate is that if the media are the main source of information, the effect of persuasion that is greater through interpersonal channels of communication. This is not to say that the media effect cannot be direct. However, empirical research has indicated that we should separate two specific functions of the media: the information effect from the convincing effect. Depending on the issue under public scrutiny, there are several channels of communication. Opinion leaders help their communities to obtain information about facts/events that are not covered by the media. Leaders are information seekers with regard to facts that are useful either in their work or in their community relationships. Opinion leaders are experts and to continue to play that role they need to be fully informed.

The "screening theory" or a "four-step model"

We proposed a new model of analysis based on the empirical evidence known as the "screening theory."[28] The central hypothesis of this theory reads as follows: "the cognitive process by which voters/citizens decide to take position on an issue is based on a constant evaluation of the forces, evaluation pondered by both structural and conjunctural determinants."[29] The process of social/political communication is based on both interpersonal influence and campaign strategies as seen through the mass media. Citizens are engaged in this communication process. Opinion leaders facilitate the creation of social coalitions. A number of structural factors, such as the economic situation, can also have an impact on the shaping of public opinion. Therefore, the social context in which these discussions take place is important. Consequently, public opinion polls can be misleading when predicting the outcome of elections or what people think about an issue.

It is suggested that the communication process is a process of social maturation in which cultural and economic factors played a role. This process is most often perceived as a four-step model: observation, evaluation, discussion and decision (see Appendix). But first of all, there should be a social consensus on the magnitude of an issue. This consensus can be described empirically as the distance between the social and individual opinions. The mathematical formula that can best describe this relationship reads as follows where pf_i stands for the degrees of agreement within the government sector and po_i stands for the degrees of agreement within the public opinion sector concerning a single policy issue:

$$\frac{n}{i} \; d = pf_i - po_i$$

My colleague Ito Youichi has suggested that if we want to compare several policy issues it might be useful to divide the result by the number of policies. Since our goal is to create an integrated model that associates the individual decision-making process with the societal decision making process, we will need to develop several valid and reliable indicators of the state of opinions concerning a single issue not only between countries but more importantly over time (a pooled cross-sectional analysis). For example, an individual can be in favor of or opposed to abortion but the government/society can be either in favor or opposed to regulations. Thus, the collective decision might differ from the sum of individual opinions. Other factors, such as the degree of dependency of citizens on governmental resources (economic arguments) can also shape opinions.

Conclusion

In this chapter, we have modestly tried to summarize the debates that emerged following the original contribution by Elihu Katz and Paul Lazarsfeld. Their "discovery" has not been completely rejected and recent work on local participation suggests that such a process of influence might still play a key role. We can briefly recapitulate, in five points, the key arguments made in this chapter:

1   Academic research has indicated that the two-step flow model is difficult to support empirically. However, from a sociological perspective,

it is debatable that community leaders and people are involved in a more complex interactive process. Therefore, the two-step flow model is not a general rule but it is possible in some situations.

2 Community leaders can limit the impact of the media.

3 Community leaders and groups can have standards, values, and opinions that differ from those proposed by the media.

4 Several models of communication are possibly based on two factors: the importance of the news and its influence on citizens/groups. Consequently, the role of all information is not necessarily to change public attitude.

5 Finally, academic researchers should attempt to distinguish between societal and personal influence by developing theoretical models that will be able to grasp both the micro- and macro-movements of opinion. The "screening theory," as it is proposed, represents such a model in an effort to amalgamate the three central components of the personal influence model: media impact, community leaders, and interpersonal effects.

Acknowledgments

I would like to thank professor Ito Youichi for his valuable comments to an earlier version of this chapter.

Notes

1 Elihu Katz and Paul F. Lazarsfeld (1955), *Personal influence. The part played by people in the flow of mass communication*, Glencoe, The Free Press. Elihu Katz (1957), "The two-step flow of communication and up-to-date report on an hypothesis" *Public Opinion Quarterly*, 21(1) (spring), pp. 61–78.

2 Elihu Katz and Paul F. Lazarsfeld, *Personal influence . . .*, op. cit., p. 31. Paul Lazarsfeld, Bernard Berelson and Hazel Gaudet (1944), *The people's choice: how the voter makes up his mind in a presidential campaign*, New York, Columbia University Press.

3 E. Katz and P. Lazarsfeld, *Personal influence . . .*, op. cit., p. 31.

4 Ibid.

5 Ibid., p. 32.

6 Ibid., p. 32.

7 French sociologist Raymond Boudon is a scholar who definitely helped disseminate the work of Katz and Lazarsfeld. See Raymond Boudon, and Paul F. Lazarsfeld (1976), *L'analyse empirique de la causalité*, Paris, Mouton, 3rd edition. François Chazel, Raymond Boudon and Paul Lazarsfeld (1970), *L'analyse des processus sociaux*, Paris, Mouton. Raymond Boudon and Paul Lazarsfeld (1965), *Le vocabulaire de science sociales: concepts et indices*, Paris, Mouton.

8 Jacques De Guise and N. Okada have both published two excellent summaries around the hypothesis of the two-step flow model. Jacques De Guise (1987), "La communication a deux paliers", *Revue de l'université Laurentienne* 19(2), 37–73. N. Okada (1986), "The process of mass communication: a review of studies of the two-step flow communication hypothesis," *Studies of Broadcasting* 22, 57–78.

9 John Stuart Mills, *On liberty*.
10 James Bryce (1911 [1st edition 1888–1889]), *The American commonwealth*, London, Macmillan. Francis G. Wilson (1939), "James Bryce on public opinion: fifty years later," *Public Opinion Quarterly*, 3(3), 420–435.
11 For a comparison of how Tocqueville and Bryce interpret public opinion, see Elisabeth Noelle-Neumann (1984), *The spiral of silence – public opinion, our social skin*, Chicago, IL, University of Chicago Press, pp. 88–93.
12 Cité par Loic Blondiaux (1998), *La fabrique de l'opinion publique – une histoire sociale des sondages*, Paris, Éditions du Seuil, 75.
13 Ibid., p. 77.
14 Elisabeth Noelle-Neumann, op. cit., p. 93.
15 Ibid., 79.
16 John R. Zaller (1992), *The nature and origins of mass opinion*, Cambridge, Cambridge University Press, p. 273.
17 The articles by M. Sheriff, (1936), "Group influence upon the formtion of norms and attitudes" (219–232), and S. E. Asch (1940), "Effects of group pressures upon the modification and distortion of judgments" (174–182), have been reproduced in E. E. Maccoby, T. H. Newcomb, and E. L. Hartley (eds) (1958), *Readings in social psychology*, New York, Holt, Reinhrat and Winston; and R. K. Merton (1948), "Patterns of influence: a study of interpersonal influence and communication behavior in a local community," *Public Opinion Quarterly* 19, 337–352.
18 Denis McQuail (2000), *McQuail's mass communication theory*, London, Sage Publications, 4th edition, p. 500.
19 See in particular G. Wallas (1908), *Human nature in politics*, London, Archibald Constable; W. Lippmann (1922), *Public opinion*, New York, Free Press; H. D. Lasswell (1927), *Propaganda technique in the World War*, New York, Knopf; and G. S. Jowett and V. O'Donnell (1986), *Propaganda and persuasion*, Beverly Hills, CA, Sage.
20 Joseph T. Klapper (1960), *The effects of mass communication*. Glencoe, IL: Free Press.
21 Thomas Patterson and Robert McClure (1976), *The unseeing eye*, New York, Putman. Thomas Patterson (1980), *The mass media election*, New York, Praeger. Shanto Iyengar, Mark Peters and Jon Krosnick (1984), "The evening news and presidential evaluations," *Journal of Personality and Social Psychology*, 46 778–787. Larry Bartels (1988), *The dynamics of presidential primaries*, Princeton, NJ, Princeton University Press. David Fan (1988), *Predictions of public opinion from the mass media*, New York, Greenwood. Benjamin Page and Robert Shapiro (1994), *The rational public*, Chicago, IL, University of Chicago Press.
22 Richard J. Hill and Charles M. Bonjean (1964), "News diffusion: a test of the regularity hypothesis," *Journalism Quarterly*, 41, 342. See also Steven N. Chaffee (1972), "The interpersonal context of mass communication," in F. Gerald Kline and Philip J. Tichenor (eds), *Current perspectives in mass communication research*, Beverly Hills, CA, Sage Publications, pp. 95–120. Steven N. Chaffee (ed.) (1975), *Political communication*, Beverly Hills, CA, Sage Publications, pp. 88–92.
23 W. Gantz, K. A. Krendl and S. R. Robertson (1986), "Diffusion of a proximate news event," *Journalism Quarterly*, 62, 282–287. J. B. Adams, J. J. Mullen and H. M. Wilson (1969), "Diffusion of a 'minor' news event," *Journalism Quarterly* 46, 545–551.
24 R. J. Hill and C. M. Bonjean (1964), "News diffusion: a test of the regularity hypothesis," *Journalism Quarterly*, 41, 336–342.

25 W. Gantz (1983), "The diffusion of news about the attempted Reagan assassination," *Journal of Communication*, 33, 56–66.
26 K. E. Rosegreen (1973), "News diffusion: an overview," *Journalism Quarterly*, 50, 83–91.
27 Guy Lachapelle (1999), "L'opinion publique compte-t-elle vraiment?" in Guy Lachapelle, Luc Bernier and Pierre P. Tremblay (eds), *Le processus budgètaire au Québec*, Québec: Presses de l'université du Québec.
28 Guy Lachapelle (1998), "Le comportement politique des Québécoises lors de la campagne référendaire de 1995: une application de la théorie du dépistage," *Politique et Sociètès* 17(1–2), 91–120.
29 Ibid., pp. 94–95.

Appendix

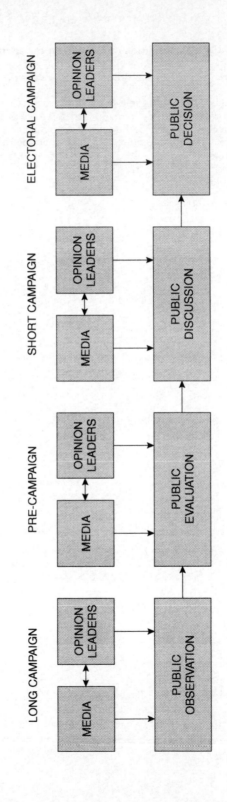

Part 2

EXPLOITING POLITICAL COMMUNICATION IN THE NEW ERA

6

POLITICAL ADVERTISING DURING ELECTION CAMPAIGNS

Christina Holtz-Bacha

The conditions under which election campaigns take place have changed considerably during past decades. The process of modernization including social and political changes on the one side and the development of the media systems on the other, have led to changes in the way the political system presents itself to the public. The latter is referred to as professionalization which in turn has brought about certain strategies and techniques that are now the characteristics of modern election campaigns. These can be grouped according to three categories: de-ideologization, personalization/ privatization, and active communication management including adaptation, distraction and attention strategies. These three categories are not independent but rather influence each other (cf. Holtz-Bacha, 2000).

While the political system predominantly depends on the media for reaching the electorate, political actors – parties and candidates – strive to keep the power to define the issues in the public's as well as the candidates' images. Active communication management serves this goal. Through adapting to the media's selection and presentation techniques the political system tries to ensure the media's attention and increase the chances of getting its messages into the media, as unchanged as possible. The risk of "distortion" is highest in the so-called mediatized formats. The media's campaign coverage is referred to as being fully mediatized because it is material that is produced by the media themselves and can only, to a very low degree, be influenced by the political actors. Partially mediatized refers to appearances by politicians in debates, interviews or talk shows, and similar programs, in which they are still in a position largely to influence the flow of events. These formats whether they be fully or partially mediatized are also called free or earned media. The non-mediatized formats finally are fully controlled by the parties or candidates while the media only serve as means of transport and have no influence on the content. (Paletz &

Vinson, 1994). This can include ads on television, in radio, or in the print media. They are often referred to as paid media though in many countries election broadcasts do not have to be paid for but time is allocated for free. Nevertheless, parties or candidates have to pay for the production of the ads.

While free media appearances are not fully in the hands of the political actors, they have the advantage of being considered as more trustworthy because their persuasive intent is not immediately recognized by the audience. Paid media on the other hand, while controlled by the parties or candidates, have the disadvantage of being directly perceived as interest-bound advertising.

The importance of the diverse campaign channels differs according to a country's political culture. In the US television is regarded as the most important medium of the election campaign with candidates spending more than half of their campaign budget on TV advertising. Most Western European countries also put a strong emphasis on television. Nonetheless, other campaign channels have kept some importance as well. A comparison of the relevance of different campaign channels for voters in twelve EC member states during the 1989 European election campaign shows that interpersonal communication as well as newspaper coverage play an important role beside television. In addition, some media have specific relevance in individual countries as for example, posters in Germany, radio in Greece, newspaper ads in Denmark, and party brochures in Great Britain (Scherer, 1995, p. 214).

The situation for electoral advertising in Western Europe changed somewhat when commercial broadcasting was introduced, leading to dual broadcasting systems with private broadcasters supplementing the traditional public stations. However, although the establishment of commercial stations brought an increase in media outlets, it did not necessarily mean deregulation of political advertising or direct access for parties through free purchase of airtime. Most European countries continue to set narrow limits for electoral advertising.

In Western Europe, only Germany allowed the parties to purchase advertising time on commercial channels in addition to allocation of free airtime on the public stations. Finland, where political ads are exclusively broadcast on the commercial channel, which only appeared in 1993, has allowed parties free purchase of advertising time (cf. Moring, 1995). Recently, the Netherlands also permitted parties to buy airtime for their electoral advertising on television. Italy permitted parties to buy airtime until in 1993 a new law banned TV spots from the hot campaign phase (cf. Mazzoleni & Roper, 1995). Another law that passed the legislature in 2000 prohibits electoral ads on television altogether during the official campaign period. Switzerland does not allow electoral ads on TV at all (Blum, 1999). So, most European countries, even with the advent of commercial broadcasting and the development of dual broadcasting systems, kept a policy of controlled allocation of advertising time thus preventing radio or TV ads becoming a more important campaign channel.

Compared to the electronic media, ads in newspapers or journals are usually less regulated. However, their role in the electoral campaign is much overshadowed by the importance that campaigners attribute to television which again is mirrored in the attention researchers give to ads in the print media.

Research overview

Due to a long story of success and the importance television and TV ads gained early in the US (cf. e.g. Diamond & Bates, 1988; Jamieson, 1996), research on content and effects of political broadcasts is also very much dominated by studies done in the US. However, the dependence of the design of the ads on a country's political and electoral system makes a generalization of findings from the US to other countries dubious. Nevertheless, modernization of campaign techniques in Western Europe and the orientation of European campaign managers towards the US model may provide for a greater similarity of political advertising across the Atlantic in the future. In fact, some studies have shown common features of electoral advertising on TV for the US and European countries (cf. Johnston, 1991; Holtz-Bacha *et al.*, 1994; Kaid & Holtz-Bacha, 1995a, b; Kaid, 1998; Holtz-Bacha, 1999a).

Typologies

Over the years several typologies of political broadcasts have been presented (e.g. Devlin, 1986; Diamond & Bates, 1988; Kern, 1989; Johnson-Cartee & Copeland, 1997). However, they usually cannot be compared. On the one hand, this is often due to a lack of documentation of the criteria that were used to differentiate the various types of ads. On the other hand, typologies are based on different perspectives using the functions ads serve during the different campaign phases, or for viewers. Other typologies apply characteristics of content or visual style to distinguish different types of ads. Sometimes the distinguishing criteria even change within a typology (e.g. Devlin, 1986).

Among the most recent typologies is the one proposed by Johnson-Cartee and Copeland (1997). It is based on four strategies underlying the use of ads during a campaign, that is they are classified according to the functions they serve for political consultants in the course of the campaign, even though broadcasts are identified by their style. Thus, the typology offered by Johnson-Cartee and Copeland is orientated toward the analysis of ad strategies and the different styles serving these strategies (cf. also

Biocca, 1991). By applying this perspective the typology focuses on the production process but at the same time comprises the perspective on the audience because these strategies are intended to have certain effects on the viewer. The typology distinguishes four types of ads. The basic classification criterion of the typology is whether ads are positive or negative (type I and II). Reactive response ads (type III) and proactive inoculation ads (type IV) are used to react upon negative ads or as a defensive measure against presumed attacks.

How the different strategies are operationalized in the specific ads varies according to different schools of consulting. Montague Kern identifies three "philosophical camps" (1989, p. 24). The emotional school where political advertising resembles commercial advertising most closely, relies heavily on visual and audio effects. The informational school, by devoting its attention to clarifying the issue stands of candidates, is more language based in its strategies. Finally, the quick-response school is least oriented to entertainment techniques and high-quality visual while applying a "factual" format (Kern, 1989, p. 24).

The strategies pursued in planning the campaign and with the production of ads do not necessarily prescribe a certain presentational format. In fact, over the years a considerable variety of formats has developed. Among these, however, are some basic formats that – so to speak – constitute the classic repertory of political TV advertising. This comprises the "talking head ad" with the candidate speaking directly into the camera; the "*cinéma verité* ad" with the candidate being filmed in real life settings interacting with people; the "documentary ad" describing the accomplishments of the candidate; "production idea spots" conveying important ideas about a candidate; and finally "testimonials" where prominent people speak on behalf of the candidate, also called "Man-in-the-street-ads" if citizens are involved (Devlin, 1986).

Further differentiation, e.g. according to positive or negative spots, does not describe presentational formats but instead refers to the concrete design of a spot and to its strategic function. The same applies to the differentiation of soft-sell and hard-sell that opposes emotional advertising and a more direct style focusing on facts or issues.

Contents

The dominant focus of content analyses in the US derives from the ongoing image-issue controversy (Shyles, 1986, p. 111). This discussion is based on a polarization between either image- or issue-oriented spot contents and at the same time expresses traditional doubts about the general possibility of presenting issue information within only 60 or even 30 seconds. Nevertheless, the history of political spot advertising on television has shown that ads became shorter and shorter. US campaigns today are dominated by the 30-second spot. This development was accelerated by the costs for the purchase of advertising time going hand in hand with the growing conviction that longer spots are not more effective than shorter ones.

The question of spots being either more image-oriented or more issue-oriented thus has become a constant of content analyses. However, the findings from several studies have proven fears unwarranted predicting the development of electoral broadcasts to mere image advertising (e.g. McClure & Patterson, 1976; Hofstetter & Zukin, 1979; Joslyn, 1980).

A study by Joslyn (1980) – representative of others – demonstrates the problems of the image concept as used in content analyses of electoral ads. Image orientation is only referring to candidates and is operationalized as personal characteristics being mentioned for the candidate. In addition, image-orientation is usually determined by analyzing the verbal spot message only, even though – as Joslyn himself admits in his study – the visuals are at least equally important for the conveyance of candidate images.

Several studies use mutually exclusive categories, determining spots as being either image- or issue-oriented. In his research overview in 1989, Aden criticizes that "scholars seem possessed with separating image and issue concerns in spots despite respective findings and observations that illustrate their interrelated nature" (Aden, 1989, p. 6). In fact, campaign strategists also use issue-oriented formats to support the image of a candidate (e.g. Rudd, 1986) and some studies have shown that issue formats can influence a candidate's image (e.g. Kaid & Sanders, 1978; Geiger & Reeves, 1991; Holtz Bacha & Kaid, 1996). On the other side, "issue-orientation" does not necessarily mean the extensive discussion of political issues as is implied in their supposed superiority in conveying information. Actually, the "real" informational content of so-called issue-oriented spots has rarely been analyzed.

Finally, the close connection of image-orientation with the presentation of candidates in the ads is very much a characteristic of the US candidate-centered political system where candidates themselves purchase broadcasting time and produce their own spots. The definition of "image-orientation" through the presence of a candidate has therefore seldom been discussed. It neglects that issues can be employed to convey a particular image of a candidate and that image advertising can be done without a candidate being present in the spot, e.g. through emotional pictures. This is meant when Shyles suggests:

> If we recognize a difference in the meaning of "image" when used to refer to graphic methods or presenting candidates (visual display), versus character attributes of candidates, then we can begin to assess more accurately the relationship between images and issues in televised political spots; perhaps then some of the controversy regarding the value of image and issue content of candidates in televised political advertising can be resolved.
>
> (Shyles, 1986, p. 115)

It was thus proposed to distinguish between a candidate just being present in the visuals or a candidate being made the topic of a spot, e.g. by talking about her/himself or by showing a biographical film. Only the latter would then be regarded as the image-oriented presentation of the candidate (cf. Holtz-Bacha & Lessinger, 1997; Holtz-Bacha *et al.*, 1998).

For a long time, content analyses mainly referred to the verbal messages of the spots. Studies only recently have begun to take the visual level into account and thus acknowledged the importance of the visual message of political advertising. Kaid and Davidson (1986, pp. 186–189) proposed the "videostyle" concept, combining three components for analyzing the self-portrayal of a candidate: the verbal content, the nonverbal content including visual and audio elements that do not have specific semantic meaning (e.g. sounds, dominant speaker, environment, body movement of the candidate, facial expression), and production techniques like spot length and various film techniques (e.g. camera shots, angles, use of music). However, the videostyle concept again is very much candidate-centered because several of the categories are only applied if a candidate is present.

Griffin and Kagan (1996) also criticize the candidate-centered research on political advertising and propose an approach to the visual analysis of political advertising that aims at explicating the cultural images embedded in campaign commercials. They define "'cultural images' as depictions that make reference to national, regional, ethnic, religious, subcultural, or class characteristics in order to evoke mythic themes, cultural archetypes, and historical associations" (Griffin & Kagan, 1996, p. 45). This approach allows for the analysis of visual strategies independent of the presence of a candidate and is better suited for the study of broadcasts that are produced by parties as in most West European countries, and not by individual candidates.

A more meaningful technique, which is at the same time better orientated toward practical questions concerning the production of political broadcasts, is the identification of strategies. Analyzing strategies goes beyond counting issue mentions or characterizations of candidates and studies their presentation in connection with rhetorical styles and presentational formats. Ideally, this combines the analysis of verbal and visual aspects. The US literature has frequently described such strategies, partly based on interviews with political consultants and their publications, partly based on content analyses of spots. However, they do not offer a systematic description of such strategies, a prerequisite for their application to future research. Instead, findings from different studies can be drawn together to a sort of catalogue.

An overview of such strategies or appeals is offered by Johnson-Cartee and Copeland (1997, p. 88). They distinguish three main types of persuasive appeals deriving from Aristotle, that is "political issue appeals" (logos), "political character appeals" (ethos), and "emotive appeals" (pathos). Again though, these categories and their various sub-forms do not lead to clear distinctions; they allow for a fairly systematic approach and also reflect the different schools of consultants with an emotional school on the one side and an informative school on the other. The third camp was identified by Kern (1989) as the quick-response school and can be regarded as a sub-form of the informative school.

Effects

In the US there is no doubt about the effectiveness of electoral ads. Aden's research overview in 1989 concludes: "The general finding emerging from the different topic areas of political spot research is that these spots work" (p. 10). In fact, US research has presented a multitude of studies on the effects of political advertising. However, they are often limited in their scope and their design. Thus, it is difficult to come up with a general statement about what kind of spots have what effect on whom.

At the same time the extensive body of research on political advertising in the US also demonstrates that the question of effects is much broader than just the possible influence on voting preference. Limiting the effectiveness of political advertising to its impact on the vote neglects the possibility of other politically relevant effects and moreover brings about considerable problems for research. In fact, the majority of studies in the US deal with effects other than the ads' (direct) impact on voting preference. Anyhow, taken together, the findings rather speak for indirect effects, that is effects on knowledge, attitudes and emotions. These in turn can affect voting intention and the actual voting decision. Thus, independent of the candidates' or parties' intention and independent of the ads' actual influence on the vote, effects here have to be understood in a much broader sense. This also includes consideration of macroscopic effects, that is on the system level, that have come to the attention of researchers only recently.

Most US studies deal with effects of political advertising on the viewer and try to assess cognitive, affective or behavioral effects. Some studies take intervening variables on the part of the viewers into account. Fewer studies consider variables based on the "stimulus," for example different presentational formats or the visual design of the ads. Only the growing prominence of negative advertising in US campaigns has attracted the attention of researchers. However, the lack of findings on the effectiveness of the various formats and other aspects of design is amazing because this is what consultants should be interested in. That seems to speak for the creation of political advertising being done intuitively rather than on the basis of findings from systematic research. This assumption is corroborated by the interviews which Diamond and Bates carried out with political consultants. For example, they cite Robert Squier who worked for Hubert Humphrey in 1968 and for Jimmy Carter in 1976 among others: "The very best people in this business probably understand only about five to seven percent of what it is that they do that works. The rest is all out the in the unknown" (Diamond & Bates, 1988, p. 353).

At least, US candidates and their consultants do not have to worry much about how to reach the audience. As opposed to European countries with their limits and special conditions for the broadcasting of electoral advertising, ads in the US are treated just like any other commercial. That means that the ads appear without further announcement and are included in advertising blocks interrupting programs. The unlimited number of spots combined with a high repetition rate increase the likelihood of reaching the voters.

Findings on different effects

Some studies dealt with effects of formal or content aspects of the spots. Formal features like length or the dynamics of an ad proved their influence on how a candidate is perceived by the audience (e.g. Kaid & Sanders, 1978; Meadow & Sigelman, 1982; Lang, 1991). Little is known about the effectiveness of different presentational formats. The consultants interviewed by Diamond and Bates (1988, p. 358) were convinced that ID-spots can be successful, provided there is enough money to secure a high repetition rate.

In the light of the issue/image controversy it is astonishing to note that there have not been more studies attempting to assess the effects of issue or image-oriented ads. Some researchers ascertained a superiority of image ads concerning the short-term recall of spot contents (e.g. Kaid & Sanders, 1978) or of the candidate's name (Kaid, 1982). Others found that recall for visual information is better for image-oriented ads while the verbal message is remembered better if an ad is issue-oriented (Geiger & Reeves, 1991). Issue-oriented spots also work better in favor of a positive evaluation of a candidate (Kaid & Sanders, 1978; Geiger & Reeves, 1991; Chanslor et al., 1992). In addition, the type of program surrounding the commercial has proven its impact on the effectiveness of an ad (Chanslor et al., 1992).

Not least because of ethical reservations, more and more studies have focused on the impact of negative advertising. The general finding for negative ads is that they work although voters do not like them. However, there is much uncertainty about the effects, in particular because negative ads sometimes have unintented effects. Therefore Diamond and Bates conclude: "as a rule negative advertising is the riskiest element of the campaign" (1988, p. 359).

Though voters judge negative ads critically they are regarded as being informative and viewers remember the verbal and visual messages of negative ads better than of positive ads (cf. e.g. Surlin & Gordon, 1977;

Newhagen & Reeves, 1991). These results correspond to findings on commercial advertising in general and are probably due to the higher emotional arousal of the viewers who therefore remember the ads better (cf. Basil *et al.*, 1991, p. 248). The risk of attacks in negative ads is due to a potential backlash effect on the attacking candidate (Garramone, 1984) or a negative effect on both the attacking and the attacked candidate (Basil *et al.*, 1991). Independent sponsorship of an ad, the viewers' perception of a negative statement as being true and the attack aiming at the issue stand of the opponent rather than at the character positively influence the effectiveness of a negative ad in the intended direction (cf. Garramone, 1984; Roddy & Garramone, 1988). As with the ads in general the campaign environment and the surrounding program play a role for the effectiveness of negative ads (Basil *et al.*, 1991; Chanslor *et al.*, 1992).

Meanwhile it is regarded as a campaign rule that attacks have to be answered. Though reaction by a positive spot is better evaluated by the audience, reaction by a counter attack proved to be more effective (Roddy & Garramone, 1988). The "inoculation theory" finally has shown that – if an attack is expected – the effects of negative spots can be weakened by pre-emptive spots that immunize the audience (cf. e.g. Pfau & Burgoon, 1988).

Among the audience variables that influence the effectivity of political ads in general, two concepts have received attention, that is selectivity and involvement (cf. Kaid, 1981). Selective exposure is usually not regarded as a problem for political advertising. Particularly the short length of the ads interrupting programs and thus taking viewers by surprise are seen as good conditions to overcome the selectivity hurdle. Particularly ads surrounded by entertainment programs reach an inadvertent audience, not expecting political messages. Ross Perot's 30-minute informercials that reached comparably high ratings during the 1992 campaign seem to show that even longer candidate broadcasts are not subject to selective exposure. This, however, may have been a curiosity effect toward a third and sometimes scurrilous candidate.

While it appears plausible that political advertising can overcome selective exposure, the question remains open of whether the same is true for selective perception and selective recall. The concentration of research on short-term effects – not least because of the methodological difficulties when studying long-term effects – leaves this a task for future research.

Involvement has proved to be a key variable for the effectiveness of advertising in general. Accordingly, advertising has a good chance of reaching its goal even if, or particularly if, involvement is low. Herbert Krugman (1965) who first applied the involvement concept to advertising during the 1960s called this "learning without involvement." That means the usual effects chain from ad message through attitude change to behavioral change (purchase of product) is reversed with behavior being affected before an attitude change takes place. The low-involvement-concept is also true for political advertising. Spots are more effective with a low-involvement audience, that is viewers with low interest in the campaign or politics in general (cf. McClure & Patterson, 1974; Rothschild & Ray, 1974; Hofstetter *et al.*, 1978; Hofstetter & Buss, 1980).

Altogether, at least at the individual level, research has clearly established the effectiveness of political advertising in the US. Viewers do learn something about the campaign, the issues, and the issue stands of candidates (cf. e.g. Atkin *et al.*, 1973; Atkin & Heald, 1976; Patterson & McClure, 1976; Schleuder *et al.*, 1991). However, the findings from studies trying to assess the relative effectiveness of ads compared to other campaign channels, are mixed (cf. Patterson & McClure, 1976; Just *et al.*, 1990; Zhao & Chaffee, 1995). Contrary to earlier research, more recent studies identified effects on candidate images from verbal and visual messages in the ads (cf. e.g. Patterson & McClure, 1976; Kaid & Sanders, 1978; Meadow & Sigelman, 1982; Cundy, 1986; Roddy & Garramone, 1988; Basil *et al.*, 1991; Geiger & Reeves, 1991; Chanslor *et al.*, 1992; Kaid & Chanslor, 1995; Kaid, 1997; West, 1997), leading Diamond and Bates to summarize that political broadcasts "can polish up a candidate's image considerably" (1988, p. 362).

The presumably most important question concerning the effects of political advertising, that is whether ads do have an impact on the voting decision, has relatively seldom been made the topic of respective research. However, most studies unspokenly assume an indirect effect of the ads on the vote via cognitive, emotive and attitude changes.

The meta-campaign and macro-level effects

Electoral ads not only aim at voters directly. They also count on the multiplicator effect of the free media's reporting about the ads. Some spots are intentionally produced to cause commentaries of newspapers and television news, others become the subject of the media's discussion unintentionally. The most prominent example for the latter is the "Daisy spot" of the Johnson campaign 1964 against Goldwater, a spot that was only broadcast once and became famous nonetheless: the spot showing a little girl counting daisy petals on a meadow until an atomic bomb explodes and thus imputing to the possibility that Goldwater might use the bomb. Meanwhile, the media have institutionalized the dissemination of spots by establishing "ad watches," originally thought to work as a kind of spot control by evaluating the statements made in an ad. However, by repeating or describing the ads in the comments, the free media help to make the candidates' message known to an even greater public. Accordingly, some studies have yielded findings showing the ads can have an effect on the audience via the ad watches (cf. Ansolabehere & Iyengar, 1995; O'Sullivan

& Geiger, 1995). Thus, campaign managers have good reason to use this indirect way of trying to influence the voters. On the one hand, the one-time or only regionally limited broadcasting of an ad hoping for further dissemination through the news media helps to reduce the costs of the advertising campaign. On the other hand, advertisers hope for a better effect because the news media's reporting is thought to have greater credibility than the ads themselves whose persuasive purpose is recognized and which may cause reactivity.

The long-term effects of electoral advertising, particularly on the system level, remain a predominantly open question. Nevertheless, there have been several suggestions as to negative consequences. These concern the rise of candidate-centered politics and at the same time a decrease in the relevance of the parties (cf. Wattenberg, 1982; Diamond & Bates, 1988, p. 379).

At the same time the question was raised whether the increase in negative advertising may be responsible for political alienation and the decline in voter turnout in the US. While Ansolabehere & Iyengar (1995) showed a relationship between viewing negative ads and the intention to vote others have raised considerable doubts as to the assumption in general and the study in particular and also hypothesized a possible mobilizing effects of negative ads (Johnson-Cartee & Copeland, 1991, p. 278; Ansolabehere *et al.*, 1997, 1999; Finkel & Geer, 1998; Kahn & Kenney, 1999; Lau *et al.*, 1999; Wattenberg & Brians, 1999). In a similar vein others fear that ads "tend to emphasize the diverting over the cerebral" (Diamond & Bates, 1988, pp. 383–384) and thus trivialize politics which in turn could lead to political alienation. This is a discussion closely connected with the image/issue controversy. Finally, the ever increasing number of ads during election campaigns has been brought into the discussion about campaign financing. This also was the rationale behind the allocation of free advertising time by the big networks during the presidential election campaign in 1996. Nevertheless, the 1996 campaign has shown that the candidates did not reduce their paid ads in spite of the availability of free time segments on the networks (cf. Holtz-Bacha, 1999a). The fact that more and more money is invested in the ad campaign may be due to findings about a correlation between amount of money spent on advertising and the chances of winning the election (cf. Prisuta, 1972; Wanat, 1974; Nowlan & Mountray, 1984).

How research is done – the methods

The study of formal aspects and content of the ads is based – if not on impressionistic descriptions – on systematic content analyses. The coding unit as a rule is the whole spot. Categories referring to the verbal or visual messages are coded for present/not present. Using the whole spot as a coding unit, however, is very much oriented toward the US situation with very short broadcasts that do not change the presentational format within one spot. Longer ads, which are common in Western Europe, often combine two or even more presentational formats. Therefore, it has been proposed to use smaller coding units as they allow for a more detailed analysis of the spot content. One such possibility is an elaborate coding scheme that considers two levels (cf. Holtz-Bacha & Lessinger, 1997; Lessinger 1997). In the first step, structural data like length or cuts, are coded for the whole spot. In the second step, formats and contents of the spots are coded according to spot sequences or scenes. Adopted from film theory, a sequence in a spot is defined as a unit containing one or multiple takes (separated by cuts or a superimpositions) that constitute a continuum connected to a unit by several criteria. These criteria either refer to the content (e.g. a continuum of location, time, action, the constellation of actors, or the topic) or to the formal features (e.g. a continuum of noise, music, speaker). Though this means splitting a (longer) spot into smaller segments, this is not so far from what Richardson (1998) proposes when he calls for a more "wholistic perspective" and proposes "genre" – which he understands as "the shared narrative and audio-visual conventions of popular culture in our times" – as the unit of analysis because these are the messages that viewers use in their reconstruction of meaning from the ads. When sequences are made the unit of analysis and these are closely connected with presentational formats, these can be understood as "genres" of political advertising as well (cf. Lessinger, 1997).

Manifold are the methods used for the study of reception of the spots and their effects. Reference is often made to the high ratings reached by the ads. However, ratings alone do not tell much about acceptance, attention and even less about effects, in particular for the ads. Ads do not have their "own" audience but usually profit from the surrounding programs. Thus, because a spot's audience is determined by the surrounding programs, ratings and socio-demographic characteristics delivered by standard audience research do not allow for a description of the audience of ads.

What is here mentioned as a problem of audience research at the same time is a great advantage for the ads: viewers are caught by chance. The factors that usually determine exposure to political broadcasts, for example, political interest or campaign interest and party preference, do not influence exposure to electoral ads. That is why high TV use can be regarded as a factor increasing the chance to be reached by campaign ads.

Attempts to assess the use of ads through survey research and then searching for correlations with attitudes and voting behavior are also confronted with difficulties. Interviews assessing the role of the media for campaigns usually ask for the use of the different campaign channels. The items are read or presented on a list and thus possibly lead to an over-estimation of the ads. It may be that respondents almost automatically name the ads when asked where they read or heard something about the campaign because ads always stand in connection with an upcoming election and are broadcast during campaigns. Thus, naming the ads always is the "right" answer. In any case, questions like these and surveys in general can hardly ascertain recall of specific ads, their sponsors and details of the ad content.

On the other side, asking respondents for the factors their voting decision may result in an underestimation of ads because people usually do not want to admit being influenced by advertising. The best way to assess the influence of ads on knowledge, attitude and voter preference is through panel studies that allow for the establishment of causal relationships. Nevertheless, panel studies, as well as surveys in general, require better, that is more detailed, instruments to measure the use of spots. These measures should provide for information about which ads were watched, how attentive viewers were, and which parts of the verbal and the visual message can be remembered.

Against this background of methodological difficulties and shortcomings it comes as no surprise that the majority of effects studies used experimental research designs. They are usually based on pre-test/post-test designs with respondents answering questionnaires before and after having watched ads. Experiments allow for far-reaching control of intervening variables which is their disadvantage at the same time because they create artificial situations. These do not correspond to the actual use of ads that are watched by chance and may be influenced by the surrounding programs or other ads, and watched less attentively. However, experimental designs best allow for the assessment of cause and effect. The frequent use of experimental designs in US research explains why many studies rely on limited numbers of subjects, often recruited from university courses, and ask narrow research questions.

However, experiments only allow for the examination of short-term effects. That again explains why findings on long-term effects are rare. At the same time this ignores the fact that political advertising may have effects that go beyond election campaigns. Independent of the ads' impact on the attitudes toward a candidate or a party political advertising has a general informative function: parties, candidates, political goals get known through the ads. The way candidates and parties present themselves during the campaign can shape the picture that people have of the political system, and not only those that are allowed to vote.

The international perspective

Political advertising on television has less importance in Western Europe than in the US. As became obvious in the section about regulations concerning electoral advertising, the US not only has the longest tradition of political advertising but the characteristics of the media system as well as a political system centering on the individual candidates much more than on parties provided the conditions for political ads to become the most important campaign channel. Contrary to the situation in the US, TV ads in Western European election campaigns are of minor importance. Even though television has assumed a dominant role for election campaigns as well, other means of speaking to the voters have maintained some importance in Western Europe as well. One aspect that greatly influenced the role played by TV ads in the electoral marketing mix of campaigners was that even after the introduction of commercial broadcasting, many West European governments refrained from opening up commercial television to electoral advertising. So, even if dual systems of public and commercial broadcasting are the rule in Western Europe now, most countries did not allow for advertising time to be purchased on commercial stations. As a consequence, political advertising during election campaigns in Western Europe mostly means the allocation of (free) broadcasting time on public television. In addition, political advertising is usually limited to electoral campaigns, in particular the last weeks before election date.

Due to the parliamentary systems and the proportional vote that dominate Western European countries, the parties play the most important role in the political system. Therefore, it is the parties that are allocated advertising time on television and not individual candidates (cf. Holtz-Bacha & Kaid, 1995). However, in some countries where the president is elected directly by the people (e.g. France) there may be additional camapigns with candidate advertising.

These are the background variables that account for considerable differences between the role TV ads play in the US electoral campaigns on the one side and Western European races on the other. The strong position of the parties in European political systems also influences the content of ads in so far as they set limits to the degree of personalization. The number of parties competing, their size (e.g. mass parties trying to address as many voters as possible compared to smaller or single-issue parties that rather address target groups; financial capacity), and the common type of government (coalition versus single-party governments) further influence the content of electoral advertising. Finally, the importance of myths and symbols for political communication and for visual communication in particular makes political advertising something that – as all advertising – has to refer to common values and cultural patterns in order to receive resonance from its audience. This is highly dependent on a country's political culture and at the same time can be regarded as an expression of the political culture. Advertising in general and political advertising as well thus become a sensitive indicator for social change (cf. Schmidt, 1995, pp. 37–38). So, when US political scientist James Combs writes about political advertising: "perhaps archeologists of the 27th century will be able to fathom trends in Americam culture by looking at changes in their ads" (1979, p. 333), this can be generalized for other countries and their specific political cultures as well.

Due to the minor importance of political advertising on television in Western European countries, research efforts here are not comparable to the US. In particular, TV ads in Europe are more often part of studies addressing wider research questions, for example, campaign communication in general, whereas much more US research concentrates on ads. Among the studies dealing with political advertising in Europe, two types can be distinguished, first those that present international comparisons, but rely on US models for analysis, and second, single-country studies. Comparisons across countries have yielded similarities for the more rough categories but necessarily have to neglect the details that probably are those most susceptible to differences in political culture (cf. Johnston, 1991; Holtz-Bacha et al., 1994; Kaid & Holtz-Bacha, 1995a; Kaid, 1998; Holtz-Bacha, 1999a). Findings about similarities in campaign communication have fueled the discussion of an "Americanization" of campaign strategies in Europe while some researchers prefer to speak about a general modernization of campaigns with the US only being the front runner (cf. e.g. Holtz-Bacha & Kaid, 1995; Mancini & Swanson, 1996). Some studies referring to individual European countries have shown an overall professionalization of campaign communication and of TV advertising in particular (for the Netherlands cf. Brants, 1995; for Italy cf. Padula, 1996; for France cf. Dauncey, 1998; for Germany cf. Holtz-Bacha, 1999b) while campaigners in other countries remain rather reluctant with TV advertising (e.g. Finland, cf. Moring, 1995), or the possibilities of political advertising on television are limited through regulations (e.g. Italy cf. Mazzoleni & Roper, 1995) or even see electoral ads on the decline (e.g. Great Britain cf. Scammell & Semetko, 1995).

Some thoughts about theory

Not much has been done to provide a theoretical background for political advertising. Instead, previous research was very much oriented toward the role of ads during campaigns and whether they reach their goal as a means of persuasive communication. Independent of their short-term purpose of influencing voters in their attitudes and voting behavior, political advertising can also be understood as a manifestation of political culture.

According to more recent concepts that go beyond the classical conceptual scheme of Almond and Verba (1963), political culture is defined as a collectively shared pattern for the everyday construction of political reality, whether in the form of ways of thinking, or emotional dispositions or in the form of habits of a common way of life (Dörner, 1995, p. 60). Political culture is thus the politically relevant conception a collectivity has of the world (Weltbild). It is a political code that conditions but not determines the thinking, acting and feeling of all political actors, professional politicians as well as citizens. As Elkins and Simeon put it: "Political culture defines the range of acceptable possible alternatives from which groups or individuals may, other circumstances permitting, choose a course of action. . . . Its explanatory power is primarily restricted to 'setting the agenda' over which political contests occur" (1979, p. 131).

Political culture comprises two dimensions, a cognitive or *normative* dimension referring to the substance of political culture, and an affective and *esthetic* dimension referring to its interpretative side (Rohe, 1990, p. 337). Subject to examination therefore is not only *what* the assumptions of a political culture are but also *how* they are expressed. Whether a political culture also receives emotional approval by its members in addition to being rationally grounded, is to a great extent dependent on its expressive dimension (Rohe, 1990, p. 338). Symbols play a decisive role for the expression of a political culture. Dittmer even equates one with the other when he defines: "Political culture is a system of political symbols" (1977, p. 566).

This function of political symbolism of creating an affective tie to a certain political culture also sheds a new light on the notion of symbolic politics. Symbolic politics has very much been defined in the sense of a substitute for "real" politics, as a means to divert attention from complex and difficult political decisions (e.g. Edelman, 1976; Sarcinelli, 1986). However, defining political symbolism as an integral part of political culture that creates an affective relation to political culture acknowledges that symbols and symbolic politics are and have always been part and parcel of everyday political life. It is through symbols and symbolic politics that a political culture is expressed and becomes visible. Thus, symbols and symbolic politics must be regarded as serving two functions: they provide orientation to the individual members of a specific political culture, but they can also be instrumentalized for specific political strategies (Dörner, 1995, p. 56).

It is against this background that political advertising can be understood as a manifestation of political culture, one of several ways through which a political culture is expressed. Political advertising is part of the *design* of a specific political system and thus offering orientation within the system as well as a chance for identification.

References

Aden, R. C. (1989). Televised political advertising: a review of literature on spots. *Political Communication,* 14(1), 1–18.

Almond, G. A. and Verba, S. (1963). *The civic culture. Political attitudes and democracy in five nations.* Princeton, NJ: Princeton University Press.

Almond, G. A. and Verba, S. (eds) (1980). *The civic culture revisited.* Newbury Park, CA: Sage.

Ansolabehere, S. and Iyengar, S. (1995). *Going negative. How political advertisements shrink and polarize the electorate.* New York: Free Press.

Ansolabehere, S., Iyengar, S. and Simon, A. (1999). Replicating experiments using aggregate and survey data: the case of negative advertising and turnout. *American Political Science Review*, 93, 901–909.

Ansolabehere, S., Iyengar, S., Simon, A. and Valentino, N. (1997). Does attack advertising demobilize the electorate? In S. Iyengar and R. Reeves (eds), *Do the media govern? Politicians, voters, and reporters in America* (pp. 195–204). Thousand Oaks, CA: Sage.

Atkin, C. K., Bowen, L. Nayman, O. B. and Sheinkopf, K. G. (1973). Quality versus quantity in televised political ads. *Public Opinion Quarterly*, 37, 309–324.

Atkin, C. and Heald, G. (1976). Effects of political advertising. *Public Opinion Quarterly*, 40, 216–228.

Basil, M., Schooler, C. and Reeves, B. (1991). Positive and negative political advertising: effectiveness of ads and perceptions of candidates. In Frank Biocca (ed.), *Television and political advertising*. Volume 1: *Psychological processes* (pp. 245–262). Hillsdale, NJ: Lawrence Erlbaum.

Biocca, F. (1991). Looking for units of meaning in political ads. In F. Biocca (ed.), *Television and political advertising*. Volume 2: *Signs, codes, and images* (pp. 17–25). Hillsdale, NJ: Lawrence Erlbaum.

Blum, R. (1999). Handicapierte politische Werbung [Handicapped political advertising]. *Neue Zürcher Zeitung*, 7 (December), pp. 23–24.

Brants, K. (1995). The blank spot: political advertising in the Netherlands. In L. L. Kaid and C. Holtz-Bacha (eds), *Political advertising in western democracies. Parties and candidates on television* (pp. 143–160). Thousand Oaks, CA: Sage.

Chanslor, M., Hovind, M. and Kaid, L. L. (1992). The influence of program and commercial type on political advertising effectiveness. Paper presented at the International Communication Association Convention, Miami, FL (May).

Combs, J. (1979). Political advertising as a popular mythmaking form. *Journal of American Culture*, 2, 331–340.

Cundy, D. T. (1986). Political commercials and candidate image. The effect can be substantial. In L. L. Kaid, D. Nimmo and K. R. Sanders (eds), *New perspectives on political advertising* (pp. 210–234). Carbondale, IL: Southern Illinois University Press.

Dauncey, H. D. (1998). Modernising French political communication: picturing French political culture in party and presidential spots in the 1990s. *Political Communication* (Special electronic issue).

Derieux, E. (1994). *Droit de la communication* [Communication law] (2nd edition). Paris: LGDJ.

Devlin, L. P. (1986). An analysis of presidential television commercials, 1952–1984. In L. L. Kaid, D. Nimmo and K. R. Sanders (eds), *New perspectives on political advertising* (pp. 21–54). Carbondale, IL: Southern Illinois University Press.

Devlin, L. P. (1995). Political commercials in American presidential elections. In L. L. Kaid and C. Holtz-Bacha (eds), *Political advertising in western democracies. Parties and candidates on television* (pp. 186–205). Thousand Oaks, CA: Sage.

Diamond, E. and Bates, S. (1988). *The spot. The rise of political advertising on television* (revised edition). Cambridge, MA: The MIT Press.

Dittmer, L. (1977). Political culture and political symbolism: toward a theoretical synthesis. *World Politics*, 29, 552–583.

Dörner, A. (1995). *Politischer Mythos und symbolische Politik: Sinnstiftung durch symbolische Formen am Beispiel des Hermannsmythos* [Political myth and symbolic politics: the creation of meaning through symbolic forms illustrated by the myth of Hermann]. Opladen: Westdeutscher Verlag.

Edelman, M. (1976). *Politik als Ritual. Die symbolische Funktion staatlicher Institutionen und politischen Handelns* [Politics as ritual. The symbolic function of state institutions and political acting]. Frankfurt a.M.: Campus.

Elkins, D. J. and Simeon, R. E. B. (1979). A cause in search of its effect, or what does political culture explain? *Comparative Politics*, 11, 127–145.

Finkel, S. E. and Geer, J. G. (1998). A spot check: casting doubt on the demobilizing effect of attack advertising. *American Journal of Political Science*, 42, 573–595.

Garramone, G. M. (1984). Voter responses to negative political ads. *Journalism Quarterly*, 61, 250–259.

Geiger, S. F. and Reeves, B. (1991). The effects of visual structure and content emphasis on the evaluation and memory for political candidates. In F. Biocca (ed.), *Television and political advertising*. Volume 1: *Psychological processes* (pp. 125–143). Hillsdale, NJ: Lawrence Erlbaum.

Griffin, M. and Kagan, S. (1996). Picturing culture in political spots: 1992 campaigns in Israel and the US. *Political Communication*, 13, 43–61.

Hofstetter, C. R. and Buss, T. F. (1980). Politics and last-minute political television. *Western Political Quarterly*, 33, 24–37.

Hofstetter, C. R. and Zukin, C. (1979). TV network news and advertising in the Nixon and McGovern campaigns. *Journalism Quarterly*, 56, 106–115, 152.

Hofstetter, C. R., Zukin, C. and Buss, T. F. (1978). Political imagery and information in an age of television. *Journalism Quarterly*, 55, 562–569.

Holtz-Bacha, C. (1999a). The American presidential election in international perspective: Europeanization of the US electoral advertising through free-time segments. In L. L. Kaid and D. Bystrom (eds), *The electronic election. Perspectives on the 1996 campaign communication* (pp. 349–361). Mahwah, NJ: Lawrence Erlbaum.

Holtz-Bacha, C. (1999b). "Wir sind bereit": Wählen Sie "Weltklasse für Deutschland". Die Wahlwerbung der Parteien im Fernsehen ["Wir sind bereit": vote for "Weltklasse für Deutschland". Political advertising of the parties on television]. In C. Holtz-Bacha (ed.), *Wahlkampf in den Medien – Wahlkampf mit den Medien. Ein Reader zum Wahljahr 1998* (pp. 69–85). Opladen: Westdeutscher Verlag.

Holtz-Bacha, C. (2000). Wahlkampf in Deutschland – Ein Fall bedingter Amerikanisierung [Campaigning in Germany – a case of limited Americanization]. In K. Kamps (ed.), *Trans-Atlantik – Trans-Portabel? Die Amerikanisierungsthese in de politischen Kommunikation* (pp. 43–55). Opladen: Westdeutscher Verlag.

Holtz-Bacha, C. and Kaid, L. L. (1995). A comparative perspective on political advertising: media and political system characteristics. In L. L. Kaid and C. Holtz-Bacha (eds), *Political advertising in western democracies. Parties and candidates on television* (pp. 8–18). Thousand Oaks, CA: Sage.

Holtz-Bacha, C. and Kaid, L. L. (1996). "Simply the best." Parteienspots im Bundestagswahlkampf 1994 – Inhalte und Rezeption ["Simply the best." Party spots during the 1994 Bundestag campaign – content and reception]. In C. Holtz-Bacha and L. L. Kaid (eds), *Wahlen und Wahlkampf in den Medien. Untersuchungen aus dem Wahljahr 1994* (pp. 177–207). Opladen: Westdeutscher Verlag.

Holtz-Bacha, C., Kaid, L. L. and Johnston, A. (1994). Political television advertising in Western democracies: a comparison of campaign broadcasts in the US, Germany and France. *Political Communication*, 11, 67–80.

Holtz-Bacha, C. and Lessinger, E.-M. (1997). *Party electoral advertising as representation of political culture.* Paper presented at the International Conference on History and Development of Political Communication on Television, Amsterdam, Netherlands, October.

Holtz-Bacha, C., Lessinger, E.-M. and Hettesheimer, M. (1998). Personalisierung als Strategie der Wahlwerbung [Personalization as strategy in electoral ads]. In K. Imhof and P. Schulz (eds), *Die Veröffentlichung des Privaten – Die Privatisierung des Öffentlichen* (pp. 240–250). Opladen: Westdeutscher Verlag.

Jamieson, K. H. (1996). *Packaging the presidency. A history and criticism of presidential campaign advertising* (3rd edition). New York: Oxford University Press.

Johnson-Cartee, K. S. and Copeland, G. A. (1991). *Negative political advertising. Coming of age.* Hillsdale, NJ: Lawrence Erlbaum.

Johnson-Cartee, K. S. and Copeland, G. A. (1997). *Manipulation of the American voter. Political campaign commercials.* New York: Praeger.

Johnston, A. (1991). Political broadcasts: an analysis of form, content, and style in presidential communication. In L. L. Kaid, J. Gerstlé and K. R. Sanders (eds), *Mediated politics in two cultures* (pp. 59–72). New York: Praeger.

Joslyn, R. (1980). The content of political spot ads. *Journalism Quarterly*, 57, 92–98.

Just, M., Crigler, A. and Wallach, L. (1990). Thirty seconds or thirty minutes: what viewers learn from spot advertisements and candidate debates. *Journal of Communication*, 40(3), 120–133.

Kahn, K. F. and Kenney, P. J. (1999). Do negative campaigns mobilize or suppress turnout? Clarifying the relationship between negativity and participation. *American Political Science Review*, 93, 877–889.

Kaid, L. L. (1981). Political advertising. In D. D. Nimmo and Keith R. Sanders (eds), *Handbook of political communication* (pp. 249–271), Beverly Hills, CA: Sage.

Kaid, L. L. (1982). Paid television advertising and candidate name identification. *Campaigns and Elections*, 3, 34–36.

Kaid, L. L. (1997). Effects of the television spots on images of Dole and Clinton. *American Behavioral Scientist*, 40, 1085–1094.

Kaid, L. L. (1998). Political television advertising: a comparative perspective on styles and effects across cultures. Paper presented at the American Political Science Association Convention, Boston, MA (September).

Kaid, L. L. and Chanslor, M. (1995). Changing candidate images: the effects of television advertising. In K. Hacker (ed.), *Candidate images in presidential election campaigns* (pp. 83–97). New York: Praeger.

Kaid, L. L. and Davidson, D. K. (1986). Elements of videostyle: candidate presentation through television advertising. In L. L. Kaid, D. Nimmo and K. R. Sanders (eds), *New perspectives on political advertising* (pp. 184–209). Carbondale, IL: Southern Illinois University Press.

Kaid, L. L. and Holtz-Bacha, C. (1995a). Political advertising across cultures: comparing content, styles, and effects. In L. L. Kaid and C. Holtz-Bacha (eds), *Political advertising in western democracies. Parties and candidates on television* (pp. 206–227). Thousand Oaks, CA: Sage.

Kaid, L. L. and Holtz-Bacha, C. (eds) (1995b). *Political advertising in western democracies. Parties and candidates on television*. Thousand Oaks, CA: Sage.

Kaid, L. L. and Sanders, K. R. (1978). Political television commercials: an experimental study of type and length. *Communication Research*, 5, 57–70.

Kern, M. (1989). *30-second politics. Political advertising in the eighties*. New York: Praeger.

Krugman, H. E. (1965). The impact of television advertising: learning without involvement. *Public Opinion Quarterly*, 29, 349–356.

Lang, A. (1991). Emotion, formal features, and memory for televised political advertisements. In F. Biocca (ed.), *Television and political advertising*. Volume 1: *Psychological processes* (pp. 221–243). Hillsdale, NJ: Lawrence Erlbaum.

Lau, R. R., Sigelman, L., Heldman, C. and Babbitt, P. (1999). The effects of negative political advertisements: a meta-analytic assessment. *American Political Science Review*, 93, 851–875.

Lessinger, E.-M. (1997). Politische Information oder Stimmenfang? Eine explorative Studie zum Kommunikationsstil in Wahlwerbespots der Bundestagswahlen 1976 bis 1994. Bochum: unpublished manuscript.

Mancini, P. and Swanson, D. L. (1996). Politics, media, and modern democracy: introduction. In D. L. Swanson and P. Mancini (eds), *Politics, media, and modern democracy. An international study of innovations in electoral campaigning and their consequences* (pp. 1–26). Westport, CT: Praeger.

Mazzoleni, G. and Roper, C. S. (1995). The presentation of Italian candidates and parties in television advertising. In L. L. Kaid and C. Holtz-Bacha (eds), *Political advertising in western democracies. Parties and candidates on television* (pp. 89–108). Thousand Oaks, CA: Sage.

McClure, R. and Patterson, T. E. (1974). Print versus network news. *Journal of Communication*, 26(2), 23–28.

Meadow, R. G. and Sigelman, L. (1982). Some effects and noneffects of campaign commercials. An experimental study. *Political Behavior*, 4, 163–175.

Moring, T. (1995). The North European exception: political advertising on TV in Finland. In L. L. Kaid and C. Holtz-Bacha (eds), *Political advertising in western democracies. Parties and candidates on television* (pp. 161–185). Thousand Oaks, CA: Sage.

Newhagen, J. E. and Reeves, B. (1991). Emotion and memory responses for negative political advertising: a study of television commercials used in the 1988 presidential election. In F. Biocca (ed.), *Television and political advertising*. Volume 1: *Psychological processes* (pp. 197–220). Hillsdale, NJ: Lawrence Erlbaum.

Nowlan, J. D. and Moutray, M. J. (1984). Broadcast advertising and party endorsements in a statewide primary. *Journal of Broadcasting*, 28, 361–363.

O'Sullivan, P. and Geiger, S. (1995). Does the watchdog bite? Newspaper ad watch articles and political attack ads. *Journalism and Mass Communication Quarterly*, 72, 771–785.

Padula, V. L. (1996). Party change and political campaigning in Italy: personalized leadership and ideology in party campaign televised ads. Paper presented at the Convention of the American Political Science Association, San Francisco, CA (August–September).

Paletz, D. L. and Vinson, C. D. (1994). Mediatisierung von Wahlkampagnen. Zur Rolle der amerikanischen Medien bei Wahlen [The mediatization of campaigns. On the role of the US media in elections]. *Media Perspektiven* (July), 362–368.

Patterson, T. E. and McClure, R. D. (1976). *The unseeing eye. The myth of television power in national elections.* New York: Paragon.

Pfau, M. and Burgoon, M. (1988). Inoculation in political campaign communication. *Human Communication Research,* 15, 91–111.

Prisuta, R. H. (1972). Broadcast advertising by candidates for the Michigan legislature. *Journal of Broadcasting,* 16, 453–459.

Richardson, G. W. Jr (1998). The popular culture context of political advertising: linkages and meanings in political information processing. *Political Communication* (Special electronic issue).

Roddy, B. L. and Garramone, G. M. (1988). Appeals and strategies of negative political advertising. *Journal of Broadcasting and Electronic Media,* 32, 415–427.

Rohe, K. (1990). Politische Kultur und ihre Analyse. Probleme und Perspektiven der politischen Kulturforschung [Political culture and its analysis. Problems and perspectives for research on political culture]. *Historische Zeitschrift,* 250, 321–346.

Rothschild, M. L. and Ray, M. Michael L. (1974). Involvement and political advertising effect: an exploratory experiment. *Communication Research,* 1, 264–285.

Rudd, R. (1986). Issues as image in political campaign commercials. *Western Journal of Speech Communication,* 50, 102–118.

Sarcinelli, U. (1986). Wahlkampfkommunikation als symbolische Politik. Überlegungen zu einer theoretischen Einordnung der Politikvermittlung im Wahlkampf [Campaign communication as symbolic politics. Thoughts about the theoretical position of political communication during election campaigns]. In H.-D. Klingemann and M. Kaase (eds), *Wahlen und politischer Prozeß. Analysen aus Anlaß der Bundestagwahl 1983* (pp. 180–200). Opladen: Westdeutscher Verlag.

Scammell, M. and Semetko, H. (1995). Political advertising on television: the British experience. In L. L. Kaid and C. Holtz-Bacha (eds), *Political advertising in western democracies. Parties and candidates on television* (pp. 19–43). Thousand Oaks, CA: Sage.

Scherer, H. (1995). Kommunikationskanäle in der Europawahl 1989 [Communication channels during the European election campaign 1989]. In L. Erbring (ed.), *Kommunikationsraum Europa* (pp. 203–221). Konstanz: UVK Medien Ölschläger.

Schleuder, J., McCombs, M. and Wanta, W. (1991). Inside the agenda-setting process: how political advertising and TV news prime viewers to think about issues and candidates. In F. Biocca (ed.), *Television and political advertising.* Volume 1: *Psychological processes* (pp. 265–309). Hillsdale, NJ: Lawrence Erlbaum.

Schmidt, S. J. (1995). Werbung zwischen Wirtschaft und Kunst [Advertising between economy and art]. In S. J. Schmidt and B. Spieß (eds), *Werbung, Medien und Kultur* (pp. 26–43). Opladen: Westdeutscher Verlag.

Shyles, L. (1986). The televised political spot advertisement: its structure, content, and role in the political system. In L. L. Kaid, D. Nimmo and K. R. Sanders (eds), *New perspectives on political advertising* (pp. 107–138). Carbondale, IL: Southern Illinois University Press.

Surlin, S. H. and Gordon, T. F. (1977). How values affect attitudes toward direct reference political advertising. *Journalism Quarterly,* 54, 89–98.

Wanat, J. (1974). Political broadcast advertising and primary election voting. *Journal of Broadcasting,* 18, 413–422.

Wattenberg, M. P. (1982). From parties to candidates: examining the role of the media. *Public Opinion Quarterly,* 46, 216–227.

Wattenberg, M. P. and Brians, C. L. (1999). Negative campaign advertising: demobilizer or mobilizer? *American Political Science Review*, 93, 891–899.

West, D. M. (1997). *Air wars. Television advertising in election campaigns 1952–1996* (2nd edition). Washington, DC: Congressional Quarterly.

Zhao, X. and Chaffee, S. H. (1995). Campaign advertisements versus television news as sources of political issue information. *Public Opinion Quarterly*, 59, 41–65.

7

STATES, INTERNATIONAL ORGANIZATIONS, AND THE NEWS MEDIA

Problems of image cultivation

Michael Kunczik

Introduction

The focus of this essay will be the field of international public relations, i.e. the problem of image cultivation of nations or international organizations (e.g. United Nations, World Bank, International Monetary Fund, Greenpeace, Amnesty International, World Wildlife Fund, etc.). Up to now most research has been done concerning images of nations. Taking the quantity of publications as an indicator, it is clear that the body of research on international organizations and the media is an area that still has large gaps. But even the relationship between news media and images of nations is not well researched, for this very reason the following discussion cannot claim to be complete. The main reason for this gap in research can be seen in the often highly sophisticated methods of states to influence world opinion, in which among others public relations agencies and even the secret services can play a decisive role in activities that very often take place far from the light of day (Kunczik, 1997). Public relations is also the art of camouflaging and deceiving, successful PR also means above all that the target groups (those to be influenced) do not notice that they have become the "victims" of a PR activity.

Because credibility is a decisive variable in the communication process, attempts are forever being made to influence media reporting by covert means to avoid the impression of manipulation. The aim of such activities is chameleonlike: to adapt to the surroundings and remain submerged. The attempt to identify the instigators of national public relations is like trying to nail pudding to a wall. Therefore, the accessibility of literature on this theme is quite poor. One cannot, after all, do a representative survey of the KGB or the CIA, although the USIA (US Information Agency) has been the subject of a published empirical study (Bogart, 1976). The borders between secret services and news agencies are often fudged, as the example of TASS, the former main Soviet agency, shows (Kruglak, 1962). Most industrial and many developing countries either have created special organizations (USIA, British Council, Maison Francaise, Goethe Institut, etc.) to improve their country's image or have commissioned PR organizations to do so.

Images of certain nations, however right or wrong they might be, seem to form, fundamentally, through a very complex communication process involving varied information sources. The process starts with one's experiences in very early life; in school; in children's books, fairytales, and other leisure literature; the theater and so on, and may include accounts by relatives, acquaintances, and friends.[1] In 1951, Jean Piaget and Anne-Marie Weil published a study "The development in children of the idea of the homeland and of relations with other countries" in which they asked children about their ideas about foreigners. A Swiss youngster aged nine and one-half made the following statements: "The French are not very serious, they don't worry about anything and it's dirty there." The child's image of the Russians was the following: "They're bad, they're always wanting to make war." The Americans also were described: "They're ever so rich and clever. They've discovered the atom bomb." Asked how the child came to know all these things, the answer was: "I don't know. . . . I've heard it . . . that's what people say." But radio and TV transmissions of international programs, newspapers, and magazines, cultural exchange programs, sports, books, news services, and so on are probably the strongest image shapers. The various communication sources are responsible for the image or images of another nation in all strata of a population. Education and travel – that is the degree of personal experience of foreign cultures – are also of extraordinary importance to image building. In his famous book, *Public opinion*, Walter Lippmann (1922) wrote: "Man . . . is learning to see with his mind vast portions of the world that he could never see, touch, smell, hear, or remember. Gradually he makes for himself a trustworthy picture inside his head of the world beyond his reach" (p. 181). The mass media (and not only the news media) are, in fact, continuously offering images of nations.

For the nation-state (and international organizations), PR means the planned and continuous distribution of interest-bound information by a state aimed (mostly) at improving the country's image abroad. Trying to distinguish among advertising, PR, and propaganda in foreign image cultivation is merely a semantic game. In Harold D. Lasswell's (1942) definition of *propaganda* as "the manipulation of symbols as a means of influencing attitudes on controversial matters" (p. 106), one could easily substitute *PR* for *propaganda*. I treat *propaganda* and *PR* as synonyms. This means, following the tradition of one of the founding fathers of PR, Edward L.

Bernays (1923), that "The only difference between 'propaganda' and 'education', really, is the point of view. The advocacy of what we believe in is education. The advocacy of what we don't believe in is propaganda" (p. 212). So, PR for the nation-state comprises persuasive communicative acts, directed at a foreign audience. But a famous comment by Lippmann (1922) applies also to the changeability of images: "For the most part we do not first see, and then define, we define first and then see" (p. 81). In other words, from the wealth of events and information available, we select those that conform to the already existing image. Furthermore can information in which one is not interested be ignored. For example, in September 1947, a six-month propaganda campaign to promote the United Nations was begun in Cincinnati (its slogan was "Peace begins with the United Nations – the United Nations begin with you"). It was largely unsuccessful because those who paid attention to the message were primarily individuals already interested in and informed about the United Nations. As Star and Hughes (1950) observed, "The conclusion is that the people reached by the campaign were those least in need of it and that the people missed by it were the new audience the plan hoped to gain" (p. 397).

Mediation of foreign policy

Public relations for states is closely connected to mediation of foreign policy. Hertz (1982) asserted: "It is perhaps no exaggeration to say that today half of power politics consists of image making. With the rising importance of publics in foreign affairs, image making has steadily increased. Today, hardly anything remains in the open conduct of foreign policy that does not have a propaganda or public relations aspect ..." (p. 187). Kepplinger (1983) concluded that the mass media, originally located outside the political system, have taken over a place within the political system. The media have become a political force that no longer just reacts, but also acts, and essentially – because the media, as an autonomous force, define the extent of the political possible – cogoverns. The functional dependencies of political institutions and the mass media in parliamentary democracies are seen as a matter of both domestic and foreign politics. Through their mediating function the mass media hold a key position in the political process. The media have the power to put themes on the agenda hitherto ignored by politics, they can help to establish contacts not possible at the level of diplomacy, and they can be used as instruments of foreign policy.

On the significance of the mass media in foreign policy, Karl (1982) wrote: "The media are increasingly a part of the process (if not the entire process) in the communication between governments and publics about international politics" (p. 144). Indeed, governments can come under pressure from what is already on media record. Thus, in the event of a potential or actual conflict, negotiated solutions could become more difficult if it seemed that such a new, conciliatory approach might, because of an earlier media-expressed hard line, involve a loss of face. To quote Karl again: "In an age of media diplomacy, statecraft may have become the hostage – if not the victim – of stagecraft. Only the media have a first-strike capability on both national and international levels" (p. 155).

The mass media of communication have broken into the traditionally exclusive sphere of diplomacy, and have themselves become an instrument of international conciliation, and mediation – and also of conflict. The mass media, by serving in the diplomatic sphere as a source of international information, can contribute to international orientation, for example by establishing a common fund of knowledge that enables or facilitates negotiations. But as to the quality of this common basis of information, many countries (especially developing countries) believe that their positions – because of the current structure of the global information system – are not receiving due attention in the world or in a certain region. Such a situation can be defined as an image crisis: the political elite of a state believes that they do not have a fair and adequate image in a foreign country; that is, they believe that they are not given adequate and unbiased media attention.

The field of diplomacy is shifting from traditional diplomacy toward public diplomacy, whereby politicians are trying to instrumentalize the mass media. Adaptation of foreign policy to the mass media means that politicians are accepting advice from PR. The dominating motive of political action is no longer the substantial quality of policy, but the creation of newsworthy events. To paraphrase Karl (1982), statecraft becomes stagecraft, and the PR practitioners know how news is selected by journalists. Bernays (1923) argued in his famous *Crystallizing public opinion*: "The counsel on public relations not only knows what news value is, but knowing it, he is in a position to make news happen. He is a creator of events" (p. 197). In his memoirs (1965) Bernays described how he advised the exiled Czech politician, Tomás Garrigue Masaryk, who had been elected president of the Czechoslovak National Council, to issue his country's declaration of independence on a Sunday for PR reasons: because Sunday was a slow news day, so it would get more space in the world's newspapers.

Important to image building are "pseudoevents" (Boorstin, 1961), events more or less deliberately staged to gain attention or create a certain impression. There are hundreds if not thousands of examples which demonstrate that the staging of pseudoevents has become routine. These make up much of media coverage. Mahatma Gandhi staged pseudoevents in his struggle for liberation from the British. In 1930 he organized the march on the salt works of Dharasana and allowed police to batter several thousand demonstrators with long sticks with steel nails embedded in the end. More than 2,000 newspapers throughout the world reported this bloodbath. World public opinion condemned the British. An American senator read the report by a UPI correspondent in Congress. Physically, the police had been the victors, but morally they were beaten.

Another example for a pseudoevent was the July 1983 action of Greenpeace in the Bering Sea. Members of Greenpeace deliberately violated Soviet territorial waters after having informed the mass media of their intention. Ostensibly, they were there to photograph illegal Soviet whaling, but in all probability their real aim was to be captured by the Soviets and thereby create a "news event". Greenpeace had earlier checked out the dangers of possible punishment by the Soviet Union. As Peter Dykstra of Greenpeace explained, "We consulted all available experts. If there had been any strong indication our people would actually have spent any time in harsh conditions of the prototypical Siberian labor camp, we'd never have taken that kind of chance" (Blyskal & Blyskal, 1985, p. 188). And, on the real objective of the PR stunt, Dykstra said, "Obviously, if the public supports what we did in the Soviet Union, they will support us with funding" (Blyskal & Blyskal, 1985, p. 188). Because of strong public opinion, clearly some countries actually feel threatened by Greenpeace actions. Grave damage to international image is done, at least in the short term, by such actions as the sinking of a Greenpeace ship by the French secret service or the subsequent treatment of those who committed the act. Relations between France and New Zealand were strained when, in 1985, French secret service agents attacked the ship *Rainbow Warrior* in the port of Auckland. The ship had not yet left port to protest the French atomic bomb testing on Mururoa Atoll when it was sunk to prevent drawing world attention to the protest. France obviously felt that its policy was endangered and worried about its image as a "grand nation".

Many countries make considerable efforts to cultivate their images abroad, especially in the US and Europe. As a rule, no precise linkage between commissioned PR activities and what appears in the mass media can be traced. Typically one can do little more than guess at what suggestions were made, which were accepted, and how they were implemented. The precise nature of the intervention remains something of a mystery. Manheim and Albritton (1984) studied the influence of the activities of PR agencies on images of nations. They examined in particular *The New York Times* coverage of six countries (the Republic of Korea, the Philippines, Yugoslavia, Argentina, Indonesia, and Rhodesia), which had entered into PR contracts in the US.[2] The major service the PR firms offered was to improve the respective governments' access to American journalists. In addition, they wrote press releases, did direct mailings, and sent out newsletters and brochures. In some cases, embassy personnel were trained how to speak about sensitive issues such as terrorism or human rights. Field trips for the press, visits with editors, and lunches with business groups were organized. One of the main effects of the PR activity was that, with the exception of

121

Indonesia, the visibility – that is, the amount of coverage – was reduced. This corresponds to research findings of research on the effects of mass communications whereby the image of a country that makes negative head-lines and also has a negative image in public opinion cannot be changed by the sudden appearance of positive reporting because this would be perceived as incredible. Withdrawal from public attention makes people forget, providing an opportunity to build slowly a positive new image.

Nevertheless, some of the emphases of the PR activities can be illus-trated (see, e.g. Cutlip, 1994; Kunczik 1997; Manheim 1994; Manheim & Albritton 1984), such as visits by heads of state, the release of political prisoners, trips for journalists organized by the respective governments or by transnational corporations, establishment of information offices, cos-metic redistribution of power within a country, scheduling of elections, sporting events, and so on. All these are events with a high likelihood of reporting in the news media. I believe it is useful to adapt some hypotheses that have been developed in news research to guide research on PR for states. For example, the hypothesis could be put forward that, the more a country depends on exportation, the more likely and the more intensely it will mount campaigns of image cultivation. Further, a state may be more likely to mount a PR campaign in another region if the reporting there is biased due to the structures of news selection. Another hypothesis could be: the more important (economically and/or politically) an entity (whether country or union, e.g. the European Community [EC]), the more likely it is that foreign countries will untertake campaigns there (e.g. most campaigns are waged in the US and Western industrialized countries). Until now, PR and/or advertising campaigns for tourism have represent the focal point of activities in the area of international PR (Kunczik & Weber, 1994).

The structural necessity of international public relations

Mass media reporting of foreign affairs often governs what kind of image of a country or a culture predominates. Johan Galtung and Mari Holmboe Ruge (1965) argued that the world comprises individual and collective actors whose actions are determined by their particular images of reality. International actions are based on the image of international reality. Although these are not shaped by the news media alone, their ubiquity and perseverance would certainly make them first-rate competitors for the number-one position as international image former. Especially in democracies, in which, at least theoretically, the individual can participate in the socially relevant decision-making processes, the mass media can exercise considerable indirect influence on a country's policies by the images they help to create with their foreign reporting. There are no data as yet, however, on how, say, foreign policy might be influenced by images so shaped. In this field, discussion consists almost totally of plausibility arguments.

Foreign reporting operates as follows: the mass media selectively perceive events in the world and, as they propagate them, distortions occur. The media image thus created is then perceived by individuals selectively and, hence, distorted further. Galtung and Ruge (1965) examined the reporting about crisis in the Congo, Cuba, and Cyprus. Overall they found that the cynical journalists' adage, "Bad news is good news," applied to the reporting they examined. International news is selected by criteria similar to those used for national news or local news: higher ranking (superpower) or geographically and/or culturally close states are most likely to be reported on. Economic, alliance, and ideological relations also generate more intensive coverage of another country. In the Foreign Images Study for the United Nations Educational, Scientific, and Cultural Organization (UNESCO), the selection of international news in twenty-nine countries was examined (Sreberny-Mohammadi, 1985). According to this study, selection is done by universally valid criteria, with particular emphasis on the unusual: disasters, unrest, coups, and so forth. Regionalism is particularly pronounced in all media systems. Hence, one cannot speak of a clear predominance of the world centers over the periphery. Thus a study of "foreign news flow in Africa" found a principle of news selection that can be described, at best, as a village pump perspective (Ume-Nwagbo, 1982). But negativism (civil war, natural disasters, debt crisis, human rights violations, electoral frauds, etc.) often remains the only important news factor dominating the coverage of developing countries in the North. Aside from this aspect, the media of the Third World do not themselves measure up to the demands made by their representatives at the international level, for they select news according to the same criteria as the Western media. Accordingly, the media of the Third World are noted for using a high proportion of non-political bad news from the industrialized nations. The crisis-oriented reporting on the Third World by the Western media corresponds to the bad picture of the Western nations in the press of those developing countries.

Given the structural conditions of the international flow of news, countries with economic or political interests in having a positive image in a certain region, including those that are at a disadvantage from the outset because of the standard processes of gathering and selecting information, must mount active publicity campaigns. Although by definition, PR for states is always interest-bound communication, it can, however, offset communication deficits due to structures. This form of PR for states, meant primarily to compensate for structural communication deficits, aims mainly to adapt the image to news values by trying to influence mass media reporting. *Structural* international PR aims at correcting the "false" images previously created by the mass media. *Manipulative PR*, on the other hand, tries to create a positive image that, in most cases, does not reflect reality, including lying and disinformation. The AIDS campaign of the KGB[3] and the disinformation campaign of the Reagan administration against Muammar Qaddafi are good examples of this.[4]

Excursus: the necessity to manipulate the news media during wartime

During wartime, the manipulation of the news media is a necessity. The first military theoretician to recognize this was the Prussian general, Carl von Clausewitz (1780–1831). In his *Vom kriege (On war)*, published posthumously in 1832, von Clausewitz argued that Napoleon's military success was due mainly to the enthusiasm of the French people. According to von Clausewitz, war is an act of violence aimed at forcing the enemy to accept our will. The central aspect of warfare, he suggested, however, is not physical force, but morale. The goal of war, then, is to break the enemy's morale. The von Clausewitz theory of war takes the following factors into consideration: (a) the government that defines the war aims, (b) the army that is fighting, and (c) the people.

Important to understanding the theoretical foundation of censorship is the environment in which military actions are taking place. This environment is characterized by danger, highest physical strain and confusion. Von Clausewitz (1832) called this *friktion*, which means that all plans developed during maneuvers have to be changed in real war. All is simple in war, but the simple is difficult and nothing is certain. Camouflage and deception are the norm. Most intelligence is not secure and very often is wrong. Indeed, von Clausewitz argued, in war most news is false. Secrecy becomes most important because the enemy has to be deceived.

According to von Clausewitz (1832/1873) lying and deceit are necessary in war. Mastery of deceit and hypocrisy is decisive for successful military actions because the aim has to be to surprise the enemy. The German sociologist Simmel (1920) argued that during war the basis of social life must be undermined. The enemy must be confronted with unexpected situations. Simmel made the following assumption: "All relationships between people are self-evidently based on their knowing something about each other" (p. 256). People have expectations regarding the behavior of others and know that those they are dealing with also have such expectations. Stable social relations are based on the formation of "expectations of expectations," which makes social behavior predictable. In a war situation, one has to deceive the enemy's expectations of one's behavior and, as a result, to undermine the foundations of human coexistence.

Communication is interaction through messages. Communication means, then, that information is passed from one person to another. In times of war, communication with the enemy means that we try to pass false intelligence to the enemy – and the enemy knows that this is our intention. It is a situation of paradoxical communication (Watzlawick, 1976). Decision making in war, then, means making paradox predictions: the higher the probability of a certain action, the lower the chance the enemy will mount it. The lower the probability of an action, the higher the probability the enemy will act that way. The art of disinformation assumes highest importance for survival in times of war. Successful disinformation means the enemy treats false information as credible. The logic of disinformation is as follows: what does the enemy think, that I think, what he thinks, and so on (Watzlawick, 1976). Reporting the truth of war might not only give the enemy advantages but also weaken the morale of one's own population and/or troops. Lying and propaganda are important instruments of warfare. If journalists can be instrumentalized, that is, can be manipulated to do propaganda, then they are useful. But reporting the truth in most cases is dangerous for the successful achievement of war aims.

Three more reasons for manipulating the media and institutionalizing censorship during wartime are (a) the morale of the soldiers, (b) the morale of the population, and (c) world public opinion. Any nation-state waging war has to find stories that justify and ennoble the cause. These are the stories to be disseminated, whereas those that tell of the horrors of war from the soldiers' point of view should be suppressed. The German sociologist Ferdinand Tönnies (1922) argued that in a country at war, people believe in the just cause of the war, which was forced upon the country by the enemy. To stabilize belligerent public opinion, the government stigmatizes the enemy as aggressor or as a nonhuman monster. President Bush, who characterized Saddam Hussein as another Hitler, argued: "Saddam tried to cast this conflict as a religious war, but it has nothing to do with religion per se. It has, on the other hand, everything to do with what religion embodies: good vs. evil, right vs. wrong" (*Time*, March 11, 1991, p. 24).

During war it is of vital interest to the supreme command or the government to control the mass media in order to hinder shifts in public opinion. It can be argued, for instance, that the US was drawn into the quagmire in Somalia under the influence of television. But television was also probably responsible for America's subsequent withdrawal from Somalia. As Considine (1994) put it, "The pictures of Michael Duran and other soldiers brutalized in Somalia set off a media and public clamour for American withdrawal. The frenzy prompted Secretary of State, Warren Christopher, to say that however useful television coverage was to national understanding, edited highlights and pictures taken out of context could not become the driving force for determining American foreign policy" (p. 11). But Considine maintained that "State Department sources had confirmed that news coverage was driving US foreign policy" (p. 11). At least the quality of foreign policy has changed under the influence of television; possibly not a turn for the better. There are indications that even warfare is being affected by media coverage. A NATO officer explained why the Allied forces declined to shoot down Serbian helicopters violating the no-fly zone: "Even if they were carrying arms, we worried that someone would stick civilian bodies in the wreckage just in time to be filmed by CNN" (*Newsweek*, March 14, 1994). Further, NATO commanders decided not to use napalm or cluster bombs, capable of clearing large swaths of terrain, in Bosnia because: "Bad TV. Napalm leaves it victims shrivelled and charred. Cluster bombs tear them into shreds. The West is worried how they might look on the nightly news" (*Newsweek*, April 25, 1994, p. 13).

Image and the international system

In literature there is no clear definitive delimitation between such concepts as attitude, stereotype, prejudices, or image. Often the terms overlap or are used differently from author to author. The term *image* became popular in the 1950s, especially in the US, and was used to describe the aura of a person in public life, a party, a product, a nation, a people, and so forth. The image is something created and cultivated by its possessor, that is, something that can be actively influenced by PR activities. By contrast, prejudices and/or stereotypes are created by the environment and are ascribed. In this sense, in the following discussion image always contains an active component. But images of nations, at least partly, can be understood as hardened prejudices; these are not suddenly there but often have grown in long historical processes. Such social prejudices can be defined as expressed convictions of a particular group (or its members) about an alien group (or individuals because of actual or assumed membership of the alien group) without consideration of their correctness.

Similarly to Boulding (1956), it is assumed here that the conception of an image means not only the conception of the image at present, but also aspects of its past and future expectations. National image, then, can be defined as the cognitive representation that a person holds of a given country, what a person believes to be true about a nation and its people. Of special importance to political action is the benevolence or malevolence imputed to other nations in the images, as well as the historical component of the image. Feelings about a country's future are important, too. Boulding (1969) defined image as "total cognitive, affective, and evaluative structure of the behavior unit, or its internal view of itself and the universe" (p. 423). The problem of what is reality or fiction in our various perceptions of the world usually plays no large part in our daily lives. One behaves as if one's perception of the world were "true." Moreover, in everyday behavior there are mechanisms leading to the discovery and remedy of mistakes. There is the possibility of moving to "near reality," as feedback leads to the elimination of errors. As Boulding (1956, 1967) argued both in science and in the area of "common beliefs" advances in recognition come from the disappointment of hopes because only through mistakes could anything new be learned; successes only confirmed existing perceptions. In this respect there are by and large, no differences between scientific learning and folk learning. Experiences that do not fit into one's perceptions can, but need not, lead to modifications of those perceptions.

Between the world of folk learning and the folk images derived from it and the world of scientific learning and scientific images, Boulding (1967) localized another image sphere, which he described as a "world of literary images" (p. 5). In this world the test of reality is the least pronounced; that is, the elimination of errors either does not take place at all or occurs only at enormous cost. It is in this world that the images of the international system are localized and in which the international decision makers mainly move. Indeed, Boulding regarded the international system as by far the most pathological and costly part of the world system (e.g. costs of military, foreign ministries, diplomatic corps, secret services, and wars). In fact, decision makers are usually aware that they are living in a world of images. As the famous French statesman Talleyrand pointed out, in politics what is believed to be true is more important than truth itself. Ronald Reagan knew that "Facts are stupid things" (*Time*, August 29, 1988, p. 52). Knorr (1980) quoted Dorothy L. Sayers (1926): "My lord, facts are like cows. If you look them in the face hard enough, they generally run away" (p. 226). Kissinger (1969) stated: "Deterrence above all depends on psychological criteria" (p. 61).

According to Boulding there are two main reasons for the pathology of the international system. First, neither folk learning nor science can shape adequate images of it. The simple feedback mechanisms that work in everyday life do not help in understanding the complexity of the international system. And scientists currently are unable to provide the information needed to build a realistic image of the international system, although there have been repeated efforts to that end. Further, as a rule, political decision makers are highly mistrustful of research findings in the social sciences. Boulding wrote (1967): "On the whole the images of the international system in the minds of its decision makers are derived by a process that I have described as 'literary' – a melange of narrative history, memories of past events, stories and conversations, etc., plus an enormous amount of usually ill-digested and carelessly collected current information. When we add to this the fact that the system produces strong hates, loves, loyalties, disloyalties, and so on, it would be surprising if any images were formed that even remotely resembled the most loosely defined realities of the case" (p. 9).

Manheim (1991) took the same position, arguing that for top decision makers in the US, "the likelihood is that most people in our government and others, even at the highest level, received at least as much information about the June 1989 massacre in Beijing's Tiananmen Square from media reports as from diplomatic or intelligence sources. They know little more than we know. We are vulnerable" (p. 130). For politicians like foreign ministers, for example, the success of their career has not been dependent on the ability to estimate correctly the images of foreign nations but to meet the demands and stereotypes of their voters: if the people believed that the Soviet Union was an "empire of evil" (as did Ronald Reagan), one can win elections only if one is of the same opinion or at least gives that impression. Although they often refuse to believe it of themselves, politicians are as prone to distorted perceptions as anyone else. When such distorted perceptions flow into political decision making, there can be very negative consequences.

Actors in the field of international public relation

It is almost impossible to differentiate clearly between international PR of nation-states, of international social/economic organizations (e.g. the World Bank, Greenpeace), of international political organizations (e.g. United Nations, NATO, etc.), and of multinational corporations (MNCs). Furthermore, the same PR agency can work for states and MNCs. The following discussion proceeds from the premise that the economy cannot be regarded as a subsystem equal in importance to others. Rather, economics is assumed to be a basic social factor that also decisively influences other subsystems; in particular I argue that economy and policy cannot be separated. All too often, people overlook the fact that MNCs are quite active in foreign policy and interact with states: I need refer here only to the oil crisis (of the 1970s) or the worldwide bribing by Lockheed. Bernays (1965), working as PR counselor to United Fruit, wrote, "I was struck by the thought that although I was advising a banana company, I was actually fighting in the Cold War" (p. 766).

Nations' worry over their image gives power to such organizations as Amnesty International. Founded in 1961 by the British jurist, Peter Benenson, its aim is obtaining the release of political and religious "prisoners of conscience" through international protest. Benenson was moved to act in 1961 when two Portuguese students were sentenced to 7 years' imprisonment each for uttering a toast to freedom. Benenson announced his campaign on May 28, 1961 in a full-page article in *The Observer*. Amnesty's aim is to stir up moral outrage. Lia Dover of the organization put it like this to *Time* (October 17, 1988, p. 23) "The fact that a crime is known and publicized has an effect on decision makers. They care about their image. Torturers go to great lengths to ensure that they are not identified, so putting them in the spotlight helps ensure it doesn't happen again." In January 1989, Amnesty International focused on violations of human rights in Turkey. This may be one of the reasons why, in June 1989, the

Table 7.1 Use of international public relations (PR)

	Public	Private
For-profit	State-owned airlines	MNCs
Non-profit	Governments, international organizations	Foundations

Turkish government hired Saatchi & Saatchi, an advertising agency known throughout the world, to improve its country's image.

A simple classification of those who use international PR can be developed using two dimensions: for-profit versus non-profit and public versus private (Table 7.1).

This is only a rough classification however. Other actors are also in the field such as international influence brokers as individuals (e.g. Henry Kissinger) and international PR agencies (e.g. holdings like Interpublic, Omnicom Group, Wire & Plastic Products (wpp) Young and Rubicam, True North Communication Inc., Saatchi & Saatchi etc.), which often give advice to influence, or at least try to influence, world politics. Walter Isaacson (1992) argued that Kissinger's comments on the crackdown of the democratic movement in China in June 1989 were based on commercial interests, because Kissinger had clients with strong business involvements in China (among them, Atlantic Richfield, ITT, and an investment partnership called China Ventures). After the Tiananmen Square crackdown, Kissinger recommended in a television interview on ABC, that the US should maintain good relations instead of imposing economic sanctions, as an indication of political maturity. Isaacson maintained, that "if the American reaction to the Tiananmen had been mild, as Kissinger urged, China Ventures would have proceeded, and Kissinger would have made a significant amount of money" (p. 749). According to Isaacson Kissinger's trip to China in November 1989 was staged to show the world that the time for ostracism was over. Kissinger met Deng Xiaoping and later reported on his meeting and the atmosphere within China to President Bush and top American leaders.

There are also voluntaristic campaigners who fight for certain goals or against certain institutions without having well-established organizational structures. Tocqueville emphasized in 1835 in his famous Democracy in America (1835/1946), "Americans of all ages, all conditions, and all dispositions constantly form associations ... If it be proposed to advance some truth, or to foster some feeling by the encouragement of a great example, they form a society" (p. 114). Tocqueville believed the Americans to be perfect campaigners, noting: "the extreme skill which the inhabitants of the US succeed in proposing a common object to the exertion of a great many men, and in getting them voluntary to pursue it" (p. 114). Examples of this kind of non-professional, spontaneous PR in nineteenth century US are the visit of Lafayette in the US and the campaign for Pope Pius IX (cf. Olasky, 1985). A more recent example of voluntaristic international PR occurred when, in September 1994, the World Bank and the International Monetary Fund (IMF) celebrated their fiftieth anniversary. In the German weekly *Die Zeit* (September 23, 1994) an advertisement by a public interest group *Entwicklung braucht Entschuldung* (development needs freedom from encumbrance) was published. It declared that there was nothing to celebrate, that the managers of the World Bank and IMF failed to control the debt explosion in the South, resulting in economic conditions in Africa worse than 15 years earlier. For instance, many of the projects supported by IMF and the World Bank resulted in ecological and social disasters (especially building of dams). The committee urged the German government to attempt to change the policy of the World Bank/IMF, that is, to control the projects of the World Bank/IMF, contending that the focus of the World Bank's activities should be the fight against poverty. They also demanded that all debts be paid.

The close interconnections between states and MNCs are demonstrated by the Mobil Corporation. In October 1981 an advertisement was published in *The New York Times.* "Saudi Arabia: Far More Than Oil" (Grunig & Hunt, 1984, p. 521). In 1986 Mobil waged a campaign in the US for the sale of missiles to Saudi Arabia, which, Mobil argued, would serve America's interests: "This week, the Senate will attempt to override President Reagan's veto [President Reagan had vetoed the resolution of the Congress to block the sale of missiles to Saudi Arabia], and kill the sale. When the crucial roll call is taken, members should remember a simple fact: they *aren't* voting on just an arms bill for Saudi Arabia. They *are* voting on an arms bill for American interests. Against such a yardstick, we trust the presidential veto will be sustained" (Onkvisit & Shaw, 1989, p. 148). Mobil also referred to the Red Menace emphasizing the Soviet interest in the turmoil in the Middle East.

The Ford Company also fought against communism. In 1951 Henry Ford took part in the Crusade for Freedom. According to Scott M. Cutlip (1994) Henry Ford II identified himself with that crusade "making an imaginative, constructive and dramatic effort to fight Communism. Uses of Ford–Lincoln–Mercury dealerships throughout the US as focal points for Crusade collections magnified this identity" (p. 698). In 1953, near the fiftieth anniversary of Ford, the film *The American Road* was produced to show that Henry Ford was an American success story. Furthermore, a fiftieth anniversary book was published, with a foreword from Henry Ford II written by the PR agency of Earl Newsom, saying, among other things, that "the growth and achievements of Ford Motor Company have been made possible by the kind of world we live in, by American democracy, and the economic opportunity to seek change and progress freely" (Cutlip, 1994, p. 698).

The German DEMAG (Deutsche Maschinenbau AG), which built the steel works in Rourkela, India, waged a three-year campaign in which the politics of industrialization of the Indian government were praised and the efficiency of German industry was emphasized. During this time, the Soviet Union built another steel works. The Soviets then waged a campaign against Germany and its industry, alleging that Germans were capitalists and exploiters trying to colonize India, and that German products were of poor quality. This fight for Indian public opinion was called "West German–Russian steel battle" (Darrow *et al.*, 1967, p. 523). DEMAG countered with its own campaign: pamphlets were distributed to journalists, to members of the congress, to teachers, and professors at universities; 20,000 diagrams explaining the production of steel and its further processing were donated to schools and universities; Radio Ceylon aired programs sponsored by DEMAG; advertisements were published in Indian newspapers; journalists of the most important Indian dailies were visited by the press secretary of DEMAG.

In recent years, Russia started its own PR activities in cooperation with capitalist companies. On April 20, 1992, an advertisement was published in *Time* for a conference to convene on April 25 and 26 in the Hotel Intercontinental in Geneva:

MEET THE NEW GOVERNMENT OF RUSSIA

The New Business Environment – Industries for sale – Foreign trade – Countertrade – Privatisation

Sponsors of the conference were *Time* and Volvo. Swissair was the official carrier, and the organizer of the conference was listed as the "Academy of National Economy in Russia, Management Network, and the Multimarketing group in cooperation with *Time* magazine". Speakers were, among others: Petr O. Aven, Minister of Foreign Economic Relations; Yegor E. Gaydar, First Prime Minister; Sergey M. Shakry, Vice Prime Minister of the government of Russia; the mayor of St Petersburg, and the director of the Trade Department of the Economic Commisssion Europe.

Even rates of exchange can become the target of PR campaigns waged by MNCs. This was the case with Eastman Kodak (Dilenschneider & Forrestal, 1989). The company knew that its competitive position in the world marketplace was hurt by the then strength of the US dollar. Kodak's communication division suggested they run a PR program targeted at this issue. Fact-finding meetings with President Reagan, high-level administration officials, and key national economic and trade groups were arranged. According to Dilenschneider and Forrestal the company funded a $150,000 study by the American Enterprise Institute, a conservative think tank (eighteen members of the Institute joined the Reagan Administration in 1981), to research the relationships between the strength of the dollar and the federal budget deficits. The Institute found a relationship between high interest rates required to finance the huge deficits and the dollar's strength. Dilenschneider and Forrestal wrote:

> Kodak believed a public affairs program could play a major role in persuading the government to pass legislation to eliminate federal budget deficit and intervene in currency exchange markets to stabilize the overvalued dollar. Kodak developed a 12-month communications program to reach members of Congress, the administration, and others in a position to influence economic policy. The message was that the overvalued dollar and escalating budget deficits were so damaging to manufacturers that a decisive action was needed.
>
> (p. 679)

The program, which received a Silver Anvil Award in the 1986 competition of the Public Relations Society of America, included a mailing to Kodak's shareholders, a "Write to Congress" campaign, consultations with leading politicians including Treasury Secretary Baker, and visits by Kodak executives to members of Congress and Cabinet members. According to Dilenschneider and Forrester the campaign played a direct role in changing the government's position and furthermore set the stage for two historic events: the September 1985 Group of Five communiqué pledging dollar stabilization, and the Gramm–Rudman–Hollings Act, aimed at eliminating federal budget deficits by 1991.

The main aim of international PR: establishment of trust

The main objective of international PR is to establish (or maintain an already existing) positive image of one's own nation, that is, to appear trustworthy to other actors in the world system. Trust is no abstract concept. In the field of international policy, trust is an important factor in mobilizing resources, for examples, in receiving political and/or material support from other nations. In other words, if other actors in the world system place their trust in one's nation, in her future because of her reliability, trust becomes the equivalent of money. Put simply: trust is money and money is trust. The positive image of a country's currency reflects confidence in that country's future. International business and currency exchange rates are not determined simply by pure economic facts (like currency reserves and gold reserves, deficit or surplus in balance of trade or balance of payment). The image of a nation-state, the rating of its business as solvent, the credibility of its politicians (i.e. can they be relied on to tame inflation by tight fiscal and monetary policies?), and so on are of decisive importance. Indeed, a country's reputation for solvency is more important to the stability of her currency than some short-term economic fluctuations.

In 1926 the French economist Albert Aftalion published his theory (Théorie psychologique du change) based on the hypothesis that the exchange rate of a country's currency is determined mainly by trust in the future of that country. A deficit of the balance of payments will not cause a devaluation of the currency as long as the belief in the future of this currency will attract foreign capital and balance the deficit. There is one main reason for the use of a certain currency as key currency: trust in the respective currency. Monetary policy is image policy. Money is an illusion, nothing more than the trust people have in their respective currency.

PR-counselor Ivy Ledbetter Lee certainly was aware of the importance of trust when he argued: "Those who handle a loan must create an atmosphere ..." (Hiebert, 1966, p. 266). Lee knew that simple statistics were not enough to market a loan. Lee handled loans for Poland, Romania, France, and other countries, but considered Hungary a difficult case because too many people in America "had a mental picture of the [Hungarian] people as a wild, Bohemian lot, instead of the agricultural, sane, and highly cultivated people that they really are" (Hiebert, 1966, p. 267). His advice to Hungary was to create the image that their country was stable and civilized. Argentina had problems attracting investors because of its image of social instability. Lee advised to them to send a polo team to the US to compete with American teams, arguing, "The vital idea is that polo is not played except where there is a very high degree of civilization and a stable society ... The galloping gentleman would tell the story more convincingly than any amount of statistics or mere statements as to the true conditions" (Hiebert 1966, p. 267).

The following are some examples of various countries' attempts to gain trust[5] in the international community:

1   On July, 1, 1994 Banco do Brasil advertised in the leading German daily *Frankfurter Allgemeine Zeitung* that Brazil now had a new and stable currency: the *real*. This monetary reform was called the most decisive turning point in the history of Brazil's economy, an unparalleled enterprise. Brazil now offered investors more opportunities than ever before. It urged investors to have confidence in the new currency of a country, which in former times was plagued by inflation. The advertisement closed with the slogan: "BANCO DO BRAZIL. Good for you. Good for Brazil."

2   Estonia published in *Time* (July 4, 1994) a country profile/advertisement: "ESTONIA: Rebirth of a Nation." According to the advertisement after years of quiet opposition to Soviet rule, Estonia seized the opportunity of the failed coup of August 1991 in Moscow to

declare full independence: "Swift and decisive actions underwrote this move: a new constitution was drawn up, free elections held, monetary reform (including a new currency) was initiated, and a fast-track policy of economic renewal was implemented." The advertisement pointed out that the change was without friction and caused ripples of consternation, but Estonia in the meantime had developed into a stable democracy with a strong currency (kroon exchange rate linked to the German mark). Estonia characterized itself as throwing open the doors to trade and being confidently braced for the shock of competition. Knowing that years of Soviet central planning distorted Estonian economy, "the imperatives of a military/industrial ideology gave rise to monolithic, uneconomic and inflexible industries." Information about the economic climate and new opportunities in the Baltics was provided, especially concerning the progress of privatization: "New ownership structures are the single most important aspect of the marketization of economic life."

3   Peru, which had a worldwide bad image due to the outbreak of cholera in 1991 and the guerrilla movement Shining Path, in 1993 published a special advertising section in the *International Herald Tribune* (November 24). President Alberto Fujimori emphasized in an interview the "dramatic moves his government has made to improve the country's economic and business climate." One article dealt with the economic comeback of the country. Privatization was described as generating cash and competition. Peru was characterized not only as a country of ancient culture but also as a whole world of opportunities.

A long list of nations have published similar advertisements. Sometimes nations are interested in projecting a negative image, at least to a target group. Mexico became the first country to practically declare itself insolvent by an ad in the *International Herald Tribune* (June 8, 1989). Luis Tellez, general director of financial planning in the Mexican ministry of finance, signed the text, in which the chairman of the Citicorp bank, John Reed, is attacked. The banker is accused of having too restricted a view of things:

> For Mexico, the debt crisis is much more than a discussion of swaps or of the return of flight capital. It is a story of adjustment, of an extraordinary effort to transform an economy and of the hopes of millions of Mexicans for an opportunity to increase their standards of living. All parties involved should begin to look at the situation from both sides. We created the debt problem together; therefore it is up to both debtors and creditors to find a way out . . . We should all realize that there is much to gain by acting together. If banks insist on keeping their eyes closed to economic realities there will be no winners.

Worth mentioning is that Kissinger, one of the most effective influence brokers in Washington, published columns on Mexico and its debt problem. The issue was of specific concern for some of his clients, including American Express and Chase Manhattan Bank. Isaacson (1992) documented that Kissinger wrote a column for the *Los Angeles Times/Washington Post* syndicate after the election of Carlos Salinas as President of Mexico. Kissinger evoked the enemy image of the international communist threat, praised Salinas, and argued that "the US can play a major role in encouraging democracy and economic reform" (p. 746). He proposed an easing of the debt problem, recommending that some of the burdens of relief should be borne by creditor governments.

Conclusion

W. I. Thomas and D. S. Thomas' (1928) famous comment is still valid: "If men define situations as real they are real in their consequences" (p. 572). The image of a country in permanent crisis or as economically unreliable, generated perhaps by continuous negative reporting, can influence economic decision-making processes and discourage investment, which in turn can exacerbate future crises. For example, the then Prime Minister of Slovakia, Vladimir Meciar (1993), complained in an interview that due to negative reporting investments had declined. Meciar said that foreign investors didn't know much about Slovakia, but from the newspapers they learned that communist dictator Meciar was ruling and that the country was not known for its stability. If he had only this distorted information about his country, allowed Meciar, he would not invest there either. Similar complaints have been heard from Malaysia (in October 1983, e.g.) and the Philippines. Due to globalization one of the main problems for so called developing countries and/or emerging markets will be their image in the world of international investors. The better the image the easier will be the access to the international capital market. If this assumption is correct, there will be a more intensive image-fight between nations with imge polishing becoming a functional equivalent to investor relations.

Notes

1   For instance, in a study of English children (Himmelweit *et al.*, 1958) those who watched TV described the French as gay and witty, reflecting the fact that nearly all the French people they saw on television were cabaret artistes. Younger viewers saw the Germans as arrogant and vicious – again a reflection of television drama, where Germans were presented mainly in the role of Nazis. Again, if no other sources of information are available, the greatest influence on the image of foreign nations is the mass media.

2   Coverage of Mexico, although it had no contract with any agency, was also monitored. *The New York Times* was chosen because it is the newspaper most

widely read by the American elite, is most frequently quoted by political decision makers, is known from previous research to have a strong agenda-setting
effect on public opinion, and provides more foreign coverage than comparable
American daily newspapers.

3   The AIDS disinformation campaign began in 1985 whereby the US was blamed
worldwide for the outbreak of the disease. This report, although dismissed as
absurd by all experts, including Soviet medical scientists, met with much positive response, especially in African countries. For example *Afrique Novelle*, a
weekly newspaper very close to the Catholic church, reported: "According to
an authorized scientific source, the AIDS virus was developed in the research
center at Fort Detrick, Maryland, where it was grown at the same time as other
viruses to be used in biological weapons. It was then tested on drug addicts
and homosexuals" (US Department of State, 1987, p. 71). In August 1986 a
study conducted by biophysicist Professor Jakob Segal, his wife Dr Lilli Segal,
and Dr Ronald Dehmlow of Humboldt University in East Berlin became public.
The study claimed that at Fort Detrick in 1977, the US had synthetically manu-
factured the AIDS virus by combining two naturally occurring viruses, VISNA
and HTLV-I. Experts agree that this hypothesis is untenable, but it circulated
nonetheless in the media of Africa, South Asia, and the Soviet Union. Indeed,
it was discussed extensively at the eighth conference of the Nonaligned
Movement at Harare in September of that year. Both *Pravda* and *Izvestiya* have
repeatedly printed articles alleging that AIDS was created in laboratories at Fort
Detrick as part of alleged attempts by the US to create new biological weapons
(Walker, 1988). The Soviet media later warned against American soldiers
spreading AIDS in other countries. The obvious intention of such reports was
to spread mistrust of the American military, but it also affected tourists, busi-
nesspeople, and so forth. Indeed, the newspaper *Sovyetskaya Rossiya* reported
on January 23, 1987 that in Western Europe AIDS was most prevalent in places
where US troops were based.

4   On August 25, 1986, a report appeared in the *Wall Street Journal* claiming
that Qadaffi was planning new attacks, that the US and Libya were again headed
for collision, and that the Pentagon was preparing plans for another bombard-
ment of Libya. The report was described as "authoritative," that is, as being
reliably sourced, by the spokesman for the White House, Larry Speakes. Other
newspapers followed with reports that Libya was sponsoring terrorist activities
and that there was the possibility of renewed confrontation with the US.
According to Hedrick Smith (1988), George Shultz, the Secretary of State,
said: "Frankly, I don't have any problems with a little psychological warfare
against Qaddafi" (p. 448), then recalled Churchill's justifying deceptions against
Hitler during World War II: "In time of war, truth is so precious, it must be
attended by a bodyguard of lies".

5   Sometimes countries want to become a negative image in certain target groups.
In 1991 Austria's Home Secretary, Franz Löschnack, published an advertisement
in the Romanian newspaper *Romania Libera*. Romanians wanting to emigrate
to Austria were warned against trying to enter Austria. Foreigners were not
allowed to work in Austria without official permission and for Romanians
no permission would be given. Romanians also had no prospects for asylum in
Austria: "There are no more shelters for people asking for asylum." The last
sentence of the advertisement was: "You don't have the slightest chance." The
compositor of *Romania Libera* protested in a subtle way: below the Austrian
ad was placed an ad for the Bucharest center for disinfection, which fought
against rat infestations and rounded up stray dogs.

References

Aftalion, A. (1929). Die jüngste Geschichte der Wechselkurse in Frankreich und die psychologische Wechselkurstheorie. *Zeitschrift für Nationalökonomie*, 1(2), 266–283.

Allport, G. W. (1958). *The nature of prejudice.* Garden City, NY: Doubleday Anchor.

Bernays, E. L. (1923). *Crystallizing public opinion.* New York: Boni and Liveright.

Bernays, E. L. (1965). *Biography of an idea: memoirs of public relations counsel Edward L. Bernays.* New York: Simon and Schuster.

Blyskal, J. and Blyskal, M. (1985). *PR: how the public relations industry writes the news.* New York: Morrow.

Bogart, L. (1976). *Premises for propaganda: the United States Information Agency's operating assumptions in the Cold War.* New York: The Free Press.

Boorstin, D. (1961). *The image: a guide to pseudo-events in America.* New York: Harper and Row.

Boulding, K. E. (1956). *The image.* Ann Arbor, MI: University of Michigan Press.

Boulding, K. E. (1967). The learning and reality-testing process in the international system. *Journal of International Affairs*, 21, 1–15.

Boulding, K. E. (1969). National images and international systems. In J. N. Rosenau (ed.), *International politics and foreign policy.* New York: The Free Press.

Clausewitz, C. P. G. von (1873). *On war.* (J. J. Graham, trans., vols. 1–3). London: N. Trübner (original work published 1832).

Considine, D. (1994). Media literacy and media education. *Telemedium: The Journal of Media Literacy*, 40.

Cutlip, S. M. (1994). *The unseen power: public relations. A history.* Hillsdale, NJ: Lawrence Erlbaum Associates.

Darrow, R. W., Forrestal, D. J. and Cookman, A. O. (1967). *The Dartnell public relations handbook* (revised edition). Chicago, IL: Dartnell.

Dilenschneider, R. L. and Forrestal, D. J. (1989). *The Dartnell public relations handbook* (3rd edn). Chicago, IL: Dartnell.

Galtung, J. and Ruge, M. H. (1965). The structure of foreign news. *Journal of Peace Research*, 1, 64–91.

Grunig, J. E. and Hunt, T. (1984). *Managing public relations.* New York: Holt, Rinehart and Winston.

Hertz, J. H. (1982). Political realism revisited. *International Studies Quarterly*, 25.

Hiebert, R. E. (1966). *Courtier to the crowd: the story of Ivy Lee and the development of public relations.* Ames, IA: Iowa State University Press.

Himmelweit, H. T., Oppenheim, A. N. and Vince, P. (1958). *Television and the child.* New York: Oxford University Press.

Isaacson, W. (1992). *Kissinger: a biography.* London: Faber and Faber.

Karl, P. M. (1982). Media diplomacy. In G. Benjamin (ed.), *The communications revolution in politics. Proceedings of the Academy of Political Science*, 34(4), 143–152.

Kepplinger, H. M. (1983). Fuktionswandel der Massenmedien. In M. Rühl and H. W. Stuiber (eds), *Kommunikationspolitik in Forschung und Anwendung.* Düsseldorf: Droste.

Kissinger, H. (1969). *American foreign policy: three essays.* New York: Norton.

Knorr, K. D. (1980). Die Fabrikation von Wissen. In N. Stehr and V. Meja (eds), *Wissenssoziologie. Kölner Zeitschrift für Soziologie und Sozialpsychologie, Sonderheft 22*. Opladen: Westdeutscher Verlag.

Kruglak, T. E. (1962). *The two faces of TASS*. Minneapolis, MN: University of Minnesota Press.

Kunczik, M. (1997). *Images of nations and international public relations*. Mahwah, NJ: Erlbaum.

Kunczik, M. and Weber, U. (1994). Public diplomacy and public relations advertisements of foreign countries in Germany. *The Journal of International Communication*, 1.

Lasswell, H. D. (1942). Communications research and politics. In D. Waples (ed.), *Print, radio, and film in a democracy*. Chicago, IL: University of Chicago Press.

Lippmann, W. (1922). *Public opinion*. New York: Harcourt Brace.

Manheim, J. B. (1991). *All of the people all the time: strategic communication and American politics*. Armonk, NY: M. E. Sharpe.

Manheim, J. B. (1994). *Strategic public diplomacy and American foreign policy: the evolution of influence*. Oxford: Oxford University Press.

Manheim, J. B. and Albritton, R. B. (1984). Changing national images: international public relations and media agenda setting. *American Political Science Review*, 78, 641–657.

Olasky, M. N. (1985). A reappraisal of 19th-century public relations. *Public Relations Review*, 11 (Spring), 3–12.

Onkvisit, S. and Shaw, J. J. (1989). *International marketing. Analysis and strategy*. Columbus, OH: Merrill.

Piaget, J. and Weil, A. M. (1951). The development in children of the idea of the homeland and of relations with other countries. *International Social Science Bulletin*, 3, 570; quoted in: Allport, G. W. (1958). *The nature of prejudice*. Garden City, NY: Doubleday Anchor, p. 44.

Sayers, D. L. (1926). *Clouds of witness*. London: Fisher Unwin.

Simmel, G. (1920). *Soziologie* [Sociology] (2nd edn). Munich: Duncker and Humblot.

Smith, H. (1988). *The power game: how Washington works*. New York: Random House.

Sreberny-Mohammadi, A. (1985). *Foreign news in the media. International reporting in 29 countries*. Paris: UNESCO.

Star, S. A. and Hughes, H. M. (1950). Report on an educational campaign: the Cincinnati plan for the United Nations. *American Journal of Sociology*, 55, 389–400.

Thomas, W. I. and Thomas, D. S. (1928). *The child in America*. New York: Knopf.

Tocqueville, A. de (1946). *Democracy in America*, vol. II. London: Oxford University Press.

Tönnies, F. (1922). *Kritik der öffentlichen Meinung*. Berlin: Springer.

Ume-Nwagbo, E. N. (1982). Foreign news flow in Africa. *Gazette*, 29, 41–56.

US Department of State (1987). *Soviet influence activities: a report on active measures and propaganda*. Washington, DC: US Government Printing Office (October).

Walker, F. E. (1988). Recent changes in the Soviet propaganda machine. *Journal of Defense and Diplomacy* (May).

Watzlawick, P. (1976). *How real is real? Confusion, disinformation, communication*. New York: Random House.

8

MEDIA, CONFLICT, AND PEACE

Gadi Wolfsfeld

The role of the news media in conflict has long been a central concern in the field of political communication. The major areas of concentration include studies that deal with the role of the media in war, in terrorism, and in protests.[1] The topic of media and peace on the other hand has barely been touched.[2] It is helpful to begin by thinking about some of the reasons for this disparity.

The most reasonable explanation is that researchers resemble journalists in their search for drama. It is not only more exciting to study terrorism and war, but a much wider audience will read the results. Even the most noble of scholars must think about "ratings."

Another possible reason, which also parallels something found in journalism, is that studying the role of the news media in a peace process may be more difficult. Most studies of media and conflict center on case studies of a particular event or set of events, which often play out over a relatively short time span. Attempts at conflict resolution, on other hand, are usually characterized by a long complex process much of which takes place behind closed doors.

Yet another explanation may be related to the fact that so much of political communication research is carried out in the US. While the US has been involved in a significant number of conflicts in recent years, it has not been involved in drawn out peace process since the end of the Vietnam War. Perhaps researchers might have studied what happened in Bosnia and Kosovo, but these cases are better considered third party interventions than peace processes.

Those who hope to understand the role the media play in conflicts must also consider the role they can play in attempts to reduce conflict. A peace process can be considered, after all, simply as another stage in a conflict. Although the change in context leads to a somewhat different set of rules, there are important overlaps between the two topics. It is also clear that by looking at both dimensions it allows researchers to develop a more dynamic and comprehensive theory.

The goal of this chapter is to present a theoretical framework that could be a useful starting point for such an effort. The political contest model was developed in a previous work (Wolfsfeld, 1997a) but looked exclusively at the role of the media in conflict. Here an attempt will be made to extend that model by also discussing the role the media can play in the course of a peace process.

The struggle over the news media

The role of the news media in political conflicts is best understood by looking at the contest over the media among antagonists. This contest, in turn, should be seen as part of a larger and more significant battle for political power. Each of the antagonists is attempting to promote a particular frame concerning the reasons for the confrontation and what needs to be done in order to resolve it. Each hopes to mobilize the news media as a means of persuading a variety of audiences to support their cause. The media can play a role in both external conflicts (say between Israel and the Palestinians) and in internal conflict (e.g. the doves and hawks within Israel).

These are ongoing contests that take place during both the most heated stages of a conflict, and when serious attempts are being made to bring peace. Leaders can attempt to promote either aggressive policies or policies designed to lower tensions between the sides. Thus, when the discussion below talks about the role of the media in "conflict," it also refers to attempts at reconciliation. There will nevertheless be some occasions when it will be helpful to distinguish between conflicts and peace processes.

The role of the news media in political conflicts and in the attempts to resolve them can be understood by looking at three major sets of variables:

1   the nature of the antagonists involved;
2   the nature of the political environment;
3   the nature of the media environment.

While this should not be considered an exhaustive list, it should provide a broad platform for building theory in this area.

The nature of the antagonists refers to the characteristics of the actors directly involved in the conflict. One would want to consider such factors as the extent of resources at the disposal of each antagonist, the cultural resonance of each antagonist's position within the more general society, collective norms concerning the use of violence, and the antagonists' level of political, social, and media status. It would also be important to distinguish between social movements, political parties, terrorist organizations, NGOs, and states.

The political environment refers to the aggregate of private and public beliefs, discourse, and behaviors concerning political matters within a particular setting and time. It is a macro concept referring to the political "situation." What issues are people talking about? What are various leaders doing and how are people reacting to these activities? How are the news media covering political issues at that particular time and place? What is the distribution of opinion on a particular issue? What are the most common interpretive frames being employed to explain and evaluate what is happening in the political realm?

The media environment refers to the laws, norms, and practices that characterize how the news media operate in a particular setting. How free are the news media to report about government activities? How much time and resources are placed in the area of investigative reporting? What are the major professional norms that dictate how editors and reporters build news stories? Who owns the news media and how does that affect the news industry? The answers to each of these questions will have an important influence on the role the media play in conflicts and in peace processes.

It is not possible within the limited framework of this essay to deal with the innumerable variables that are contained within each of these broad divisions. Instead, the analysis will center on a single example from each category that will illustrate the utility of this approach. The discussion will focus on the impact of three constructs: the relative power of the antagonists, the level of political consensus in support of government policies, and the level of sensationalism that characterizes the media environment.

A number of rules will be developed that attempt to demonstrate the impact these factors have on the role of the news media. Support for these propositions comes from research carried out by both the author and others. Although these propositions can be applied to a broad range of conflicts and peace process, most of my own work has dealt with the Arab–Israeli conflict, and thus many of the examples come from that setting. I have also done research in the US on the role of the media in the Gulf War and more recently in Northern Ireland. The quotes that will be used as illustrations come from interviews that were carried out with leaders, spokespeople, and journalists involved in each of these conflicts.[3]

The relative power of the antagonists

One of the most important determinants of the way journalists interact with antagonists has to do with the actor's level of political power. The reason for this is that the greater the antagonist's power the more dependent the news media are on the actor for information. Weaker antagonists, on the other hand, are forced to adapt themselves to media demands in order to gain access. In addition, such actors have a much greater need for publicity, for without it they are unlikely to have any influence on the political process. This pattern of dependency leads to the first rule concerning the role of the media in political conflicts: *the weaker the antagonists, the more likely the news media will have an influence on their behavior and their chances of political success.*

The best demonstration of the relationship between power and access is to look at who chases whom. At the top of the power ladder one finds a large number of reporters competing for the privilege of gaining access to these elites. As one moves down it is the political actors who find themselves competing for access to the media.

The only way for weaker antagonists to compete for media attention is to provide some form of drama or novelty. While the powerful can gain access to the media through the front door, the powerless are required to enter through the back door (Wolfsfeld, 1997a). The right to enter through the back door is based on a group's level of deviancy; the greater the level of deviancy, the greater the exposure. The media's rules of access for weaker antagonists encourage disorder and violence. Leaders of social movements and terrorist organizations realize that they must pay the dues of disorder to achieve public standing. The weaker the group the higher the dues they are expected to pay. While those who have received a certain amount of political standing can attempt to use acts that are merely novel, more peripheral groups are forced to choose between violence and political oblivion.

Gitlin's (1980) classic work on the anti-Vietnam SDS movement provides important illustrations of this point. The news media raised the internal and external status of the more radical leaders who were providing the necessary drama. This had a profound impact on the movement's ideological and strategic direction. Leaders also found themselves under pressure to continually escalate their tactics in order to meet the rising threshold for drama. What had been considered extreme in the early days of protest against the war was soon considered routine.

Although Gitlin was concerned with anti-war movements, the same principle can also be applied to groups attempting to derail a peace process. There were a large number of Israeli movements, for example, who were opposed to the Oslo peace process when the Rabin government in 1993 proposed it. Many of the more moderate movements found it difficult to compete with the more radical groups for media attention.

One such group was the "Professors' Circle" who were opposed to using any extremist tactics (Wolfsfeld, 1997a). Interviews with the leaders of that group are full of frustration and anger about their inability to make a dent. Consider for example the comments of one of the leaders in an interview that was carried out the day after the Hebron massacre in which a Jewish settler murdered thirty-nine Palestinians.

> Access to the media is very difficult. This morning is a classic example. No matter how much you phone. I'm sitting here hoping

that despite it all somebody will get back to me. You explain to people: "look what happened Friday morning [the massacre], maybe this is the time to show that there is another way to express dissent." But if every time you bring it in another way they don't relate to you, then you understand why people take more drastic action. ... The media wants to see the action [action said in English].

(February 28, 1994)

Despite these rules of access, most political movements avoid using violence for both moral and pragmatic reasons. Although the publicity associated with violence can increase antagonists' standing, they must pay a heavy cost in terms of public legitimacy. This is the dilemma that confronts challengers around the world.

Terrorism is also rooted in weakness. An ideological decision to turn to terrorism is based on a belief that there are no other means to achieve one's political goals. One of the reasons why terrorism can be so effective is because it is considered major news (Nacos, 1994; Paletz & Shmid, 1992; Weimann & Winn, 1994). This allows such groups to take a least temporary control over the national agenda. It is by far the quickest and most effective way to achieve political standing. Anonymous movements are instantly transformed into major players. The most stunning example of this is the speech in which the name of Al Qaeda became recognized around the world after September 11, 2001.

Although the topic of media and terrorism has generated a large number of studies, very few provide a theoretical contribution to the field. One explanation for this problem is that the vast majority of these studies look at the issue of media and terrorism as an isolated topic. It makes more sense to examine this issue within a broader context in which terrorism is seen as an extreme point on a long continuum of political actions. Many of the rules that explain the role of the news media in political conflicts can also be applied to the topic of terrorism.

All of this brings us to a second rule relating to the relative power of the antagonists: *the news media have the greatest impact on political conflicts and peace processes when they provide extensive publicity for weaker antagonists.* The most profound impact the news media can have on a conflict is to change the balance of power among the antagonists. When weaker antagonists get extensive publicity it can both increase their level of political standing and enable them to bring third parties into the process.

Media standing can often be converted to political standing and this can change the course of the political process. A good example of this can be found by looking at the case of the Islamic Fundamentalist movement, Hamas. They were extremely successful at using terrorism as an instrument for establishing political standing during the long negotiations between Israel and the PLO leadership concerning the Oslo peace accords. The group was not part of that process and if not for the violence would have been ignored. One Hamas leader talked about the role the Israeli press played in their struggle.

> The enemy can sometimes serve us indirectly. We don't have any large news institutions that will publicize and cover the things that we're interested in ... So in the end, the Hamas actions force the media to report and relate to the activities and positions of the movement. I want to use the military actions to prove my abilities on both the local and regional level. The Israeli press helps with this. Therefore, through my military action I am trying to pass a message that Hamas is a central force among the Palestinians and it is impossible to ignore it.
>
> (June 8, 1995)

The second way is for underdogs to use publicity as a means of getting other actors involved in the conflict. Challengers are constantly attempting to bring in third parties – especially the US and Europe – in order to level the playing field. This is the reason why so many groups make a concerted effort to attract the attention of the foreign press. Although the news media generally give preference to the more powerful actors, they also have an important space reserved for victims. Becoming a victim is one of the only ways in which weaker antagonists can be considered both newsworthy *and* legitimate. This is one of the reasons why a strategy of civil disobedience often makes more sense from a media perspective than one that relies on political violence.

The role of the news media in the conflict over civil rights in Birmingham, Alabama in the early 1960s offers a good example (Gamson, 1990; Garrow, 1978; Paletz and Entman, 1981). The stories and pictures of the Birmingham police using dogs, clubs, and water hoses on the protesters resonated around the world. These stories remained on the front pages of the *New York Times* and the *Washington Post* for almost two weeks in May of 1963 (Garrow, 1978). President Kennedy reportedly said that the photo of dogs attacking the demonstrators had made him "sick" (Garrow, 1978; p. 141). The civil rights leaders were well aware how important this publicity was to their cause.

More recent examples of this phenomenon would include the role of the news media in the first *Intifada* (Cohen & Wolfsfeld, 1993, Wolfsfeld, 1997a), in the second *Intifada* (Wolfsfeld, 2001a), in the decision of the Americans to intervene in Northern Iraq after the Gulf War, and in Bosnia, Somalia, and Kosovo. While there were clearly other important forces at work in each of these cases, the massive amounts of publicity granted to the weaker side had to be taken into account by both the antagonists themselves and decision makers around the world.

Much of popular and scholarly discussion of this issue falls under the rubric of the "CNN" effect. The conventional wisdom is that massive coverage of victims forces Western leaders to intervene in conflicts they would otherwise avoid. However, a more careful analysis demonstrates that political leaders maintain a considerable amount of discretion concerning where and when to intervene (Livingston, 1997; Strobel, 1997). This helps explain why it is critical for researchers to better explain the circumstances in which the news media *do* become a major factor.

The news media are less likely to play an independent role when they either ignore the weaker side or become servants for the more powerful antagonist. The role of the news media in Gulf War (Bennett & Paletz, 1994; Wolfsfeld, 1997a) provides a good illustration of this point. The American and allied news media were extremely supportive of the war effort and played a role in maintaining international support for the campaign against Saddam Hussein. It was, however, a dependent role in which the news media could be considered merely one more tool in the allies' arsenal. The battle was decided on the ground. The fact that news media mostly refused to treat the Iraqis as victims meant that the war could take its natural course: the powerful defeating the weak.

These same principles can be applied then to the media's role in both intensive conflict and attempts to bring about peace. In both cases the news media can limit the ability of the more powerful antagonists to implement their policies by giving extensive publicity to challengers. In times of conflict the press can make it more difficult for the powerful to defeat weaker adversaries. When leaders are trying to promote peace the news media can play a similar role by giving a good deal of attention to opponents, making it more difficult to mobilize the necessary support for moving forward. These are the cases in which political leaders will find themselves most frustrated about their inability to promote their messages to the media.

Given these principles, the interesting issue for researchers is to better understand those circumstances in which the news media breaks free of the more powerful antagonists and become independent actors. The next set of variables provides at least a partial answer to that question.

The nature of the political environment

The impact of the political environment on the role of the news media was a central topic in the initial presentation of the political contest model (Wolfsfeld, 1997a). It was argued that the authorities' ability to take control over the political environment was a key factor in explaining their ability to promote their messages to the news media. In other words, political control leads to media control.

A major reason for this relationship is that the construction of news is a mostly reactive process. Editors and reporters respond to stimuli that are provided by a multitude of sources and events and then attempt to provide their audience with a report about the state of their world. It is a process of social construction not only because of how these inputs are turned into news, but also because of what the sources are saying and doing. Major changes in the tone and content of news coverage reflect shifts in the political process.

One particularly important aspect of the political environment concerns the level of political consensus concerning a particular government's policies. The news media are extremely sensitive to the amount of political consensus surrounding such policies and this has direct influence on coverage. When there is a high level of consensus the news media not only reflect that climate of opinion, they also reinforce it. As pointed about by Hallin (1986) when the mainstream media enter this mode of reporting they feel no obligation to present opposing views because such attitudes are considered marginal and inconsequential.

The news media play a different role when covering controversial political issues. In democratic countries, the media often serve as agents for intensifying internal disputes. The conflict *over* the conflict becomes a major news story and this makes it more difficult for the government to implement its policies. These principles lead to a third rule: *the lower the level of political consensus concerning either conflicts or efforts to bring peace, the more likely the news media will serve as obstacles to the implementation of government policies.*

One of the best-known examples of this concerns the role of the American news media in the Vietnam War. Hallin (1986) convincingly documents how supportive the US media were in the early days of that conflict when there was a high degree of consensus about the need to "stop the spread of communism." As the war dragged on however, there were a growing number of elite voices expressing dissent and news coverage became much more critical of the war effort. It is important to note that the argument states that changes in the level of consensus normally *precede* changes in the content and tone of coverage.

Just as the news media tend to exaggerate the level of agreement concerning popular policies, they also overstate and intensify the level of disagreement concerning less popular policies. This is because the media have a vested interest in such conflicts. Editors and journalists are constantly on the lookout for a good fight. While points of agreement are considered boring, discord is always newsworthy.

The news media, I would argue, not only reflected the change in the American mood concerning the Vietnam War, they amplified and accelerated it. The dramatic change in the story line not only signified an important change in the political environment it also contributed to it. As protests and other forms of dissent became increasingly newsworthy, this provided an important incentive for others to get involved in the anti-war

146

movement. The Johnson administration grew increasingly defensive about the war, despite the fact that opinion polls showed a majority in support of its policies.

A similar conclusion emerges from a study (Wolfsfeld, 1997b) that compares the role of the news media in Israel's peace process with Jordan, with their role in the Oslo peace process with the Palestinians. There was a tremendous degree of consensus concerning the peace agreement with Jordan. The peace process was a relatively short, painless affair, and there were no major political parties who were opposed to the agreement. The Knesset vote ratifying the agreement was overwhelming: ninety-one in favor and only three opposed.

This provided the Rabin government with an unprecedented opportunity to promote the peace process with the Israeli news media as an enthusiastic partner. The coverage of these events was pure celebration. The height of this enthusiasm occurred during the signing ceremony in the Arava desert that took place in October, 1994. Journalists talked of shedding tears and several newspapers prepared special pullout sections filled with pictures of the ceremony. It was a telling sign that the major television news anchor was willing to serve as the Master of Ceremonies at that ceremony.

A content analysis of the newspaper articles that appeared during the major period of coverage confirms the extremely supportive role played by the news media.[4] Seventy-four percent of all articles were positive, twenty one percent were mixed or neutral, an only five percent could be considered negative news about the agreement. The news media had no need to even feign impartiality.

A more independent, critical press could have raised endless questions about the substance of the agreement. Israel, after all, was giving up enormous amounts of water that many believed would someday become more precious than oil. The leaders were also relinquishing sovereignty over land where Israelis had produced millions of dollars of valuable crops. Finally, the agreement recognized King Hussein's "historic role" regarding Jerusalem's holy places. Several smaller opposition parties did their best to make this a major point of contention. The press however, was operating in full celebration mode, and criticism was considered out of place.[5]

The Israeli news media played a very different role in the Oslo peace process with the Palestinians (Wolfsfeld, 1997b, 1997c). The amount of negative news about the peace process constantly outnumbered the amount of positive news items. News coverage of terrorism was especially sensationalist and interviews reveal that Prime Minister Rabin grew increasingly frustrated about what he saw as the disproportionate amount of attention given to these incidents. As discussed earlier, the news media also intensified the internal conflict over the accords by frequently giving preference to radical voices over moderate ones.

The claim being made here is that the news media often play the role of catalysts in political conflicts and in attempts at making peace. The story line is rooted in journalists' beliefs about the nature of the political environment. This assessment provides a starting point for the construction of a story line. Story lines however must be both clear and dramatic and devoid of subtleties or complexities. In addition, because conflict is such a central element of news, the impact of the press will be especially important when support is declining. The news media are fair weather friends. The minute they spot clouds on the horizon, they begin an intensive search for storms.

The impact of the level of consensus on the role of the news media can also be illustrated by looking at the peace process in Northern Ireland (Wolfsfeld, 2001b). The signing of the Good Friday agreement in April of 1998 marked an important turning point in the conflict between Protestants and Catholics. It was the most inclusive agreement ever and 71 percent of the population voted in favor of the accords. Equally important was the fact that the vast majority of political parties also supported the agreement.

This had a profound impact on the role the news media played. Interviews with political leaders and journalists all indicate that the news media played a very positive role in this process. A good example of this is the fact that the editors of the leading Unionist and Nationalist newspapers decided to write a number of joint editorials in favor of the process that were published in both papers. Such cooperation would have been impossible if there hadn't been such a high level of consensus surrounding the agreement.

A second example provides an even better illustration of the influence that political consensus can have on the construction of news stories. A few months after the signing of the Good Friday accords a group known as the "Real IRA" carried out a horrendous terrorist attack in the city of Omagh, killing twenty-nine people. Sinn Fein, who many see as the political wing of the IRA issued a clear condemnation of the attack and this was an important indicator of the consensus that had been forged in support of the peace process. The front-page of the major Unionist newspaper the *Belfast Telegraph* contained the following message:

> Let our entire community unite against this evil. Let us commit ourselves to peace and peace alone. Let us back the forces of law and order. Let us resolve to build a new future together, unionist and nationalist alike. Let this be our sincere and lasting tribute to the victims of Omagh.
>
> (August 17, 1998, p. 1)

The interviews carried out in Northern Ireland confirmed that this was the message that was being conveyed by both leaders and the other news media. The major lesson to be learned from Omagh was the proper response to violence is to move the peace process forward.

When similar attacks occurred in Israel, it was always considered a major setback for the government's attempts to mobilize support for the peace process. The news media turned antagonistic towards the government and the streets filled with anti-agreement protesters. This comparison between the two peace processes provides a graphic demonstration of how and why the level of political consensus has such an important impact on the media's role in such situations. The greater the level of public support for peace the more likely the media will interpret events in ways that move the process forward.

The impact of sensationalism

The level of sensationalism that characterizes a particular media environment can also have an important influence on the role the press will play in conflicts and peace processes. While all news media attempt to raise audience interest by emphasizing drama, some are more extreme than others. This is an important variable because the news media are important agents in setting the tone for public debate about issues concerning conflict.

The fourth and final rule states: *the more sensationalist the media environment the more likely the news media will serve to escalate conflicts and to obstruct attempts at peace making*. When sensationalism is considered a central news value it influences every stage of the news production process. Journalists search for the most dramatic and emotional stories while photographers and cameramen attempt to capture the most shocking images. The more dramatic the story the more likely editors will place it near the top of the news. Those responsible for layout and graphics also contribute to this process by using formats and headlines that magnify the intensity and importance of stories.

The more sensationalist the news media the more they have a vested interested in conflict. The best-known historical example of this phenomenon is the flagrant attempts by publisher William Randolf Hearst to stir American anger against Spain at the end of the nineteenth century. The oft-repeated story claims that a bored photographer asked to come home from Cuba because "there will be no war." Hearst alleged reply was: "You furnish the pictures and I'll furnish the war." While some have questioned the veracity of the story, there is no dispute about the fact that Hearst and others were able to significantly increase circulation by sensationalizing the Spanish–American conflict.

One reason for researchers to focus on sensationalism is to show how the role of the news media can change over time and circumstance. The change in the Israeli news media in recent years provides a useful illustration. For many years the Israeli media adopted a relatively restrained and subdued tone of coverage, even when they covered acts of terrorism. The media environment became increasingly competitive in the 1980s and 1990s and sensationalism gradually became the rule rather than the exception. Every sign of tension was considered a crisis, and acts of terrorism were often treated as if they were major threats to the existence of the state.

This change in the tone of reporting made it much more difficult for the Rabin government to proceed with the Oslo peace process. Rabin himself talked about the change in reporting, complaining that even minor incidents received bigger headlines than the outbreak of the six-day war (Rabin, 1996). One of Rabin's chief advisors, who had once worked as a journalist, talked about the extent of the change:

> There's no comparison between the coverage today and what it was like in the past. Twenty-four soldiers once died in an ammunition truck after a mission in Egypt. . . . There was an ordinary headline in *Yediot Ahronot*. Nothing like what you have today. There were two pictures, a list of the dead that was it. Two days after that there was nothing. Today with all of the picture, the headlines, and the color, it a completely different world . . . I once wrote about a bomb that went off at the central bus station in Tel Aviv. It was a one-page story. One and a half pages in *Yediot Ahronot* and that was the end of the story. People were killed. Today a bomb in the central bus station in Tel Aviv would be like the end of the world.
>
> (March 19, 1995)

The cynical saying associated with this form of journalism is: "if it bleeds it leads." This practice has both long and short-term implications for political conflicts and peacemaking. The world constructed by sensationalist journalism is a frightening place filled with threats and violence, one in which leaders and citizens must be constantly concerned with security. Enemies appear to be powerful and unwilling to compromise. Given this atmosphere, those promoting peace and reconciliation appear, at best, naïve.

A peace process is also a rather tedious affair. It involves long, drawn out negotiations over a long period of time. There may be a few celebrations along the way but leaders have little to provide journalists during the long periods in between. Those opposed to peace, on the other hand, are often in a better position to provide drama. Political violence is always newsworthy, but when drama becomes the central news value it has a major impact on both the quantity and quality of news stories.

The more serious news media give additional weight to political *substance*. Their approach will be more analytical and editors will attempt to place the day's events within a broader perspective. There is only one major Israeli newspaper, *Ha'aretz* that can be considered a broadsheet. This difference in style is reflected in how that newspaper covers the Arab–Israeli conflict. The coverage of violence is more restrained and the coverage of the peace process provides more in-depth information about policies, institutions, and Palestinian perspectives. The paper however, pays a serious price for this approach. While the newspaper is read by Israeli elites, it has little appeal among the mass public.

The influence of sensationalism on political conflicts can be better understood by examining the role the media can play during negotiations. Negotiations about peace are usually difficult and there are always setbacks along the way. When these setbacks occur, leaders will often turn to the press in order to attribute blame. The more heated the media environment the more likely the press is to turn each setback into a major crisis. Journalists will intentionally search for extreme statements from all sides and this will provide the basis for large glaring headlines. The conflict between the two sides will escalate and negotiators will find themselves spending valuable time attempting to defuse the situation.

Another way of demonstrating the impact of the media environment is through comparative research. The news media in Northern Ireland are considerably less sensationalist than those in Israel. While the London tabloids do have a high circulation in Northern Ireland, these are not the major sources of information about the peace process. The major sources are the local BBC affiliates and the three major newspapers.

Interviews with journalists and political leaders reveal a very different media environment in Northern Ireland than one finds in Israel. The local newspapers, radio, and television are all modeled on the more serious news media that appear in England. Journalists have developed an extensive set of norms and guidelines to insure that they do nothing that could inflame the conflict between Protestants and Catholics. Reporters attempt, for example, to avoid situations in which their presence might inflame the conflict. One of the reporters for local radio talked about this policy.

> It's commercially problematic, but I think regardless of the commercial function that you're trying to fill, you've got to be responsible and that's what I think is the bottom line for any reporting in Northern Ireland. Sensationalism can cost lives although that's perhaps being over-dramatic. You just don't want to play into that.
>
> (April 14, 1999)

In general then, a sensationalist news media serves to intensify political conflicts and to make peace more difficult. The only exceptions to this rule have to do with the coverage of peace ceremonies where such media become exceptionally euphoric in tone (Wolfsfeld, 1996b). This too, however, may prove to be a disservice to the peace camps for it only makes the subsequent crises appear that much more dramatic and surprising.

Leaders attempting to mobilize citizens for war, however, will find the sensationalist press to be eager allies.

Conclusion

The goal of this paper was to suggest a theoretical approach that could provide researchers with some guidelines for understanding the changing role of the news media in conflicts and in peace processes. The central argument focused on three sets of variables: the nature of the antagonists involved, the nature of the political environment, and the nature of the media environment. Each of these factors has a major impact on the inter-actions between political actors and journalists, on the construction of news, and the impact of the media on the political process.

Four rules were put forth to demonstrate how such an approach could be used. The first rule was: *the weaker the antagonist, the more likely the news media will have an influence on their behavior and their chances of political success.* The relations between political actors and journalists are, to a certain extent, a question of power. Weaker antagonists must adapt themselves to media demands because they suffer from two disadvantages: they have little to offer the media, and little chance of success unless they attain some coverage. This dynamic has been labeled the principle of cumu-lative inequality – those that need the news media the most are the ones that find it hardest to gain access (Wolfsfeld, 1997a).

The second rule also relates to the relative power of the two sides: *the news media have the greatest impact on political conflicts and on peace processes when they provide extensive publicity for weaker antagonists.* When the weaker side does achieve coverage, especially sympathetic coverage, it changes the balance of power between the two sides. The weaker side becomes a player to be reckoned with and has the potential to mobilize third parties into the conflict. It is in these situations that the news media become partici-pants and make it more difficult for leaders to take control. When, on the other hand, the news media allow the stronger antagonist to dominate media coverage, they are best thought of as conduits for reinforcing existing gaps in power. This too may be an important type of influence to study, but those cases in which the news media have an independent influence on conflicts provide an especially significant area of inquiry.

The third rule deals with the nature of the political environment: *the lower the level of political consensus concerning either conflicts or efforts to bring peace, the more likely the news media will serve as obstacles to the imple-mentation of government policies in these areas.* The news media are constantly on the lookout for disputes and confrontations because they have a vested interest in conflict. When governments are unable to mobilize a wide level of support for their efforts, the news media make things worse for them by emphasizing the extent of discord and by being especially attentive to negative developments. This makes it difficult for leaders to carry out long-range policies in the areas of peace and war because the political environment will become increasingly hostile over time.

The fourth and final rule deals with one aspect of the media environment: *the more sensationalist the media environment the more likely the news media will serve to escalate conflicts and to obstruct attempts at peace making.* This rule is an important reminder that news values vary among different media and that this will have a significant impact on the role they will play in political conflicts and peace processes. The more the media in a particular context move toward a sensationalist format the more dangerous they become. The world portrayed by tabloid journalism is a frightening place. Every dispute becomes a crisis and every danger a serious threat. If, as some argue, the news media in Western countries are becoming increasingly oriented towards entertainment, one can expect this problem to become even more acute.

The principles developed here provide guidelines for future work in this area. Many useful questions can be formulated by thinking about different types of antagonists, political environments, and media environments. How do political ideologies influence a group's willingness to adapt to media demands? How do the media assess changes in the political environment? How do different media ownership patterns influence the role the media will play in conflicts and peace processes?

The key to success in this field is to examine as many different types of conflicts and peace processes. The comparative approach must look at conflicts in different countries, different conflicts within the same cultural setting, and variations that occur in the course of a conflict. As the role of the news media is constantly changing it makes little sense to carry out single case studies.

One can also hope that more researchers will become interested in this field. There are very few political scientists who do work in this area, and even in the field of political communication, interest appears limited to the outbreak of major conflicts and bouts of terrorism. Although studying the role of the media in conflict and peace may be more daunting than other topics in the field, the political importance of the topic justifies the effort.

Notes

1 A listing of some of the most important literature in this area can be found in Wolfsfeld (1997a).
2 There are a number of studies that deal with such topics as the role of the media in foreign policy and diplomacy (Cohen, 1986; Cohen, 1987; Fromm *et al.*, 1992; Gilboa, 1998; Gowing, 1996; Henderson, 1973; O'Heffernan, 1993, 1991; Serfaty, 1991; Strobel, 1997), several that relate to the problems peace movements face in attempting to mobilize the news media (Gitlin, 1980; Glasgow University Media Group, 1985; Hackett, 1991; Ryan, 1991; Small,

1987), a few articles that deal with the role of the news media in disarmament and international cooperation (Bruck, 1988, 1989; Dorman *et al.*, 1988; Gamson & Stuart, 1992), and several that have to do with images of the enemy (Ayres, 1997; Becker, 1996; Eckhardt, 1991; Ottosen, 1995). There is also some work on the topic of "peace journalism," which talks about the need to change journalists' norms and routines for covering peace and conflict (Adam & Thamotheram, 1996; Bruck & Roach, 1993; Galtung, 1998; Himmelfarb, 1998; Lynch, 1998; Manoff, 1996, 1997, 1998; Roach, 1993; Shinar, 2000).

3 These were all semi-structured interviews that use a central core of questions, but provide flexibility for moving in different directions within each session. Methodological details can be found in the publications that are associated with each study that is noted.

4 For details of the content analysis see Wolfsfeld (1997b).

5 It is important to note that looking at this issue over a longer period of time provides a more complex picture. Once formal peace was established between the two countries, the Israeli press mostly ignored Jordan, unless something dramatic (and usually negative) took place (Wolfsfeld *et al.*, 2002). Editors assumed that the Israeli public had little interest in Jordan

References

Adam, G. F. and Thomotheram, R. (1996). The media's role in conflict: report reviewing international experience in the use of mass media for promoting conflict prevention, peace and reconciliation. Geneva: Media Action International.

Ayres, R. W. (1997). Mediating international conflicts: is image change necessary? *Journal of Peace Research*, 34, 431–447.

Becker, J. A. (1996). A disappearing enemy: the image of the US in Soviet political cartoons. *Journalism and Mass Communication Quarterly* 73, 609–619.

Bennett W. L. and Paletz, D. L. (eds) (1994). *Taken by storm: the media, public opinion, and US foreign policy in the Gulf War*. Chicago, IL: University of Chicago Press.

Bruck, P. A. (ed.) (1988). *A proxy for knowledge: the news media as agents in arms control and verification*. Ottawa: Carleton International Proceedings.

Bruck, P. A. (1989). Strategies for peace, strategies for news research. *Journal of communication*, 39, 108–129.

Bruck, P. A. and Roach, C. (1993). Dealing with reality: the news media and the promotion of peace. In C. Roach (ed.), *Communication and culture in war and peace*. Newbury Park, CA: Sage.

Cohen, R. (1987). *Theatre of power: the art of diplomatic signalling*. London: Longman.

Cohen, Y. (1986). *Media diplomacy: the foreign office in the mass communications age*. London: Frank Cass.

Cohen A. and Wolfsfeld, G. (1993). *Framing the Intifada: media and people*. Norwood, NJ: Ablex Press.

Dorman, W., Manoff, R. K. and Weeks, J. (1988). *American press coverage of US–Soviet relations, the Soviet Union, nuclear weapons, arms control, and national security: a bibliography*. New York: Center for War Peace and the News Media.

Eckhardt, W. (1991). Making and breaking enemy images. *Bulletin of Peace Proposals* 22, 87–95.

Fromm, J., Gart, M., Hughes, T. L., Rodman, P. and Tanzer, L. (1992). The media impact on foreign policy. In H. Smiln (ed.), *The media and the Gulf War*, Washington, DC: Seven Locks Press.

Galtung, J. (1998). High road, low road: charting the course for peace journalism. *Track Two*, 7, 7–10.

Gamson, W. A. (1990). *The strategy of social protest*, Belmont, CA: Wadsworth Publishing Company.

Gamson, W. A. and Stuart, D. (1992). Media discourse as a symbolic contest: the bomb in political cartoons. *Sociological Forum*, 7, 55–86.

Garrow, D. J. (1978). *Protest at Selma*. New Haven, CT: Yale University Press.

Gilboa, E. (1998). Media diplomacy: conceptual divergence and applications. *Harvard International Journal of Press/Politics*, 3, 56–75.

Gitlin, T. (1980). *The whole world is watching*. Berkeley, CA: University of California Press.

Glasgow University Media Group (1985). *War and peace news*. Philadelphia, PA: Open University Press.

Gowing, N. (1996). Media coverage: help or hindrance in conflict prevention? (unpublished paper). New York: Carnegie Commission on Preventing Deadly Conflicts.

Hackett, R. (1991). *News and dissent: the press and politics of peace in Canada*, Norwood, NJ: Ablex Publishing.

Hallin, D. (1986). *The uncensored war*. New York: Oxford University Press.

Henderson, G. (ed.) (1973). *Public diplomacy and political change: four case studies, Okinawa, Peru, Czachosolvakia, Guinea*. New York: Praeger.

Himmelfarb, S. (1998). Impact is the mantra: the "common ground" approach to the media. *Track Two*, 7, 38–40.

Livingston, S. (1997). Clarifying the CNN effect: an examination of media effects according to the type of military intervention, Research Paper R-18, Cambridge, MA: The Joan Shorenstein Center on the Press, Politics, and Public Policy, Kennedy School of Government, Harvard University.

Lynch, J. (1998). Findings of the conflict and peace journalism forum (unpublished manuscript). Tablow Court, Talow, Buckinghamshire, England.

Manoff, R. (1996). The mass media and social violence: is there a role for the media in preventing and moderating ethnic, national, and religious conflict? (unpublished paper). New York: Center for War, Peace, and the News Media, New York University.

Manoff, R. (1997). The media's role in preventing and moderating conflict. *Crossroads Global Report*, March/April, 24–27.

Manoff, R. (1998). Role plays: potential media roles in conflict prevention and management. *Track Two*, 7, 11–16.

Nacos, B. L. (1994). *Terrorism and the media: from the Iran hostage crisis to the World Trade Center bombing*. New York: Columbia University Press.

O'Heffernan, P. (1991). *Mass media and American foreign policy*. Norwich, NJ: Ablex.

O'Heffernan, P. (1993). Mass media and US foreign policy: a mutual exploitation model of media influence in US foreign policy. In R. J. Spitzer *Media and public policy*. Westport, CT: Praeger.

Ottosen, R. (1995). Enemy images and the journalistic process. *Journal of Peace Research*, 32, 97–112.

Paletz, D. L. and A. P. Shmid (eds) (1992). *Terrorism and the media*. Newbury Park, CA: Sage.

Paletz, D. and Entman, R. (1981). *Media, power, politics*. New York: Free Press.

Rabin, Y. (1996). The promise and problems of the Israeli press: in conversation with Marvin Kalb. *Harvard International Journal of Press/Politics*, 1, 106–112.

Roach, C. (1993). Information and culture in war and peace: overview. In C. Roach (ed.), *Communication and culture in war and peace*. Newbury Park, CA: Sage.

Ryan, C. (1991). *Prime time activism: media strategies for grassroots organizing*. Boston, MA: South End Press.

Serfaty, S. (ed.) (1991). *The mass media and foreign policy*. New York: St. Martin's Press.

Shinar, D. (2000). Media diplomacy and "peace talk": the Middle East and Northern Ireland. *Gazette*, 62, 83–97.

Small, M. (1987). Influencing the decision-makers: the Vietnam experience. *Journal of Peace Research*, 24, 185–198.

Strobel, W. P. (1997). *Late breaking foreign policy: the news media's influence on peace operations*. Washington, DC: The US Institute of Peace.

Weimann, G. and Winn, C. (1994). *The theater of terror: mass media and international terrorism*. Reading, MA: Addison-Wesley.

Wolfsfeld, G. (1997a). *Media and political conflict: news from the Middle East*, Cambridge: Cambridge University Press.

Wolfsfeld, G. (1997b). Fair weather friends: the varying role of the news media in the Arab–Israeli peace process. *Political Communication*, 14, 29–48.

Wolfsfeld, G. (1997c). Promoting peace through the news media: some initial lessons from the peace process. *Harvard International Journal of Press/Politics*, 2, 52–70.

Wolfsfeld, G. (2001a). The news media and the second Intifada: some initial lessons. *The Harvard Journal of Press/Politics*, 6, 113–118.

Wolfsfeld, G. (2001b). *Media and peace: from the Middle East to Northern Ireland*. Peace Works No. 37. Washington, DC: The US Institute of Peace.

Wolfsfeld, G., Khouri, R. and Peri, Y. (2002). News about the other in Jordan and Israel: does peace make a difference? *Political Communication*, 19, 189–210.

9

GOVERNMENT COMMUNICATION TO THE PUBLIC AND POLITICAL COMMUNICATION

Philippe J. Maarek

Government communication to the public is in a sense the oldest form of political communication. Looking at the origins of politics, and of the art of rhetoric, one immediately remembers the skills of political communication in the Agora of ancient Greece, notably Athens at its peak. Government bodies have also for long known how to advertise their territories in order to attract tourists, but, until recently, they have never consciously started to organize and rationalize their communication with their citizens. Within the frame of the growth of the centralized states apparatus during the past two centuries, government communication at large has followed.

In the last two decades, the communication flow emanating from local and national government bodies has arisen considerably in most of the Western countries, at least. Local particularities have been risen again, as a centrifuge counter-reaction to the nineteenth and twentieth centuries' strengthening of the "Nation-States": local territories and political forces are trying to assert more clearly their existence and actions to the eyes of the citizen. The communication flow coming from transnational administrative bodies is also growing, while the pressure groups and other formerly less organized voices are now part of the communication public sphere – thanks notably to the emergence of new media technologies, which means that the process is more complex.

In this chapter, we are first going to try and evaluate the main reasons of that evolution, and notably of the recent increase of the local and national government communication flow. Then, using the current state of literature and research, and looking in more detail to the case study of France, we are going to try and assess how closely government communication to the public is related to political communication, either as a part of it, or as an increasingly independent field by itself.

157

PHILIPPE J. MAAREK

Some grounds for the recent increase of the local and national government communication flow

The generalization of decentralization

After the expansion of so-called "Nation-Sates" in the nineteenth and twentieth centuries, the reflux of centrally governed administrative apparatus has led to an increase of decentralization in most of the democratic states. In France, Italy or the UK an increasing part of political power is given back to local government bodies, when in other democratic countries like the US, or Brazil, the local governments leeway, which has always remained important, is yet to be tarnished.[1]

In most of the so-called "democratic countries," the acceleration of the decentralization process started at the beginning of the 1980s. In France, it came with the Socialist government of François Mitterrand, in 1981, and culminated as soon as the following year with an important array of legal measures transferring many competencies of the central government ministries to decentralized bodies; in the UK, the need for an increase of local government came as a reaction to the excesses of central government during the Thatcher era;[2] in Italy, the same movement was accelerated by the weakness of the central government through decades of political instability, etc.

In countries with a looser territory administrative structure, the level of autonomy of the local governing bodies has also never been as noteworthy. In Spain, the autonomy of the provinces is seemingly endlessly growing, different sub-language being now officially admitted in some of them. In Brazil, in 1998, some State Governors and parliaments for some time led some kind of a tax secession, in refusing to pay taxes owed to the Federal Government of Brasilia, not to speak about the Argentinian situation where each provincial governor acts as a feudal lord, etc. Somehow, this trend corresponds to the slow decline of the nineteenth and twentieth century "Nation-State," the strengthening of local government links filling the gap left open.[3]

An automatic consequence of this increase of decentralization has been the increase of the communication flow emanating from local government bodies: whether recently created, or having now extended capacities, they needed to communicate to the citizens more about their new activities or even about their new existence. In countries like France, where a new category of local administrative bodies, the "region," has even been created by the 1982 set of regulations and laws, some kind of competition between the different kind of local government bodies have even started to arise![4]

The influence of new ideas about government management in local and national government agencies

Another strong trend of administrative government in recent years in most democratic countries has been the evolution of its relationship with the citizen, which has led to a considerable increase of the communication flow, local government following this general trend.

The last three or four decades of the twentieth century have caused a considerable change in the government managing processes, probably as a consequence of the enormous increase in the general media flux. Formerly, the individual citizen used to get his/her information from ear-to-ear through a personal communication network, or, at best, through a few selected mass media channels (radio and newspapers). Today, the proliferation of the media channels (television, then numerous cable and satellite channels) and now the emergence of new media, notably the Internet, has considerably increased the level of *visibility* of administrative actions. Now, no change in budget, no new policy, can be enacted without being immediately literally dissected by the different kind of media, which make immediately the general public aware of their consequences.

Starting in the US in the 1960s with the consumer movement (notably thanks to Ralph Nader), this public exposition of governing bodies decisions has led to a much stronger control of government activities by the citizen through the media. In the US, no one can now be appointed by the President without being screened for hours by the Senate, his records being put into question through the tiniest detail. In France, since Valery Giscard d'Estaing instated a surveys cell in the "Palais de l'Elysée" in 1974, no government or President has been known to directly advocate policies which were not at least in one way or another popular with a majority of the alleged "public opinion" supposedly revealed by surveys, while the first Acts on administrative transparency were also issued at the end of the 1970s.[5]

The comparison with the communication of private enterprises with their customers (now called consumers) has encouraged this evolution of the government communication to the public, especially in countries of Western Europe. Here, longstanding state owned enterprises were constantly privatized during the 1980s and the 1990s, first in the UK, during the Margaret Thatcher era, then in Italy and in France, making the border between the public and the private sector more and more permeable. Thus citizens were expecting more communication to emanate from the public sector, exactly in the way they were receiving a much more important communication flow from the private sector, in response to consumerist actions. This development is also happening in politics at large and therefore in political communication: hence the rise of the ecological parties in countries like Germany, or more recently France, and the inclusion of some of the environmental protection stands in the "traditional" parties' programs.

159

The move to an increase and an admittance of the role of government communication to the public (still often called government public relations, though much more elaborate) has then been a general consequence of that increase of visibility of political decisions and of that trend of comparing government and private originated communication. Since government management was put on the agenda, communication was needed to reinforce the new decisions and to help them to be put through.

To that effect, most of the evolutions of government management led to an increase in the flow of communication:[6]

- previously strictly hierarchical decisions needed only orders and a plain public notice publication, now delegation and personal responsibility need internal and external flows of communication;
- today, quality becomes an issue, it has to be properly advocated, then enacted, again through communication with civil servants and citizens;
- when the citizen starts to think as a consumer rather than a service user, again it increases the communication flow.

Like central government agencies or ministries around the world, local government bodies have followed this general trend of evolution from the formerly hierarchical secretive or hardly advertised administrative decisions to the more modern administrative management methods. This provoked inevitably an expansion of the communication flows emanating from the governing bodies. An "International City Management Association" has even been created in order to exchange experiences among civil servants in charge of these programs.

The influence of new ideas about management in government in local government agencies has led to considerable changes in administrative actions, all creating more "transparency" in the local government activities, namely an increase of the communication flow.

The "politicization" of local government

Another consequence of the general trend to decentralization and to local government increased competencies has been the greater role played by politicians at this level. A side effect has therefore been the extension of the communication flow emanating from local government agencies.

Since politicians are usually directly accountable for their activities, they have encouraged local government bodies to expand their communication: when the latter put forward the policies enacted by the politicians who are leading them, they indirectly promote them. Of course, everyone is aware that it helps the incumbent politicians to be acknowledged by the citizens and reelected by them at the next elections . . .

The greater importance of local government offices for politicians has been a general trend, notably since the fall of the Berlin Wall, at the end of the 1980s. From this period, nationwide politics seem to have become more and more lackluster: the "Cold War" is over, and ideology is no more an issue, leading to a lack of interest about national politics[7]. A clear sign of that process is the decline in voting participation rates: abstention from elections has never been higher than the beginning of the twenty-first century, in countries like the US where political participation is traditionally low, and in European countries, where not so long ago it used to be higher.[8] The greater level of expenses needed by national elections for politicians or political parties has also led to excesses in spending which have caused many scandals, contributing to the low esteem level of politicians as a whole. For instance, Bill Clinton's inflated sexual misconduct has somehow created a caricature of this new general trend of low esteem for politicians in democracies today.

In this regard, politicians who only care for local government have been using their positions as a stronghold for future activities, benefiting from their skills in dealing with local affairs without any ideological background. The campaign positioning of George W. Bush Jr during the 2000 presidential race in the US seems to be the best example: an emphasis on his local career as governor with an open disdain for Washington political turmoil, and a personal commitment without any clear political standpoints or program.

Paradoxically, this apparent de-politicization of local government elected officers makes for a stronger politicization of local government than ever: even if a politician claims to be elected or reelected thanks to personal skills only, rather than thanks to any political ideas, or to his partisan belonging, he needs to perform efficiently in the eye of the citizen who is going to vote, which makes for a reinforced political communication flow, inevitably linked to the local government communication flow.

The use of media and local government communication means as a method of helping the incumbent politician to achieve his personal goals is debatable, and frequently explains why this communication flow is rather (mis)used in order to soothe the mood of the people, rather than for its possible efficiency in actually helping the enactment of local policy decisions, when properly devised and used. At any rate, the general movement towards a global increase of local government communication included in the politicization process is in no doubt.

The influence of the evolution of media

The final main cause of growth of local government communication to the citizen probably lies in the transformation of modern media. At the beginning of the third millennium, the McLuhanian "Global village" has probably found its true meaning: the individual can stay at home and get fully connected to what happens all around the world, not only through a unidirectional communication means, like television, but even through bi-directional communication means, from telephone and mobile phone to more and more versatile media like Internet.

With Internet, from a desk in any household, one can now directly influence the world much more efficiently than any mass media ever did. The Lewinsky/Clinton affair was disclosed through the Net, and this trend will probably increase when television channels will be carried through the Internet thanks to the fast Internet Protocol soon to come. Within a few years, it seems that phone, television, web surfing, and e-mailing (plus probably many other things we still cannot imagine) are going to be accessed within the same electronic device, which will be the new main media of tomorrow.

As a consequence of this evolution, the "traditional" communication networks have been steadily weakening: the modern citizen knows better the face, uses, and way of speech, of the well-known politicians who are frequently on television than those of the politicians who directly rule his local vicinity: they scarcely gets access to television or the other mass media. This clearly means that local government communication has had to expand and also to become more and more sophisticated in order to compensate for this weakening of the traditional local communication network – and of the traditional urban meeting modes.[9]

Altogether, then, the expansion of Local Government Communication to the citizen, which is in no doubt, is clearly based on some strong grounds coming from the evolution of media and the change in modern politics. It has joined the flow of national government communication – initially made up as "propaganda" at the beginning of the twentieth century.

We are now going to try and assess if national and local government communication are being granted an autonomous status among the other kinds of communication processes.

National and local government communication to the public as a research field: a statute in being and an autonomy in building

We have previously established some grounds for the growth of the local government communication flow to the public, and of the more ancient government communication. Does this phenomenon constitute a specific field in communication sciences by itself, or is it mainly a by-product of either political communication, or organizational communication? We are going to see that the autonomy of government communication seems to be hardly a matter of interest among many Anglo-Saxon scholars, while a different conception of state administration seems to be encouraging an emergence of a separate field in France and some Latin countries – while not unanimously acknowledged there.

Government communication to the public in Anglo-Saxon literature

Reading American or English originated literature makes one dubious about the originality and autonomy of government communication to the public as a field *per se*. Government communication to the public as a whole is rarely even considered as separate from organizational communication. When Doris Graber writes, for instance, that "public organizations are expected to operate in an atmosphere of openness,"[10] she sums up a common understanding of the progress of government communication as an improvement of information management, rather than a complete autonomous communication process.

The common understanding is that two separate kinds of communication coexist in government communication. The communication of policy decisions, in the line of Karl Deutsch's reasoning, is linked to political communication, while the communication of civil servants and administrative bodies applying policy decisions is plainly understood as a banal process in every way similar to the same process concerning enterprises from the private sector communicating to their customers. The specific problems of the communication of administrative bodies are only seen as small variations to the general model (like the difficulties in convincing civil servants to be more "transparent" in their relationships with citizens, or the particular problems of credibility caused by the proximity to the "user/citizen/customer" in the case of local government communication).

Most of the literature in the Anglo-Saxon world follows this trend, even in countries like Germany where a different tradition of civil service might have led to other conclusions.

University courses frequently follow the same trend and do not build up government bodies' communication to the public as a field distinguishable from other organizations communicating from the business sector. National and local government communication to the public is generally included in public relations studies as a case-study within organizations or institutional communication fields. In the Free University of Berlin, for instance, the specific problems of government communication to the public is included in "Government Public Relations" (*Regierung Öffentlichkeitsarbeit*) separated from "Political communication" as a teaching field (*Kommunikationspolitik*).

Similarly, government communication is often included as one of the components of government management in many of the writings – Garnett (1992). Sometimes it's even completely absent – Rice and Atkin (1989).

Autonomy of government communication to the public in France: wishful thinking or practical reality?

Communication Sciences themselves have only recently been established as a separate field by French scholars, and this split from other Human Sciences is yet to be fully accepted: they are strongly linked to other more "established" fields, from Sociology or Social Psychology to Political Science, and many scholars do not grant them much autonomy as a separate field of Social Sciences. Of course, we do not share these views and join researchers like Philippe Breton, who convincingly assesses the right of existence to communication sciences, which, after all, are direct heirs of Rhetoric, "womb of Human Sciences."[11]

At the end of the 1970s and the beginning of the 1980s, communication from the Town Hall to citizens was still considered to be unilateral, and most of the literature in the field linked local government communication to the citizens to plain "information" processes, in the same way that government communication was – and sometime still is – assimilated to propaganda. Researches – and books – on this topic were rare, and reduced the scope of government communication to the citizen to a limited frame of disclosing information to the public through more or less traditional channels, from the official releases to slightly more elaborate public relations.[12] Government communication was frequently narrowed to the relationship between Ministers and Mayors and journalists, who were globally seen as opinion relays in the purest Lazarsfeld sense, a public relations understanding of the communication flow neighboring the Anglo-Saxon one.

Strangely enough, the main demand for recognition of government communication to the public as a separate matter came first in France from professionals from the field.

One of the first to try and obtain some kind of recognition from both the French administration apparatus and the scholars was State Councilor Pierre Zémor, a former communication advisor of previous Prime Minister Michel Rocard. He first wrote a "White paper," a special report to the government, on the organization of public service communication to the public in France.[13] He put forward that civil servants (or agents under contract) working as communications officers for administrative bodies (national or local), were doing a job quite different from what the public relations people helping politicians in their political communication were doing, and that this job was to be called "communication publique" (public service communication).

Pierre Zémor clearly pointed out in his report that the tasks of these communication officers were much more complex than those of a "plain" press office chief: public service communication officers should not only prepare information for citizens, but also organize a relationship with them, and set marketing campaigns to help carrying on public services and enacting local and national government policies, not forgetting the organization of civic and institutional campaigns, etc. He also pointed out that these professionals from the field should try and obtain an autonomy from the politicians who hire them, thus tempting a break, away from "political" communication.

Under Pierre Zémor's chairmanship, "Communication Publique" was then constituted as an association of the main officers acting as communication directors in the most important local and national government bodies. Very active and relatively wealthy (thanks to pretty high dues!), "Communication Publique" has since been organizing several meetings a year. Its members get to meet with scholars and university professors, but also with communication professionals from the private sector, in order to evaluate their practices. After a funding text in 1991,[14] "Communication Publique" put out in 1995 a thick practical handbook mostly written by professionals from the field, with various chapters giving mostly well-thought practical texts and expert accounts on the different standpoints of government communication to the public.[15]

Quite similarly, another practical book, specifically dedicated to local government communication to the public, was written under the auspices of one of the advisors of CNFPT, the center for training civil servants specializing in local government in France, and was mainly intended to them[16] (not counting the many "how to's" written by communication or marketing consultants trying to get more customers in a not too subtle way).[17]

It is then quite interesting to see that the autonomy of government communication to the public as a field per se in France is mainly built from the inside, meaning as a symbolic construction which gives a sense of belonging to the civil servants (or temporary hired agents) in charge of communication in that sector. Between 1995 and 1999 several surveys led by the Center for Comparative Studies in Political and Public Communication (CECCOPOP) have clearly pointed out this rising awareness.[18]

But, like most Anglo-Saxon literature, scholars are still more reserved on the level of autonomy of the self-styled "communication publique" – public service communication. Several well-known texts by searchers in communication or in political sciences are only describing the processes of French government communication to the public without really making a point of its autonomy.

Many still don't disconnect government communication to the citizen from political communication coming from the elected officers. A good example is a special issue on local communication of *Mots*, the review of the prestigious "Ecole Normale supérieure de Fontenay/Saint Cloud", where one hardly reads the word "communication publique"[19] and where its autonomy is neither really investigated nor even discussed.

From another perspective, Isabelle Pailliart, a well-known communication scholar specializing in local communication processes, relates local government communication to the local communication networks which are part of the existence of the individuals on a given territory.[20] She clearly analyzes local government communication as looking for an identity separating it from the three other communications models active in territories, private enterprise communication, political communication, and "local communication".[21] The autonomy from the politicians and from political communication processes is firmly denied here.[22]

Similarly, many political scientists do not leave much autonomy to government communication to the citizen, which they find too closely connected to the politicians who helm the institutions. One of the most significant cases of that kind is the (excellent) book which sums up research done in a well-known French Research Center, CURAPP:[23] here, some of the best political scientists deal with the problems of government communication(s) to the public, while using as title for the book *Political communication!*[24]

Some researchers, like Jean-François Têtu, even criticize strongly the development of local government bodies communication, arguing that it works against local democracy, in trying to impose on the citizen prospects, standpoints and ideas which are not his, but are created by the institution itself, in a tautological process denying the freedom, and nearly the existence of the individual citizen – and therefore democracy.[25]

Very few researchers, like Bernard Miège, accept a true autonomy of "public communication" in opposition to political communication, or institutional communication[26] and join the professionals from the field.

In looking at other Latin countries, like when crossing the Alps, we do find an understanding of public service communication as a field *per se*. In Italy, the same trend of building up an issue of separating local and national government communication to the public from political communication, or organizational communication, seems to be operating.[27]

As a temporary conclusion . . .

The "electronic town hall" of tomorrow is not a plain product of the evolution of communication, neither a complete by-product of government management techniques. Although the increase of the communication flow emanating from government bodies is clearly a strong tendency of modern government management, its grounds and its limits are yet to be clearly defined. The quantitative need of local and national government bodies to communicate more and more to the citizen is clear, the qualitative necessity of communicating better and better, in order to hold the comparison with communication in the private sector, is certain, but the reality of the autonomy of a so-called "public sector communication" in regards to political communication, or organizational communication, is less blatant.

This autonomy is even more difficult to achieve in the case of local government communication to the public. Since local government bodies are usually headed around the world by politicians holding a mayor or governor office (or similar), then, inevitably, their influence is bound to put pressure on civil servants or on other people managing the communication offices of the local government body: they have a hard time obtaining some kind of leeway since they have to obey him. Here, politics clearly restrain the autonomy of the field.

So, in a paradoxical way, democracy is a victim of democracy: in most countries, in order to achieve a respectable goal of having an elected officer hold office at the helm of government structures, one knows that the autonomy of communication of the body itself is going to be bound by the political communication flow coming from the same politician. Since, of course, we can only accept as a democratic strong point that politicians holding offices have to be elected, and thus, do have to strengthen their political communication to that effect, then we have to take it into account in the evaluation of the autonomy left to the communication emanating from the local government body which the politician heads, or wants to head when elected.

As a temporary conclusion, we could suggest that government communication to the public might be inextricably linked to political communication in order to create a proper communication flow answering the various needs of the citizen, exactly as the two separate branches of DNA are inextricably linked and equally needed in order to carry the genome of the species.

Notes

1 In a way, the centrifugal forces currently in action in many less politically stabilized countries, from the former USSR to Africa, are part of the same phenomenon, although quite differently in form.
2 Even charismatic Prime Minister Tony Blair indirectly conceded defeat in the May 2000 London local election when the candidate he supported lost against then dissident Ken Livingstone . . .
3 See Badie (1995); Habermas (2000); also special issue of *Quaderni*, 34, "L'incertitude des territoire."
4 In some cases, the level of local management has even gone to much smaller areas than the traditional administrative precincts. In France, many cities are now splitting their communication policies according to the different neighborhoods, and some politicians are even contemplating a division of some of the bigger administrative units, the "*departements*" in so-called "*pays*" (counties) closer to the inhabitants' characteristics; on the evolution of the political understanding of the longstanding "territories," notably the "nation-state," see Badie (1995).
5 Notably a July 1978 Law on access and transparency of administrative acts and documents, and a January 1978 Law on the protection of the citizen against personal computerized data in government administration, but also in the private sector.

6 On the generalization of the new management methods, see Burns *et al.*, (1994).
7 On that matter, the September 11 consequences are yet to be fully understood, and maybe even to be known.
8 The June 1999 elections for the European Parliament have been at the lowest in regards to participation to the vote all through Europe; in the US, the Gore/Bush election did not really improve voting participation in spite of a huge campaigning budget and its bumpy ending is certainly not going to increase the American voters' trust in politics.
9 On the consequences of the expanded capacities of electronic media, see Rodota (1999).
10 Graber (1992), p. 12.
11 Philippe Breton, La naissance des sciences de la communication (à la recherche d'un programme de séparation), in *Quaderni*, 23, Spring, 1994, *Sciences de la Communication*.
12 See Mabileau and Tudesq (1980); Péron (1983).
13 See Zémor (1992).
14 La Communication Publique, in *La Revue française d'administration publique*, 58.
15 Marianne Messager and Communication Publique (1995); see also Zémor (1995).
16 André Hartereau (1996).
17 We won't cite these basic writings which generally lack any depth and just focus on which communication tools and methods to apply.
18 CECCOPOP (1995), (1996), (1997), (1998) and (1999); see also Maarek (1998).
19 *Voix de la politique locale* (1990).
20 Isabelle Pailliart (1992).
21 Idem, p. 94.
22 Ibidem, p. 98.
23 This is also known as the Centre Universitaire de Recherches Administratives et Politiques de Picardie.
24 La Communication Politique (1991).
25 Têtu (1995).
26 Miège (1990), p. 120.
27 See Mancini (1996).

References

Badie, Bertrand (1995). *La fin des territoires (essai sur le désordre international et sur l'utilité sociale du respect)*. Paris: Fayard.
Burns, Danny, Hambelton, Robin and Hoggett, Paul (1994). *The politics of decentralisation (revitalising local democracy)*. London: Macmillan
Cardy, Hélène and Maarek, Philippe, J. (1997). *Le Discours de voeux de l'élu territorial: concepts, méthode, pratiques*, éditions de La Lettre du Cadre Territorial, coll. Dossiers d'experts, France.
CECCOPOP (1995). Survey data included in "L'inflation de communicateurs politiques et publics: symphonie ou cacophonie?" ("Inflation of political and public communicators: symphony or cacophony?"). Published by CECCOPOP, Créteil/ Université Paris 12, 1997.

CECCOPOP (1996). Survey data included in "Quelles priorités pour la communication publique aujourd'hui?" ("What priorities for public communication today?"). Published by CECCOPOP, Créteil/Université Paris 12, 1998.

CECCOPOP (1997). Survey data included in "La loi du 15 janvier 1990 et la communication des institutions publiques" ("The law of January 15th, 1990 and communication of public insitutions?"). Published by CECCOPOP, Créteil/Université Paris 12, 1999.

CECCOPOP (1998). Survey data included in "Communication publique et médias: antagonisme ou partenariat?" ("Public communication and media: antagonism or partnership?"). Published by CECCOPOP, Créteil/Université Paris 12, 2000.

CECCOPOP (1999). Survey data included in "La communication publique et la construction de l'identité territoriale" ("Public communication and the build up of territorial identity"). Published by CECCOPOP, Créteil/Université Paris 12, 2001.

La communication politique (1991a). CURAPP, Paris: Presses Universitaires de France.

La communication publique (1991b). *Revue française d'administration publique*, 58, April–June, Paris.

Deutsch, Karl, W. (1966). *The nerves of government: models of political communication and control*. New York: Free Press.

Garnett, James, L. (1992). *Communicating for results in government (a strategic approach for public managers)*. San Francisco: Jossey-Bass.

Graber, Doris (1992). *Public sector communication (how organizations manage information)*. Washington DC: CQ Press.

Habermas, Jürgen (2000). *Après la crise de l'Etat-Nation*. Paris: Fayard.

Hartereau, André (1996). *La communication publique teritoriale (repères conceptuels, méthodologiques, professionnels)*. Paris: CNFPT.

L'incertitude des territoires (1997–1998). *Quaderni*, 34, Winter, Paris.

Maarek, Philippe, J. (1991). *Communication et Marketing de l'homme politique*. Paris: Litec.

Maarek, Philippe, J. (1995). *Political Marketing and Communication*. London: John Libbey.

Maarek, Philippe, J. (1998). Communicating for local government in France: the rise of communication departments. Communication at the Jerusalem Congress of the International Communication Association (ICA), July.

Mabileau, Albert and Tudesq, André-Jean (eds) (1980). *L'Information locale*. Paris: Pédone.

Mancini, Paolo (1996). *Manuale di comunicazione pubblica*. Rome: Laterza/Bari.

Messager, Marianne and Communication Publique (1995). *La Communication Publique en pratique*. Paris: Les editions d'organisation.

Miege, Bernard (1990). *La Société conquise par la communication*. Grenoble: Presses Universitaires de Grenoble.

Pailliart, Isabelle (1992). *Les territoires de la communication*. Grenoble: Presses Universitaires de Grenoble.

Péron, Daniel (1983). *Relations publiques et information dans les communes*. Paris: Sirey.

Rice, Ronald, E. and Atkin, Charles K. (1989). *Public communication campaigns*. London: Sage.

Rodota, Stefano (1999). *La Démocratie électronique (de nouveaux concepts et expéri-ences politiques)*. Rennes: Apogée.

Sciences de la communication (1994). *Quaderni*, 23, Spring, Paris.

Têtu, Jean-François (1995). L'espace public local et ses médiations, in *Com-munication et politiques, Hermès* 17/18. Paris: CNRS Editions.

Voix de la politique locale (1990) *Mots*, 25, December. Paris: Presses de la Fondation Nationale des Sciences Politiques.

Zemor, Pierre (1995). *La communication publique*. Paris: PUF, Collection *Que sais-je*.

Zemor, Pierre (1992). *Le sens de la relation (organisation de la communication de service public)*. Paris: La Documentation Française.

10

LOCAL POLITICAL COMMUNICATION AND CITIZEN PARTICIPATION

Sabine Lang

Introduction

Local political communication research looks like a rather disparate subfield within the context of political communication studies. In many textbooks or major works on political communication it does not even exist. This is even more surprising since the local, as a category of analysis, has in the last decade spurred an impressive body of research in sociology, political science and geography (see Parry *et al.*, 1992; Berry, 1993; Judge *et al.*, 1995; Mayer, 1996; Pratchett & Wilson, 1996). While for some time it seemed that with the rise of globalization the local would turn into a negligible quantity, recent globalization research exposed a renewed interest in the local (see Castells, 1996; Sassen, 1996; Rosenau, 1998). The local, at the turn of the century, seems to have become the marker for reality against virtuality, for presence against abstraction, for citizen participation against the hegemony of global capital interests, and for the space of "real places" against the vague "space of flows" (Castells, 1996, p. 425). Yet this renewed interest in the local not only as a counterforce but also as a site of the global has not as yet taken root in communication research. Those researchers who are concerned with local aspects of political communication are therefore almost unequivocally critical of the lack of sufficient representation of the local within the field (see Cox & Morgan, 1973; Franklin & Murphy, 1991; Kaniss, 1991; Graber, 1997, p. 313).[1]

Historically, one can distinguish three stages of local political communication research. First, the research of the 1950s and 1960s, which focused optimistically on local political communication processes as a harbinger of democracy and small town community (i.e. Janowitz, 1952; Vidich & Bensman, 1958; Wood, 1959).[2] Second, the research in the 1970s and 1980s, which conceptualized local political communication as a part of mass media communication studies and therefore concentrated on the local press, radio, and television as well as new technologies (see Cox & Morgan, 1973; Murphy 1976). The third research phase, starting in the late 1980s, reconnected local political communication via electronic media to broader questions of local democracy and participation (see Dubois, 1993; McLeod et al., 1996; Cohen, 1998; Salvador & Sias, 1998). A fourth stage of political communication research at present redefines the space and the actors of local political communication in relation to the categories of local and transnational governance. Local as well as transnational governance rely on new local actors and new modes of interaction that change the local public sphere and its established political communication culture.

Most of the research up until the 1980s took the position that analyzing local political communication made sense only within narrow geographical margins (see Rager & Schibrani, 1981). The nation state was the largest topographical framework for comparative local analysis. While this chapter will put forward evidence that broader, transnational, generalizations about the local are necessary in order to analyze trends in the changing topography of the local public sphere, it is equally important to keep in mind that options and venues for local political communication depend also on the specific institutional arrangements of political systems and on specific political cultures.[3]

A second problem in local political communication research is a definitional one: the majority of studies do not conceptualize local political communication in its full scope, but concentrate on – albeit important – aspects of mass communication processes within a local geographical setting (see Rager & Schibrani, 1981, p. 498). Yet political communication entails a wider range of activities than our focus on mass media suggests. We use political communication skills when explaining to a friend why we voted for a specific party or engage in specific causes. We communicate politically in neighborhood initiatives, in parent–teacher-associations, at business round-tables or in town meetings.

In the definition put forward in this article, local political communication involves all communicative situations in which political claims are being made, which either concern the local public, or originate within its confines. Central actors of political communication within a local public sphere are individual citizens as well as parties, interest groups, non-governmental organizations, the media, government and business. These actors and institutions use four differently aggregated types of communication, which reflect different forms of political interaction (see Lang, 2001):

- individual political statements or actions in non-institutionalized settings (i.e. a restaurant, or a political discussion at home);
- collective acts of political communication or actions, which take place on a continuum from spontaneous (i.e. protests) to semi-institutionalized (i.e. round-tables) to highly institutionalized (i.e. local parliaments);

- professional communication means (PR, press releases, videos, etc.);
- mass communication means and processes.

Which forms political actors choose for any given purpose depends on access, resources, mobilization, and organization potential, specificity of issues, social influence and power. Most of the time, political communication types appear in a combination, such as a parliamentary debate being a collective act of face-to-face communication while, at the same time, being the site of press releases and radio/TV media presence. And yet, each type of political communication will produce its own event and tell a different story. The advantage of such a typology of political communication is that it makes us understand the construction of the local via political communication – a construction in which the role of the media is important yet not hegemonic.

What is "local" about local political communication?

What are the topographical units that we think of as "local"? Is it the village, the district, the city, or the region? Does the local refer to a spatial locality? Is it bound to the city limits of Bombay or to the village of Verviers? Or is it a cultural or ethnic locality, i.e. Chinatown in San Francisco or the Turkish neighborhood in Berlin? Or is the local a political category that correlates with the borders of the smallest governmental unit? Depending on whether one constructs the local as a geographical, cultural or political category – meaning whether one puts emphasis on common processes, a common culture, or shared institutional and political structures – the local might encompass between ten and 10 million local people.[4] One should therefore caution against romanticizing the local. The local public sphere is not necessarily small, not necessarily an emphatic community and certainly not unaffected by the speed of capitalist culture.

Keeping this precarious nature of the definition of locality in mind, we can nevertheless trace certain characteristics of the local that make it a distinct category of analysis in political communication research.

First, everybody has a subjective notion of himself/herself as a member of a local community. This notion of locality rests on assumptions about shared culture, shared societal processes and/or shared institutional frameworks.

Second, the local is distinct from other units of analysis by allowing for *relatively* more shared experiences and common knowledge than other units of communication analysis.

Third, the local is a sphere which encompasses *relatively* more face-to-face interactions and interpersonal communication practices than larger units of political communication.

Fourth, the local, simply by measurement of scale and size, is *relatively* better equipped than other political units to enhance representative democracy with participatory elements which involve specific communication practices.

Yet these distinctive characteristics of the local do not make it a space with fixed boundaries, as traditional local political communication research claimed (see Dorsch, 1978, p. 190; Jarren, 1984). To treat the sphere of local political communication as a closed system meant to analyze the relationships between its actors and institutions as being independent from outside variables beyond the confines of the local unit. Yet what constitutes the local is not only about what is specific and particular to the local situation: the local public sphere is becoming more and more infused with agendas that are being drawn up within national and transnational political institutions. But while the idea of an autonomous local political system is a fiction, the specificities of a local public will infuse political communication process and its outcomes with local color.

Local political communication at work: frameworks, actors, and issues

We distinguish two forms of political communication: face-to-face and media organized types of communication (Kurp, 1994; Lang, 2001). Whereas face-to-face communication on the local level has traditionally not attracted much research (exceptions being the New England town meeting and, in recent years, discourse analysis of community meetings or round-table formats),[5] the media have taken center stage in local communication research.

Local print media

Until the early 1970s, "local media" and "local newspapers" were treated as interchangeable terms (Franklin & Murphy, 1998, p. 7). Local newspapers were the primary suppliers and the single most potent communicators of political information in the local community. They were the only medium that guaranteed the publication of communal issues on an up-to-date informational level as well as on a regular basis (Kurp, 1994, p. 135). At the same time, the local paper served as the communicative reference point for many other communication processes as citizens read the same accounts of political events in the paper and often referred to these accounts when staking out their own positions. This powerful leverage of the local newspaper has been undercut since the 1980s by several developments, which have changed the number, format and content of the local news media. The main trends that have altered the role of the local print media have been concentration, proliferation of new formats and declining readership due to competition with electronic media.

174

Concentration of the press within larger media conglomerates[6] and competition with other localized media has led to a decrease of truly local publications and an increase of regional or large metropolitan print media (see Dorsch, 1978; Jarren, 1984; Graber, 1997; Franklin & Murphy, 1998).[7] Concentration has also resulted in a rise of local newspaper monopolies. Single local newspaper markets in Germany quadrupled between 1954 and 1990.[8] One third of all local and regional newspaper readers have only access to one local print media source (Schatz 1995, p. 365). Concentration does not only happen vertically, whenever stronger news corporations buy smaller papers. There is also evidence of horizontal concentration processes on the local media markets with local papers buying shares in local/regional radio or TV stations and making use of diverse news formats for political communication (Franklin & Murphy, 1991, p. 13; 1998, p. 18).

Besides metropolitan daily newspapers with local sections and local dailies, local communities usually have an array of local print media for specialized interests, i.e. city magazines, school magazines, church bulletins, or consumer reports, which are part of the local political communication network.[9] These "sub-local" media (Dorsch, 1978, p. 193) also target various culturally diverse readerships, i.e. gay, lesbian, ethnic, or racial groups (Graber, 1997, p. 315). Especially in metropolitan areas, sub-local alternative media are flourishing. Although the majority do not survive long and depend heavily on voluntary work, sub-local media are the primary means of political information and mobilization among respective subcultures.

The 1990s have also seen a proliferation of "free newspapers" throughout Europe and the US (Franklin & Murphy, 1991, p. 10; 1998, p. 11). In Western Europe, there are research estimates of as many as 4,000 free newspaper titles distributing 200 million copies per week (Franklin & Murphy, 1991, p. 10). These local papers, which are financed mostly through advertisements, range in variety from mere commercial bulletins or personal advertising magazines to political community newspapers.[10] The success of free papers, including high advertising revenues and high profit margins, has led in Great Britain already to major acquisition initiatives: nine of the ten largest free papers have been purchased by traditional newspaper publishing houses; they make up about half of free newspaper production (Franklin & Murphy, 1998, p. 13). In addition to free papers and alternative newspapers, some countries have a tradition of free municipal newspapers, which are published by local authorities to inform the public about local politics. In England, Scotland and Wales, for example, Franklin and Murphy count seventy-four of such municipal newspapers, which are published between two and ten times a year. Forty-seven percent of these papers were founded after 1986 (Franklin & Murphy, 1991, p. 137 and Appendix I) and are part of governmental initiatives to place their agendas within the discursive context of the community. In Germany, rural audiences especially rely on an "Amts- und Gemeindeblatt" for detailed information on local government activities. In general, though, government newspapers have lacked professionalism and consumer attractiveness; only recently have there been efforts made by local governments to increase and professionalize their public relations strategies (Maarek, 1995).

Not enough attention has been given in local political communication research to the peculiar relationships between the local press and more specifically local journalists and government authorities. Studies indicated as early as the 1970s, that the local press did not live up to normative expectations of being the nurturer of a local "political public." On the contrary, evidence was mounting that local print media were acting more as transmission agencies for political authorities (Zoll, 1974 in Rager & Schibrani, 1981, p. 498; Kaniss, 1991, p. 90; Murphy, 1976, pp. 135f.; Neveu, 1998, p. 452). Not only was political agenda-setting firmly in the hands of government, but also political decision-making processes were not analyzed and made transparent to local readers. Instead, politics was communicated in a factual way, and controversies were much less reported than outcomes and agreements (Rager & Schibrani, 1981, p. 498). From the perspective of the late 1990s it seems that while commentaries and interpretive pieces have somewhat increased, political agenda-setting still originates largely in government offfices.[11] Phyllis Kaniss observed: "While there is much in the news and editorial columns that is critical of local officials, this criticism is limited when compared with the amount of information that is taken directly, and almost unquestioningly, from official bureaucratic sources" (Kaniss, 1991, pp. 90f.).

A central problem for local journalists is that their roles as journalists, private persons, and citizens are harder to keep separate than the roles of employees of national or regional news media (Dorsch, 1978, p. 195; Graber, 1997, p. 333). Reporters are believed to be soft on local elites whom they know personally and whom they must keep as sources for future reporting. In return, control of the local media does not merely happen via an abstract reader/listenership, but is performed in the local public sphere by friends and acquaintances, one's social environment and by the local ruling representatives. Local journalists are part of the local elite and are therefore integrated into a socially stratified web of relations, which can conflict with demands for journalistic independence. Journalistic independence is also indirectly threatened by heightened job insecurity. Throughout Western Europe and the US there is a tendency to replace steady jobs for journalists with freelance work (Franklin & Murphy, 1998, p. 9). Specifically in rural areas the majority of news is gathered by freelance staffers, and the local reporter has been mutating into an editor of submitted stories. Yet also in urban areas with competing media sources, the flexible personality – capable of flexibility between and within jobs – will be a requirement of the future journalistic profile. The "ideal type" of a local journalist is described by an editor of a British local media conglomerate as such: "One journalist should be capable of covering a story for the company's newspaper, cable, TV, and radio output and we will be moving down this route" (J. Morgan, op. cit.; Franklin & Murphy, 1998, p. 17).

Numbers of local print media and local readership expose a long-term downward trend in the US and Western Europe.[12] In the US, where the lack of a strong national press has traditionally encouraged local print media, subscription to daily papers fell from almost 100 percent of all households in 1970 to less than two-thirds in the mid-1990s (Koschnick, 1995, p. 1951).[13] The decline in readership corresponds to a weakening of identification with the print media. The local paper is treated as a consumer product, and readers tend to become active communicators only under very special circumstances, i.e. if challenged by the paper (Dorsch, 1978, p. 198).[14] While some research attributes the decline of the print media to increasing popularity of the electronic media, others argue against media usage as a zero-sum game. The effects of the new competitive environment created by the introduction of local electronic media have not been analyzed in full scope (McLeod et al., 1996, p. 202). Kaniss, who has so far delivered the most substantiated account of the changes in local media culture, summarizes that

> by 1990, the metropolitan newspaper has come to confront a dramatically new structure of competition. While the number of metropolitanwide newspapers within any one city has decreased, the survivors have had to contend with increased competition for audiences and advertisers from other media, including television, radio, suburban daily and weekly newspapers, and free shoppers.
> (Kaniss, 1991, p. 43)

In sum, local print media research has been able to gather and support evidence that print media concentration and competition with other political news media have contributed less to a diversified political news market and more to uniformity in political content. Reporting on political issues has suffered from shifts towards "human touch," lifestyle, and public security issues. When compared to national political news media, local media still exhibit an underrepresentation of commentary sections on political issues as opposed to small news formats. The reliance of local print media on information from local governments has been identified as a major problem of agenda-setting and has been related to the lack of resources for investigative journalism as well as to the predominance of established information channels as opposed to new and less prominent sources of information. Decline in local print media readership and advertising revenue contribute to the precarious status of the local newspaper. And yet the assets of the local press, specifically in highly competitive markets, have not been addressed in detail by existing research. The local paper materializes as a daily symbol of common identity and community. In contrast to electronic media, it can be used relatively free of time constraints, and the relative autonomy of the reader is in general higher than that of the listener or the viewer. Therefore speculations about the end of the printed press seem far-fetched to the observer of the local media market.[15]

Cable and satellite radio and television

The rise of cable and satellite technology in the late 1970s produced new hopes about participatory democracy and critical journalism on the local level (see Jarren, 1981, p. 426). Electronic media were thought to create faster and more visible local public information venues and to have a leverage in terms of actuality over the print media. Claims were also made that electronic local media enhanced a specific quality of dialogical interaction between citizens. Whereas the local paper usually would do one interview with an expert on an issue at a time, radio and TV could gather local experts from different sides, i.e. business, citizen action committees, local government, interest groups, at one table and thereby establish fora for communication and contact, which went at times far beyond the hour of discussion in the production studio (see Hamm *et al.*, 1989, p. 53). Today, researchers of local radio and TV caution high expectations about the participatory quality of traditional local electronic media. In the US and Europe, the vast majority of transmission is entertainment-centered, de-contextualized "light programming," and only narrow segments of the local electronic market are used for local political news transmission and participatory formats.

While there have been notable differences among countries as to the primacy of development of cable or satellite electronic media,[16] their respective imprint on the local media markets shows similar patterns. Local radio has been a success story all over Europe and the US, and evidence suggests that it serves well in developing countries as a means to enhance political participation (see below). In 1992, Western Europe had 7,934 radio stations of which about 90 percent were local or regional private providers (Koschnik, 1995, p. 781).[17] Yet while the vast majority of local radio stations tend to focus on entertainment, music and culture with interspersed political news programs, and political talk shows, some Western European countries have seen the establishment and proliferation of local radio channels with a strong informational bias.[18] The most prominent and also most professional actor in local news programming is the BBC. The company decided in the early 1990s to expand its public service to local programming, introducing thirty-nine local radio stations in England and several more in Scotland, Northern Ireland, and Wales (Crisell, 1998,

p. 31). Focus of the BBC is on programming for underrepresented minorities, thus advocating program formats and content which generally do not sell well to advertisers. Eighty percent of the transmission is supposed to be speech. Over 20 percent of the UK's adult population listens to local BBC radio; its market share is around 15 percent. Yet competition with private commercial radios which operate on the local or regional level and which keep gaining higher advertising shares have made it difficult for local BBC to stick to a truly political information format.[19]

While BBC stands for local programming as a service *to* the locality, but not necessarily one which originates *from* it (ibid.), other local radio channels have tried to find a niche as producers with strong roots in the local community. Their most radical form, the so called "open radio channels" as a citizen-activating medium which blossomed in the late 1970s, seems to have been overrated under democratic premises (Jarren, 1981, pp. 426f.). While expectations ran high with the advent of citizen-initiated local programming, research has indicated that open channels are only a marginal and negligible side effect of the introduction of electronic cable media. Open channels do have democratic user value, but mostly for those who are already organized within the local community on the level of parties, clubs, social, or ecological organizations. For those actors the production process in the open channel has primarily the internal effect of goal finding and the establishing of a common cause identity. Only secondarily does it produce the external effect of giving the larger populace a voice in local issues, and of creating advocacy in the community (Jarren, 1981, p. 429). Some local governments, primarily in the US and in the Netherlands, now make use of community access cable channels to transmit city council meetings and committee work (see Graber, 1997, p. 314). But research has not yet produced evidence of viewer segments and informational effects of these transmissions.

Hopes that were instilled in the early 1990s into local talk radio formats as sites for democratic deliberation have also to be cautioned (Davis & Owen, 1998, p. 9). While especially in urban radio markets like Chicago, San Francisco, and Boston, local talk radio is the most listened to radio program (ibid., p. 10), it can hardly fulfill the normative claim of being "the ultimate arena for free speech" (ibid.). Most successful local talk radio hosts do not define their role as mediating a citizen agora, but more often the talk show format is used as a site for unmediated and spectacular clashes of opinions with high cleavage potential. Some local talk show hosts have combined verbal rhetoric and action, and have for example, initiated rallies or led campaigns for urban development initiatives. In sum, though, local talk radio formats, while giving citizens an active role and amplifying a certain spectrum of public voices, are not as much deliberative sites as creators of public spectacle and production sites for exaggerated opinions.

SABINE LANG

The US are also at the forefront of local television programming: at present, there are 740 different local television stations in the US (Klite et al., 1997, p. 102). They devote 39.8 percent of air time to newscasting components, of which again 30.2 percent go to crime stories and only 11.3 percent to government related stories (ibid., p. 103). Thirty-seven percent of the lead stories are on crime and 10 percent are on government policies (ibid., p. 104). Local TV production operates under severe financial constraints. Extended research or investigative reporting formats have lost out to mostly re-active news production. A recent content analysis of fourteen TV stations from five market segments in the US found that only 1.4 percent of over 3,000 analyzed stories included some form of commentary (Bernstein & Lacy, 1992, p. 338). Almost 50 percent of local television news stories in the US were obtained, according to a study by David Altheide, from press releases and related announcements, while almost another 50 percent were taken from police and fire department reports (Altheide, 1976, pp. 61ff.). In their coverage of political issues, local TV reveals the same bias towards government authority information as local radio and the print media (Murphy, 1976, p. 62).[20]

In the US, local television news have even surpassed news on the national networks as the number one information medium for the population (Klite et al., 1997, pp. 102f.). Sixty-seven percent of the adult population watches local news daily as compared to 49 percent who watch daily news on one of the national networks (Graber, 1997, p. 326). Local media also devote more time to the coverage of national issues from a local angle. Access possibilities via satellite or microwave technology enable local stations to report "live" from Washington and for example interview national representatives of their district without drawing on the sources of the national networks (see Graber, 1997, p. 328). This extension of the local is replicated by the interest of national politicians to cater to voters on the local level (Kern & Wicks, 1994, p. 191). In the US, presidents, senators as well as congressmen and women believe and fully practice the mantra that "all politics is local" and that elections are won not in Washington but in citizens' backyards in their home districts. Local TV has capitalized on this insight by increasing coverage of candidates in Washington under specific local angles (see Kiolbassa, 1997).[21]

But even though still three-quarters of local TV news originate locally, their emphasis on crime, drugs and disasters as well as entertainment and lifestyle issues, sports and the weather undercuts their potential (ibid.).[22] Kaniss in a study of the local news market in Philadelphia cites numerous examples of how news, which deal with urban political or social conflicts within the community, are neglected because they are, as a local Philadelphia TV journalist stated "more difficult to show on TV ... all you get are people talking" (Kaniss, 1991, p. 117). In sum:

The need to appeal to a mass audience, the cult of personality, the limited number of reporters and their reliance on routine chan- nels of information, the importance of dramatic video and sound bites, and the element of timeliness, all lead to a distinctive defi- nition of what is "local news" (1991, p. 113).

In as much as local political actors try to adapt to these imperatives of "events" in video and sound-bite culture, political communication patterns, and issue orientation will in all likelihood be affected. While on the one hand, electronic media might force local political institutions into more and faster transparency about their decision-making processes (see Hamm *et al.*, 1989, p. 65), on the other hand there is also a trend towards increasing "symbolic politics" on the local level. Staging events to fulfill expectations in terms of visualization goes in part at the expense of content and complexity of political communication.

Because so few state and local stories are intrinsically interesting to media audiences, the pressure to make stories entertaining is heightened. That means featuring colorful, charismatic politicians who speak well in ten-second sound bites or well-known key offi- cials in major cities. It means bypassing opportunities for more ample exposition of problems because carefully calibrated, fact-rich pronouncements are boring for most members of the audience.

(Graber, 1997, p. 320)

Proliferation of local electronic media therefore is as such no guarantee for a strengthening of the local political public. Local TV and radio, if treated exclusively as part of the private consumer market, are pressed by similar burdens, as are national stations. They have to cater to advertisers' needs, deploy easy listening formats, and deal with scarcity of investigative resources. While cable technology might strengthen the public voice of the citizen minority who is already engaged in local political life, technology as such is not a sufficient means for broader democratic participation. Only if new technological means are employed for the explicit purpose of partici patory democracy and are equipped with adequate resources to investigate and communicate political issues, and only, as we shall see below, if their purpose goes beyond creating outlets for individual voices, are technolog- ical means a valuable asset for citizen participation.

Power and access in local political communication

The relevance which local political communication processes acquire for citizens largely depends on how much decision-making power rests within the local community – ultimately it depends on the structure of the state itself. In highly centralized political systems where the local levels of govern-ment have little budget autonomy and decision-making power, local political communication is less influential than in decentralized systems with a high degree of autonomy on the local level as the US. The local arena "provides a framework for the exercise of individual and group participation, but it can do so only if significant decisions are taken at the local level" (Hill, 1994, p. 238). The more there is to decide on the local level, the more groups claim the right to participate and the more the local public becomes contested ground. Therefore the advocacy of more community control over local political communication processes and institutions seems far-fetched if these processes and institutions are themselves powerless (Davidson, 1979, p. 11).

A second important variable in assessing the strength of local political communication in relation to participation is the local institutional polit-ical system. Opinions of citizens on local issues will be, as Berry explains, "heard loud and clear at city hall, not by osmosis, but by institutional arrangements that facilitate input (Berry *et al.*, 1993, p. 288). How successful the ideal type of "rich, dense communication networks" (ibid.) between government, local political groups and citizens can work, depends not just on the general will of those involved, but also on the institutional particularities of the respective political system. In France, for example, even more than in Britain, local decision-making power is highly concen-trated. Compared with France the situation in Britain does allow for a certain limited dispersal of power that permits citizens to exercise some influence (Mabileau *et al.*, 1989, p. 246). This impact of specific institu-tional arrangements is also exemplified in the fact that, compared to most European countries, the local party system in the US is relatively weak and therefore opens up comparatively easy access venues for citizen councils and initiatives (see Smith & Borghorst, 1979, p. 192). In countries such as Germany or Sweden where strong local parties and neo-corporatist arrangements dominate decision-making processes, alternative actors seem to have less chance to become involved in political communication processes with the local authorities (see Lang, 2000).

"Access" to fora of institutionalized deliberation as well as decision-making therefore is an important axiom that constitutes the relationship between local political communication and political processes (Mabileau, 1989, p. 252). And yet general accessibility in and of itself does not say much about the *quality* of discourse that evolves in a local public. One of the few comparative studies of political communication processes (Asard & Bennett, 1997) comes to the conclusion that in the US with its weak parties but strong interest group involvement and a more reactive, drama-oriented media system, qualities like personalization and negativity in public communication are encouraged (1997, p. 181). In comparison, Sweden with its strong party system and a long tradition of neo-corporatist arrangements, coupled with a publicly financed election system and with strong public media, has at the same time generated higher quality in its deliberative processes (ibid.). The quality of political communication processes therefore depends on the decision-power, the permeability of the institutional system as well as on assets of the respective political culture like consensus orientation in Sweden.

Access to certain means of communication has been a central topic in the discourse on local democracy in developing countries. "Communication in the service of community" is a concept that has revitalized communication policies and media in Latin American, Asian, and African communities (see Valle, 1995, p. 209). Alternative communication practices, first developed in the 1950s, became in the 1970s a central focus of democratization policies in states like Bolivia, Venezuela, Brazil, Tanzania, and the Phillipines. Examples range from the miners' radio initiatives in Bolivia (see Valle, 1995, p. 209), which were financed by unionized miners themselves, to the "dawn peasants" radio in Peru, which uses established channels in the early morning to broadcast in rural languages and play local music (see Tealdo, 1989), to Nigerian use of video technology for political communication in largely illiterate parts of the country (see Okunna, 1995).

The general demand for "better access" of citizens to the local media therefore needs contextualization. Access is important to gain public visibility and to develop "common cause identity." Yet in and of itself broader citizen access does not guarantee high quality of deliberation or reshape the media system as a whole. Other factors, specifically the embeddedness of participatory media in the general media culture, the permeability of the institutional system and the decision-making capacities on the local level, are crucial in evaluation of citizen access to local public communication processes.

Participatory democracy and local political communication – preliminary conclusions

The link between citizenship and locality has a long theoretical tradition which involves three axioms: first, citizenship is based on community identification and membership; second, participation and civic action are concentrated at the local level; and finally, local governance in its broadest form provides the moral learning ground for citizenship (see Lowndes, 1995, p. 161).[23] Research indicates that the bulk of political participation happens on the local level and around local issues (see Mabileau et al., 1989, p. 251; Phillips 1996, pp. 26f.; Stoker, 1996, pp. 188f.) Among these practices of political engagement, voting is the most common, yet also the most sporadic, feature.[24] An even more limited number of citizens is part of the process of "formulation, passage and implementation" of politics and policies (Parry et al., 1992, pp. 16f.). Yet defined in more general terms, participation can have many "faces": it can involve "contacting politicians or government officials, joining pressure groups, attending meetings, signing petitions or demonstrating". It can refer to the "right of citizens to be involved in the processes of government – to express views, to have them listened to, to be informed of decisions and the reasons behind them, to criticize and complain" (Prior & Walsh, 1993, p. 7; Lowndes, 1995, p. 165). Ultimately, participation has to materialize in decision-making processes. This transformation of communication into results is an important, albeit in deliberative theories often neglected, aspect of participation.

Research has shown that it is not primarily the sense of community and moral obligation that fosters participation on the local level, but rather the frequency of interaction – even in the absence of community sentiment – that stimulates citizen involvement. "Face-to-face contact" is according to Berry the single most important feature of mobilization that was encountered in the five US cities included in their research (Berry *et al.*, 1993).[25] Political communication research in the light of participatory democracy therefore has to ask where, how, how often, to what purpose and with what chance of material success interaction between citizens, local interest groups, the media, and local government takes place. Crucial are also the goals of interaction: are they merely to give voice to an individual opinion, or to publicly deliberate, to decide, or to control decision making? Important is finally the spatiality of local political communication processes: there is communication that leads citizens beyond the local in order to achieve local aims – and there is communication that citizens initiate locally in order to achieve results in their state or transnationally – the WTO protests in Seattle in 1999 being a case in point.

Research until a decade ago put the print media as well as electronic media center stage within the local public. While the traditional print media, especially local dailies, have suffered from increasing market concentration and competition with other media, we have also witnessed a proliferation of new forms of advertisement-sponsored free papers and alternative print media. Yet these developments have not resulted in diversified political news markets, but have accelerated the tendency towards "human touch," lifestyle, and public security topics. The same tendencies are visible in local radio and TV programming. Privatized local electronic media have to cater to advertisers' needs, deploy easy listening formats and deal with scarcity of investigative resources. Privatized media tend to enhance fragmentation and polarization in the public sphere while the medias' potential to integrate social forces decreases (Holtz-Bacha, 1997). Even though cable technology has the potential to empower citizens, it is not as such a guarantee for broader democratic participation. Although government-run channels in most cases facilitate access to information and sometimes serve as deliberative forums, it has become increasingly clear that it is not the technological possibility as such which leads to participatory empowerment, but it is a complex interplay of technology, access, interaction possibilities, framing of issues, as well as institutional responsiveness.

Framing the local as a closed communication system is less and less appropriate. New electronic resources, i.e. the Internet, and new local actors, i.e. NGOs, underscore a more complex picture of the local as being embedded in and connected to other localities as well as national and transnational structures and institutions. This increasing embeddedness in and dependency of the local on other levels of governance changes local communicative practices as well as the possibility for citizen participation. Traditional neo-corporatist local systems are forced to be open to new sources of knowledge and influence, leading for example to increases in deployment of electronic town hall formats. Yet again such formats vary: they can be mere political bulletin boards, informative and well-prepared platforms for public discourse, or direct decision-making assemblies. Further and close-up empirical research is necessary to substantiate statements about their respective participatory qualities. What seems to be obvious is that for electronic town halls to achieve the purpose of facilitating deliberation by informed citizens, local authorities, and citizens will have to invest substantial resources in developing adequate institutionalized structures, informational links and procedural techniques. Whether they are willing and prepared to do so, remains an open question. Comparative studies are lacking in regard to classic communication media as well as in regard to ICT related media, government responses and user potential.

ICT media can empower marginalized local groups to create communication channels within and beyond the local level as well as to campaign more effectively for their specific needs and interests. Therefore, the traditional focus on mass media on the local level has to be supplemented with research on other aspects of political communication: communication between NGOs and citizens lacks consideration as much as interaction between established local actors as well as with the media. Finally, the relationship between communication, participation and decision-making in institutional settings needs more substantial scrutiny. How much of a chance of making a difference must there be in order for citizens to choose to become involved in the political public? There is evidence that complex communication technology will only be made use of widely if there is a realistic chance of influencing policy decisions. Electronic media can provide the means for dialogue, networking, cooperation within and beyond the local sphere, but technology cannot fill the void that structural de-politicization has produced. Culturally specific institutional processes regulate, channel, activate or de-activate public communication processes. "Reinventing Communication by Reforming Institutions" (Asard & Bennett, 1997) is therefore not simply a programmatic scheme, but captures the tight connection between communication processes and the institutional structures in which they are performed.

Acknowledgments

I am grateful to the organizers of and contributors to the 1999 IPSA Political Communication Workshop in Québec for helpful comments on an earlier draft. For their encouragement to pursue local political communication processes and valuable discussions I wish to thank Lance Bennett, Aaron Cicourel, Barbara Pfetsch, and Michael Schudson.

Notes

1 Franklin and Murphy (1991) criticize the "scant attention which academics have paid to the local media in general, and to the local press in particular, since the mid-1970s. Around that date, a flurry of academic activity produced a useful crop of detailed studies, typically focused on the way the local press reported, or more accurately failed to report, local politics. Subsequently, however, media research has become increasingly national in its focus and relatively unconcerned with the press . . ." (Franklin & Murphy, 1991, p. 3). Doris Graber perceives the lack of research activity on the local in mass media studies as the result of the glamour and importance which is attributed to the national, even though "it is an axiom of American politics that 'all politics is local'" (Graber, 1997, p. 313).

2 Local government and elite studies at the time were concerned with influence, power and decision-making processes in local settings and thus, without claiming to be "communication studies" contributed to the field (see Hunter, 1953; Rossi, 1958; Dahl, 1960).

3 This "caveat" is important because this paper exposes a significant Western European and Anglo-Saxon bias that is due to language skills and research options. Local political communication research for example on African and Asian countries is either non-existent or – and this is more likely – has not found its way into major Western libraries.

4 See for a discussion of the differences between rural and urban localities Mabileau *et al.* (1989) and Stamm (1985, pp. 137f.).

5 Most of these studies focus on questions of participatory democracy, but analyze communication processes in-depth. For a communication-centered analysis of town meetings see Mansbridge (1980) and Bryan (1999).

6 In Great Britain, concentration of ownership led to 89 percent of the market of local newspapers now being controlled by twenty publishers (see Franklin & Murphy, 1998, p. 19).

7 In Germany, the number of daily papers has shrunk by one third between 1954 and 1978 and since then remained stable. In 1999, 367 daily newspapers produced 1,578 local editions (Bundesverband Deutscher Zeitungsverleger, 1999). Doris Graber states for the US that "the numbers of newspapers have shrunk so that most cities are now served by a single newspaper, and many communities no longer have a paper of their own." Some metropolitan dailies "reach people in fifty counties. Typically their domain then includes some 1,300 government units, whose politics should be reported because they involve important public issues . . . Given the many active political units that require media attention, reporting, of necessity, is highly selective and superficial" (Graber, 1997, p. 313).

8 This figure applies only to West Germany (Schatz, 1995, p. 365).

9 For the US, Kaniss and Graber support the model of James N. Rosse, who perceives an "umbrella competition pattern" of the local print media (op. cit.;

Kaniss, 1991, p. 43; Graber, 1997). Under one umbrella, "smaller units operate within the area covered simultaneously by the larger units." This umbrella pattern has four layers: (1) large metropolitan dailies with dominance of international, national and regional coverage; (2) smaller satellite dailies with more weight given to local news; (3) suburban dailies with an emphasis on mostly non-political local news; and (4) free local papers (Kaniss, 1991, p. 43).

10 Franklin and Murphy identify for Great Britain a growth in free papers from 185 titles in 1975 to almost 900 in 1986 (Franklin and Murphy 1998, p. 13).

11 Graber reports a study of three economically weak network affiliates in the US west, where 75 percent of the news came from handouts, 20 percent had their origin in a tip and only 5 percent came as ideas from reporters. For larger and economically strieving stations those figures were 50 percent, 36 percent, and 13 percent. (Graber, 1997, p. 332).

12 In Great Britain, morning newspapers suffered a 6.5 percent decrease in circulation numbers between 1981 and 1996; evening daily papers went down 27 percent in the same time span. Weekly local papers decreased by 35.6 percent. The only local genres which increased during that time are Sunday papers (increase of 25.6 percent) and free weeklies (increase of 83.1 percent) (Franklin & Murphy, 1998, p. 10).

13 Young readers are especially irregular daily paper consumers. In 1990, only 21 percent of young Americans below 35 responded positively when asked whether they had read a daily paper the day before (Koschnick, 1995, p. 1951). In France, readership of dailies among youth age 15 to 19 is down to 26 percent (ibid.).

14 The paper might have reported something wrong, or the paper might stimulates reader response specifically by special invitation to comment, write on certain issues or might invite its readers to contribute articles or statements to a specific community issue.

15 In Great Britain, still 41 percent of households inform themselves of local news via newspapers, followed by television (32 percent), and radio with 13 percent (Slattery, 1997, p. 57).

16 While in Germany 70 percent of households had cable access in 1991 (Jäckel & Schenk, 1991), in the UK only 20 percent had cable in 1994 (Williams, 1998, p. 52).

17 Italy and France are with 2,500 and 1,612 radio stations the top providers for radio transmission, the Netherlands and Austria with twenty-one and four radio stations were at the bottom end. Yet the media monopoly of the Austrian Broadcasting Corporation ended in 1994, and since then private radio stations are establishing themselves (Koschnick, 1995, pp. 785ff.).

18 In Germany local radio programming by public broadcasting companies under heavy competition from private local stations has changed its philosophy from political and cultural service programs to entertaining formats with interspersed political news.

19 Competition between public radio and privately by advertisements funded radio has led in Germany already in the 1980s to demands to limit the number of private radio channels. As Jarren argues, "private, local radio which is funded through advertising can neither guarantee nor re-institute pluralism of public voices in cities and districts" (1985, pp. 36–7; translation S.L.).

20 This bias might be also the result of what Mark Fishman has identified as the heavy reliance of local electronic media on the print media for their selection of news. Specifically in policy related matters, local print media are the agenda setters for reports, while TV stations pick them up (Fishman, 1978, pp. 531ff.).

21 The reciprocity of this development is analyzed by Kiolbassa, who distinguishes two types of technologcal usage: "station controlled and candidate controlled, the former includes live reports via satellite and video services like network feeds, the latter includes campaign-supplied video and candidate interviews with local stations conducted over satellite. Video services and satellite reports can guarantee access to campaign and White House events and are not dependent on a candidate granting special permission. In contrast, campaigns govern access to campaign-supplied video and satellite interviews" (Kiolbassa, 1997, p. 91).

22 Gilliam *et al.* (1996) have analyzed local TV news and point to the intensity and racialization of crime reporting in the US at the local level. In consequence "television's fixation on crime means that it cannot provide adequate coverage to a number of other important social and politial issues" (ibid., p. 19).

23 It is therefore not surprising that literature about democratization via electronic media chooses terms like the creation of a new "body politic", the "internet community", or the "chat room" – all terms symbolizing narrowly confined localities.

24 Even though national elections and debates are generally perceived as being more important than local election processes, there is evidence that watching a debate and a race on the local level is more politically stimulating and more resonant with the experience and the informational background of citizens than performing as a national voter (see Lichtenstein, 1982; Johnson, 1990, p. 335).

25 This is supported by research of Parry *et al.* in the UK, who found participation to be higher in inner city areas where there was a high level interaction but low levels of community sentiment than in areas with high community identification but less frequent interaction (see Parry *et al.*, 1992; Lowdnes, 1995, pp. 167f.).

References

Altheide, David (1976). *Creating reality: how television news distorts events.* Beverly Hills, CA: Sage Publications.

Åsard, Erik and Bennett, W. Lance (1997). *Democracy and the marketplace of ideas. Communication and government in Sweden and the US.* Cambridge: Cambridge University Press.

Barlow, James (1995). *Public participation in urban development – the European experience.* London: Policies Studies Institute.

Bennett, W. Lance (1993). A policy research paradigm for the news media and democracy. *Journal of Communication,* 43(3), 180–189.

Bernstein, James M. and Lacy, Stephen (1992). Contextual coverage of government by local television news. *Journalism Quarterly,* 69(2), 329–341.

Berry, Jeffrey M., Portney, Kent E. and Thomson, Ken (1993). *The rebirth of urban democracy.* Washington, DC: Brookings Institution.

Box, Richard C. (1998). *Citizen governance. Leading American communities into the 21st century.* Thousand Oaks, CA: Sage Publications.

Brants, Kees, Huizenga, Martine and Van Meerten, Reineke (1996). The new canals of Amsterdam: an exercise in local electronic democracy. *Media, Culture and Society,* 18, 233–247.

Bryan, Frank M. (1999). Direct democracy and civic competence: the case of town meeting. In Stephen L. Elkin and Karol Edward Soltan (eds), *Citizen competence and democratic institutions* (pp. 195–224). University Park, PA: The Pennsylvania State University Press.

Bundesverband Deutscher Zeitungsverlager/Schaffelt, Burkhard (1999). Stelung-nahme: ein mittel gegen verkrustung und redaktionsbeamtentum. In Frank Meik *et al.*, *Redaktionen outsourcen? Die outgesourcte lokalredaktion* (pp. 19–22). Marburg: Selbstverlag.

Castells, Manuel (1996). *The rise of the network society.* Volume I: *The information age: economy, society and culture.* Oxford: Blackwell.

Cohen, Joli E. (1998). The significance of critical communication skills in a democracy. In Michael Salvador and Patricia M. Sias (eds), *The public voice in a democracy at risk* (pp. 41–56). Westport, CN: Praeger Publishers.

Cox, Harvey and Morgan, David (1973). *City politics and the press. Journalists and the governing of Merseyside.* Cambridge: University of Cambridge Press.

Crisell, Andrew (1998). Local radio: attuned to the times or filling time with tunes? In Bob Franklin and David Murphy (eds), *Making local news. Local journalism in context* (pp. 24–35). London, New York: Routledge.

Dahl, Robert A. (1960). The analysis of influence in local communities. In Charles Adrian (ed.), *Social science and communuity action* (pp. 26f.). East Lansing, MI: State University of Michigan.

Davidson, Jeffrey L. (1979). *Political partnerships. neighborhood residents and their council members.* London: Sage Publications.

Davis, Richard and Owen, Diana (1998). *New media and American politics.* Oxford: Oxford University Press.

Dorsch, Petra E. (1978). Lokalkommunikation. Ergebnisse und Defizite der Forschung. *Publizistik*, 3, 189–199.

Dubois, D. (1993). *Les politiques de communiation des collectivités territoriales.* Université d'Amiens.

Fishman, Mark (1978). Crime waves as ideology. *Social Problems*, 25, 531–543.

Franklin, Bob and Murphy, David (1991). *The market, politics and the local press.* London, New York: Routledge.

Franklin, Bob and Murphy, David (eds) (1998). *Making local news. Local journalism in context.* London, New York: Routledge.

Frederick, Howard H. (1992). Computer communications in cross-border coalition-building. North American NGO networking against NAFTA. *Gazette*, 50, 217–241.

Gilliam, Franklin D., Iyengar, Shanto, Simon, Adam and Wright, Oliver (1996). Crime in black and white. The violent, scary world of local news. *Press/Politics*, 1(2), 6–23.

Graber, Doris A. (1997). *Mass media and American politics* (5th edn). Washington, DC: Congressional Quarterly Press.

Hamm, Ingrid, Hasebrink, Uwe and Jarren, Otfried *et al.* (1989). Lokale Kommunikation in Dortmund. Journalistisches Handeln, publizistisches Angebot und "politische Kultur" nach der Einführung des lokalen Rundfunks. *Rundfink und Fernsehen*, 1, 47–69.

Hill, Dilys M. (1994). *Citizens and cities. Urban policy in the 1990s.* New York: Harvester Wheatsheaf.

Hollander, Richard (1985). *Video democracy: the vote-from-home revolution.* Mt Airy, MD: Lomond.

Holtz-Bacha, Christina (1997). Das fragmentierte mendien-publikum. Folgen für das politische system. *Aus Politik und Zeitgeschichte*, B42, 13–21.

Hunter, Floyd (1953). *Community power structure*, Chapel Hill, NC: University of North Carolina Press.

Jäckel, Michael and Schnek, Michael (eds) (1991). *Kabelfernsehen in Deutschland. Pilotprojekte, Programmvermehrung, private Konkurrenz, Ergebnisse und Perspektiven.* München: R. Fischer Verlag.

Janowitz, M. (1952). *The community press in an urban setting: The social elements of urbanism.* Chicago, IL: Chicago University Press.

Jarren, Otfried (1984). *Kommunale Kommunikation.* München: Minerva.

Jarren, Otfried (1985). Lokaler Hörfunk für die Bundesrepublik. In Otfried Jarren and Peter Widlok (eds), *Lokalradio* (pp. 15–42). Berlin: Vistas Verlag.

Jarren, Otfried (1989). Lokaler Rundfunk und Politische Kultur. Auswirkungen lokaler elektronischer Medienangebote auf Institutionen und institutionelles Handeln. *Publizistik*, 4, 424–436.

Jarren, Otfried (1991). Neue politik durch neue medien? Zur bedeutung lokaler elektronischer medien für die politische kultur in der kommune. In Bernhard Blanke (ed.), *Staat und Stadt*, special edition of *Politische Vierteijahresschrift*, 32(22), 422–439.

Johnson, Anne (1990). Trends in political communication: a selective review of research in the 1980s. In David L. Swanson, and Dan Nimmo (eds), *New directions in political communication* (pp. 329–362). Newbury Park, CA and London: Sage.

Judge, David, Stroker, Gery and Wolman, Harold (1995). *Theories of urban politics.* London: Sage Publications.

Kaniss, Phyllis (1991). *Making local news.* Chicago, IL and London: University of Chicago Press.

Kern, Montague and Wicks, Robert H. (1994). Television news and the advertising-driven new mass media election: a more significant local role in 1992? In Robert E. Denton Jr (ed.), *The 1992 presidential campaign. A communication perspective* (pp. 189–206). Westport, CT: Praeger.

Kiolbassa, Jolene (1997). Is local TV news still local? Coverage of presidential and senate races in Los Angeles. *Press/Politics*, 2(1), 79–95.

Klite, Paul, Bardwell, Robert A. and Salzman, Jason (1997). Local TV news: getting away with murder. *Press/Politics*, 2(2), 102–112.

Koschnick, Wolfgang J. (1995). Standard-lexicon für medienplanung und mediaforschung in Deutschland (2nd edn). München: K. Saur Verlag.

Kurp, Matthias (1994). *Lokale Medien und kommunale Eliten.* Partizipatorische Potentiale des Lokaljurnalismus bei Printmedien und Hörfunk in Nordrhein-Westfalen. Opladen: Westdeutscher Verlag.

Lang, Sabine (1997). The NGOization of feminism. In Joan W. Scott, Cora Kaplan and Debra Keates (eds), *Transitions, environments, translations. Feminisms in international politics* (pp. 101–120). London, New York: Routledge.

Lang, Sabine (2000). NGOs, local governance and political communication processes in Germany. *Political Communication*, 17(4), 383–388.

Lang, Sabine (2001). *Politische Öffentlichkeit und moderner Staat.* Baden-Baden: Nomos Verlag.

Lichtenstein, A. (1982). Differences in impact between local and national political candidates' debates. *Western Journal of Speech Communication*, 46, 291–298.

Lowndes, Vivien (1995). Citizenship and urban politics. In David Judge, Gerry Stroker and Harold Wolman (eds), *Theories of urban politics* (pp. 160–181). London: Sage Publications.

Maarek, Philippe J. (1995). *Political marketing and communication*. London: J. Libbey Publications.

Mabileau, Albert, Moyser, George, Parry, Geraint and Quantin, Patrick (1989). *Local politics and participation in Britain and France*. Cambridge: Cambridge University Press.

Mansbridge, Jane (1980). *Beyond adversary democracy*. Chicago, IL: The University of Chicago Press.

Mayer, Margit (1996). Social movements in European cities: transitions from the 1970s to the 1990s. Berlin (unpublished manuscript).

McLeod, Jack M., Daily, Katie, Guo, Zhongshi, and Eveland, William P. Jr (1996). Community integration, local media use, and democratic processes. *Communication Research*, 23(2), 179–209.

Murphy, David (1976). *The silent watchdog. The press in local politics*. London: Constable Press.

Neveu, Erik (1998). Media and politics in French political science. *The European Journal of Political Research*, 33, 439–458.

Okunna, Chinyere Stella (1995). Small participatory media technology as an agent of social change in Nigeria: a non-existent option? *Media, Culture and Society*, 17, 615–627.

Parry, G., Moyser, G. and Day, N. (1992). *Political participation and democracy in Britain*. Cambridge: Cambridge University Press.

Percy-Smith, Janie (1995). Downloading democracy? Information and communication technologies in local politics. *Policy and Politics*, 24(1), 43–56.

Phillips, Anne (1996). Why does local democracy matter? In Lawrence Pratchett and David Wilson (eds), *Local democracy and local government* (pp. 20–37). New York: St Martin's Press.

Pratchett, Lawrence and Wilson, David (eds) (1996). *Local democracy and local government*. New York: St. Martin's Press.

Prior, D. and Walsh, K. (1993). *Citizenship and the quality of local government*. Birmingham: Institute of Local Government Studies.

Rager, Günther and Schibrani, Harald (1981). Das Lokale als Gegenstand der Kommunikationsforschung. Bericht über den Stand der Forschung in der Bundesrepubik. *Rundfunk und Fernsehen*, 29(4), 498–508.

Rosenau, James N. (1998). Governance and democracy in a globalizing world. In Daniele Archibugi, David Held and Martin Köhler (eds), *Re-imagining political community. Studies in cosmopolitan democracy* (pp. 28–57). Cambridge, London: Polity Press.

Rossi, Peter (1958). Community decision making. In Roland Young (ed.), *Approaches to the study of politics* (pp. 359ff.). Evanston IL: Northwestern University Press.

Salvador, Michael and Sias, Patricia M. (eds) (1998). *The public voice in a democracy at risk*. Westport, CN: Praeger Publishers.

Sassen, Saskia (1996). Cities and communities in the global economy. *American Behavioral Scientist*, 39(5), 629–639.

Saxer, Ulrich (1980). Lokale Kommunikation – Bilanz der Forschung. In Wolfgang R. Langenbucher (ed.), *Lokalkommunikation. Analysen, Beispiele, Alternativen* (pp. 24–30). München: Olschlager.

Schatz, Heribert (1995). Massenmedien. In Uwe Andersen and Wichard Woyke (eds), *Handwörterbuch des politischen Systems der Bundesrepublik Deutschland* (pp. 361–371). Bonn: Bundeszentrale für Politische Bildung.

Schönbach, Klaus (1978). Die isolierte Welt des Lokalen. Tageszeitungen und ihre Berichterstattung über Mannheim. *Rundfunk und Fersehen*, 26(3), 260–277.

Slattery, J. (1997). Television tops for world news but trailing locally. *Gazette*, 25 April, 11.

Smith, Michael P. and Borghorst, Hermann (1979). Strategien der Stadtsanierungseliten in den US und in der Bundesrepublik. *Zeitschrift für Parlamentsfragen*, 2, 179–192.

Stamm, Keith R. (1985). *Newspaper use and community ties: toward a dynamic theory*. Norwood, NJ: Ablex Publishing.

Stroker, Gerry (1996). Redefining local democracy. In Lawrence Pratchett and David Wilson (eds), *Local democracy and local government* (pp. 188–209). New York: St. Martin's Press.

Tealdo, Ana Rosa (1989). *Radio y Democracia*. Lima: IPAL.

Valle, Carlos A. (1995). Communication: international debate and community-based initiatives. In Philip Lee (ed.), *The democratization of communication* (pp. 199–216). Cardiff: University of Wales Press.

Vidich, A. J. and Bensman, J. (1958). *Small town in mass society: class, power, and religion in a rural community*. Princeton, NJ: Princeton University Press.

Williams, Granville (1998). Cable television: the new local medium? In Bob Franklin and David Murphy (eds), *Making local news. Local journalism in context* (pp. 51–62). London, New York: Routledge.

Wood, Robert C. (1959). *Suburbia: its people and their politics*. Boston, MA: Houghton Mifflin.

Yankelovitch, D. (1991). *Coming to public judgement*. Syracuse, NY: Syracuse University Press.

Zimmerman, Joseph F. (1970). The town meeting: an evaluation. In Joseph F. Zimmerman (ed.), *Subnational politics. Readings in state and local government* (pp. 239–252). New York: Holt, Rinehart and Winston Inc.

INDEX

THE ADVENTURES OF
Captain Pugwash

The Painting Contest

RED FOX

A Red Fox Book

Published by Random House Children's Books
20 Vauxhall Bridge Road, London SW1V 2SA

A division of The Random House Group Ltd
London Melbourne Sydney Auckland
Johannesburg and agencies throughout the world

The Adventures of Captain Pugwash
Created by John Ryan
© Britt Allcroft (Development) Limited 2000
All rights worldwide Britt Allcroft (Development) Limited
CAPTAIN PUGWASH is a trademark of Britt Allcroft (Development) Limited
THE BRITT ALLCROFT COMPANY is a trademark of The Britt Allcroft Company plc

Cover illustration by Ian Hillyard
Inside illustrations by Red Central Limited

Text adapted by Sally Byford from the original TV story

1 3 5 7 9 10 8 6 4 2

THE RANDOM HOUSE GROUP Limited Reg. No. 954009

www.randomhouse.co.uk

ISBN 0 09 940816 3

Portobello town was buzzing with excitement. The Governor was holding a painting competition, and everyone was invited to paint a picture of their favourite person.

Captain Pugwash wasn't a bit interested, until he heard that the prize for the winner was two hundred gold doubloons. "Clattering canvasses!" he cried. "Let's get painting."

Pugwash and his crew hurried to the town square where Boris Roubles, a famous Russian artist, was teaching the people of Portobello how to paint. While they had their lesson, Tom talked to his friend Toni.

"Mr Roubles comes to our café every day," she said. "We're great friends. He's been teaching everyone for the competition. Who is the Captain going to paint?"

"I've suggested the Governor," said Tom, "as he's the judge."

They didn't know that Dook, one of Cut-throat Jake's crew, had been listening to them.

Dook quickly sneaked away and met the rest of his crew in a dark doorway.

"Pugwash is painting a picture of the Governor for the competition," he whispered.

"I'm not going to let him win," hissed Jake. "I'll enter a picture of the Governor, too. But first I must find someone to do the painting for me."

They heard footsteps coming closer and Jake peered out. "Haha-r-r-h! It's that artist," he growled. "Just what I need!"

When Mr Roubles walked past them, Jake's crew leapt on him and dragged him into the doorway.

"Help! Help!" cried Mr Roubles.

Quickly, Swine gagged him.

"Take him to the Flying Dustman," ordered Jake. "Now I have a real artist to do my painting, I'm sure to win."

The next day, Captain Pugwash and his crew were painting on board the Black Pig.

"My picture is bound to please the Governor," said Pugwash, adding a splash of red paint. "But come along, crew, let's see what you've done."

Willy, Jonah and the Mate held up their pictures, feeling very silly.

"Stuttering starfish," said Pugwash. "You've all painted me!"

"That's right," said Willy. "Your turn now."

"I've painted my most favourite person of all," smiled Pugwash, holding up his picture.

The crew were speechless. Pugwash had painted himself!

"Top-hole art!" said Pugwash. "Parcel it up, Mr Mate, and put on my special mark. Then take it straight to the Governor's house. I'm sure it's going to win."

Tom wasn't so sure. It was the most terrible picture he had ever seen, and he was worried that everyone would laugh at the Captain. He wondered whether Mr Roubles could help.

Tom ran to the café to look for Mr Roubles, but Toni hadn't seen him all day.

"Mamma said that Dook was hanging around here yesterday," said Toni. "Maybe Cut-throat Jake has something to do with Mr Roubles' disappearance."

"I bet you're right," said Tom. "Come on, let's find out." Together, they set off towards the harbour.

On the Flying Dustman, Cut-throat Jake was forcing Mr Roubles to paint a picture of the Governor. The artist was doing an excellent job.

"When it's dry, wrap it up and take it to the Governor's house," Jake ordered his men. "Pugwash doesn't stand a chance now!"

Tom and Toni watched as Dook, Swine and Stinka left their ship carrying a large parcel.

"If it's a good painting, we'll know that Jake must have taken Mr Roubles prisoner," said Toni.

"Let's get into the Governor's house tonight, and take a look," said Tom. "I know a secret way in."

That night, Tom and Toni climbed onto the roof of the
Governor's house. Tom led the way to an open skylight and
they lowered themselves down on ropes.

They crept silently through the dark rooms until they found
the paintings. They were all covered with curtains.

"There's Jake's painting," whispered Toni, spotting the
pirate's mark. They both peeped behind the curtain.

"Just as we thought," said Tom. "This has been done by
Mr Roubles. Cut-throat Jake must have kidnapped him and
forced him to paint it!"

"We can't let Cut-throat Jake win," said Toni.

Quickly they swapped Jake's mark for Pugwash's mark.

"Captain Pugwash will definitely win now," said Tom.

Then they left the Governor's house as quickly and quietly as they had come.

On the day of the competition, Toni waited until Cut-throat
Jake and his crew had left for the Governor's house. Then she
crept onto the Flying Dustman to rescue Mr Roubles. She
found him tied up on the deck.

"We must go to the Governor's house quickly," said Toni,
untying him. "Then we can tell everyone who really painted
Cut-throat Jake's picture."

At the Governor's house, Lieutenant Scratchwood was unveiling the pictures.

"My favourite person, by Captain Horatio Pugwash," announced Scratchwood, pulling back the curtain.

Everyone cheered when they saw the amazing picture of the Governor. Pugwash smiled and bowed. He didn't notice it was the wrong picture.

"That's my painting!" bellowed Cut-throat Jake, but for once no one heard him.

At the next painting, Scratchwood announced, "My favourite person, by Cut-throat Jake." Everyone laughed and booed.

"This is monstrous!" cried Pugwash, as he realised what had happened.

"That's not my painting and he's not my favourite person!" roared Jake. "He's my worst enemy!" Jake grabbed Pugwash by the neck. The crowd screamed.

"Silence!" shouted Scratchwood. "The Governor is here to announce the winner."

The Governor looked at the picture of Captain Pugwash. "Very interesting," he said kindly, to Jake. Then he moved on to the picture of himself. "However, the winning picture is this excellent work painted by Captain Horatio Pugwash."

"That's my picture!" roared Jake, as Pugwash stepped forward to take the prize.

At that moment, Mr Roubles and Toni burst into the room.

"There's been a mistake!" cried Mr Roubles. "That's my picture. Cut-throat Jake kidnapped me and forced me to paint it for him."

The Governor was horrified. "You will go to jail, Jake," he said. "And the prize money belongs to you, Mr Roubles."

"Oh no," said Mr Roubles. "Brave Captain Pugwash must have the prize. His friends saved my life. I'd like him to have my painting, too. You can have his own interesting picture for your art gallery."

Captain Pugwash was delighted. "A triumph, me hearties,"
he cried. "Two hundred gold doubloons, a painting worth a
fortune, my picture hung in the Governor's gallery and, to cap
it all, Cut-throat Jake out of the way for a very long time."

Then he and his crew went back to the Black Pig for a
top-hole celebratory tea.